The Campaigns of Sir William Waller, 1642–1645

Laurence Spring

Helion & Company

Helion & Company Limited
Unit 8 Amherst Business Centre
Budbrooke Road
Warwick
CV34 5WE
England
Tel. 01926 499 619
Email: info@helion.co.uk
Website: www.helion.co.uk
Twitter: @helionbooks
Visit our blog at http://blog.helion.co.uk/

Published by Helion & Company 2019
Designed and typeset by Mach 3 Solutions Ltd (www.mach3solutions.co.uk)
Cover designed by Paul Hewitt, Battlefield Design (www.battlefield-design.co.uk)

ISBN 978-1-912866-56-4

British Library Cataloguing-in-Publication Data.
A catalogue record for this book is available from the British Library.

For details of other military history titles published by Helion & Company Limited, contact the above address, or visit our website: http://www.helion.co.uk

We always welcome receiving book proposals from prospective authors.

Contents

List of Illustrations

List of Maps

Acknowledgements

I would like to thank the staff of the British Library, the National Archives at Kew, East Sussex Record Office and the Hampshire Record Office, without whose assistance this book would not have been possible.

The Series Editor would like to thank Terry Harris, Serena Jones, Nicola and Alan Turton, Michel Paradowski and David Wilton, for their help and support in supplying photographs and illustrations for this book.

Introduction

Nothing sums up the tragedy of the Civil War more than the friendship between Sir William Waller and his friend and opponent Sir Ralph Hopton, as 'this war without an enemy.' He was born on 3 December 1598, the son of Sir Thomas and Margaret Waller of Knole in Kent. As a young man of about 20 he entered the Venetian Army and was involved in several skirmishes. Then in 1618 the Defenestration of Prague marked the beginning of the Thirty Years' War, and the following year the Bohemian rebels offered Frederick, Elector Palatine, the Bohemian Throne. Frederick's wife, Elizabeth, was the daughter of King James I and sister to the future Charles I, but James would have nothing to do with the war. To the English, James may have been seen as Scottish, but the nobility adored Elizabeth and many volunteered to serve in her lifeguard, including Waller and Hopton. The latter called her the 'Queen of women'. Her lifeguard took part in several engagements, but missed the battle of the White Mountain, which took place near Prague on 8 November 1620, since unbeknown to Frederick and Elizabeth, with members of her lifeguard were having lunch in Prague. With their army defeated Frederick and Elizabeth fled Bohemia. At first their coach was escorted by her lifeguard, but when the coach got stuck in the snow Elizabeth – who was about eight months pregnant with the future Prince Maurice – is said to have ridden behind Hopton on his horse for about 40 miles.[1] With the failure of the Bohemian Revolt many English continued to fight, first to protect Frederick's Palatinate, and then to protect the Protestant religion; they included Sir Walter Waller, William's brother, who was killed in 1625.

However in 1621 William Waller returned to England and would not take up the sword again until the outbreak of the Civil War. He was not even an MP when Charles tried to arrest the Five Members on 5 January 1642, which included Sir Arthur Heselrige. He had tried to become an MP in 1641, but it was not until the following April 1642 that he became the Member for Andover.

Unfortunately, like so many who supported either King or Parliament in the war we do not know why he joined the Parliamentarian cause. After the

1 John Adair, *Roundhead General: a military biography of Sir William Waller* (London: MacDonald, 1969), p.25.

Restoration, which he helped bring about, he wrote that he had no wish to harm the King;

> Or the diminution of his just power and greatness, and that I would sooner have perished ten thousand times, then to have touched the lap of his garment, otherwise, then with honour. All the ends I had in carrying on of that service were but to bring things to a fair and peaceable issue, that there might have been a general payment of all duties. That God might have had his fear; the King his honour; the Houses of Parliament their privileges; the people of the kingdom their liberties and properties; and nothing might have remained upon the score among us, but that debt which must be ever paying and ever owing, love.[2]

Certainly the Earl of Clarendon believed that why Waller sided with Parliament was more a case of honour since he had been insulted by his first wife's cousin, Thomas Reynell. who was also held the 'Office of the king's Cupbearer'. However, this seems unlikely. Waller's second wife, Lady Anne, was known to have been a strict Puritan and despite him being mocked by the Royalist broadsheets for being under his wife's thumb, there was an underlying belief that he might change sides if the occasion arose. Despite the Royalists offering him an olive branch on several occasions he remained loyal to the Parliament's cause.

Waller was generally respected by both sides. The Royalist officer Walter Slingsby, described him as 'the Fox' and the 'best shifter and chooser of ground when he was not master of the field'. The Parliamentarian John Vicars in his *England's Worthies*, published in 1647, refers to him as 'one of the most impregnable offensive and defensive walls of the kingdom.' His victories in 1642 and early 1643 earned him the nickname of 'William the Conqueror' and the 'Night Owl', due to his tactic of marching by night to surprise his enemy, although he was not the only commander to master this difficult manoeuvre.

He would also continue his campaigns long after other armies had settled into 'winter quarters', and as his biographer, John Adair, recalls, by March 1645, 'Waller had led an army in the service of Parliament almost continuously for two years. No officer had done more than him to stave off defeat or to win victory.'[3] Brigadier Peter Young is more harsh on Waller, 'having lost his first army at Roundway Down, had won an important victory at Cheriton with his second. This however, had achieved little or nothing since its defeat at Cropredy Bridge.'[4] This is a little unfair, since after Cropredy Bridge he had to reinforce the garrisons in the south-west of England which still held out for Parliament, and early in 1645 he was given the task of defending these garrisons without the means to do so.

2 Sir William Waller, *Vindication of the Character and Conduct of Sir William Waller Knight... Explanatory of His Conduct in taking up arms against King Charles the First* (London: J Debrett, 1793), pp.303–304.

3 Adair, *Roundhead General*, p.11.

4 Brigadier Peter Young, *Naseby 1645: The Campaign and the Battle* (London: Century Publishing, 1985), p.183.

1

Waller's Early Campaigns, 1642

On 22 August 1642 Charles raised his standard at Nottingham marking the beginning of the English Civil War, but few men flocked to his cause, and it appeared that he would not be able to fight a war. However, in other parts of the country there were glimmers of hope for Charles' cause, not least in Hampshire where on 2 August Colonel George Goring, the governor of Portsmouth, declared for the King. Two days later it was reported in Parliament that Goring had 'put the town in a posture of defence and shut the gates'. His recruiting parties had gathered 500 'Papists and others that are ill affected to the parliament in the town to assist him'.[1]

Sir William Waller, an engraving by George Perfect Harding, based on an earlier work. (The Turton Collection)

Parliament ordered Robert Devereux, the 3rd Earl of Essex who had recently been appointed Lord General of the Parliamentarian Army was to raise a force 'and forthwith to march with them before Portsmouth to kill, and slay all that oppose their passage and to demand Portsmouth and the castle to be delivered up to them and to demand Colonel Goring and to apprehend him as guilty of high treason.'[2] However, before Essex could raise this force, the Parliamentarian Committee of Hampshire decided to deal with the situation themselves and sent Waller, who had been appointed a captain of a troop of horse on 15 July 1642, with a force to recapture Portsmouth.[3]

1 *A True relation of the several passages and proceedings of Colonel Goring at Portsmouth* (London: E.G. for John Benson, 1642).

2 *A True relation of the several passages and proceedings of Colonel Goring at Portsmouth* (London: E G for John Benson, 1642).

3 The National Archives [hereafter TNA], SP 28/261/9, Warrant for payment of £105 12 shillings to Captain Sir William Waller's troop of horse, 6 August 1642.

Robert Devereux, Earl of Essex, on foot, by Wenceslaus Hollar. (The Wenceslaus Hollar Collection, University of Toronto Library)

By 12 August Waller assisted by the Hampshire Trained bands and the navy, which had declared for Parliament laid seized Portsbridge which controlled the entrance to Portsea Island, thus preventing any assistance reaching Portsmouth from land, while Robert Earl of Warwick who commanded a squadron of Parliament's navy blockaded the town by sea. Waller ordered gun platforms to be erected at Gosport and on 28 August he called on Goring to surrender. Despite many of the Royalist garrison having deserted Goring refused, so the Parliamentarian guns began to bombard the town. The following day a night assault captured Southsea Castle and its guns were also turned towards Portsmouth. With the town surrounded and with little hope of relief, on 7 September Goring surrendered, but instead of being tried for high treason he was allowed to leave England for the Netherlands.

The Hampshire Committee and Waller seem to have been unaware of Parliament's order to Essex, because Waller, writing after the war in his *Recollections*, sees the siege as being the cause of friction between Essex and himself which was to last for most of the war:

> It was about this time that those misunderstandings grew between me and the Lord General Essex which were afterwards noticed in some sort by the Parliament; and there were those who fomented our discord for their own advancement. Some whom I at that time commanded, but who have since sat in a higher seat, were not wanting to misrepresent and to inflame on either side; and the country did suffer for these things, which the Parliament well knew, but thought it not convenient at all times to notice.[4]

By now events were moving swiftly in the national arena. The Royalists had an early success at Powick Bridge near Worcester on 23 September, when Rupert's cavalry routed a party of Parliamentarian horse and the following month fought the Earl of Essex, the commander of the Parliamentarian army, to a draw at the battle of Edgehill. By now Waller had become a colonel and was present at the battle where his regiment was placed on the left wing under Sir James Ramsay; it is said to have been formed of 24 troops of horse, possibly 12 troops forming the front line and 12 the second. Usually two or three troops would have formed a squadron, so each line would have been formed of between four and six squadrons.The composition of Waller's regiment is not known at this stage but Horatio Carey is listed as its major in 1642, as well as Sir Faithful Fortescue. Ramsay's cavalry were supported by

4 Waller, *Recollections*, p.121.

600 musketeers from Colonel Denzil Holles' and Thomas Ballard's foot regiments, and some pieces of artillery which were designed to break up the attack of the advancing Royalist cavalry, which were led by Prince Rupert. Rupert's cavalry included his own, his brother's Prince Maurice's, the Prince of Wales and the King's Lifeguard, plus Colonel Usher's regiment of dragoons.

To encourage the men under his command Sir James Ramsay gave a rousing speech to each squadron:

Prince Rupert with Boy, from Parliamentarian pamphlet satirising the Prince following his rampage through Birmingham in early 1643. (Public domain)

> exhorting them to magnanimity and resolution, showing them the worth of their ancestors, desiring them to show themselves worthy [of] such noble progenitors, and putting before them the justness of the cause, that it was the purity of religion, the liberty of the subject and the King and Parliament's honour, that drew them into the field, and no man's private quarrel; and the more to encourage them I did lay before them the unworthiness of the adverse party, who were advancing to charge us, and commanding ours to receive them resolutely.[5]

Despite this encouragement nothing could prepare them for the sight of thousands of cavalrymen advancing towards them. Even though James, Duke of York was only nine years old in 1642, he later wrote an account of the battle in which he describes Rupert's cavalry:

> Marched up with all the gallantry and resolution imaginable, especially the right wing led by Prince Rupert; though while they advanced, the enemy's cannon continually played upon them, as did the small divisions of their foot, which were betwixt their squadrons, neither of which did in the least discompose them so much as to mend their pace. Thus they continued moving, till they came up close to the enemy's cavalry, which after having spent their first fire, immediately turned their backs, the Royalists pursuing them with great eagerness.[6]

Lord Bernard Stuart who commanded the King's Lifeguard confirms James' account:

> Upon our approach they gave fire with their cannon lined amongst their horse, dragooners, carbines and pistols, but finding that did noting [too] dismay the

5 British Library, Thomason Tracts [hereafter BL TT], 669 f.6, *The Vindication and Clearing of Sir James Ramsay* (London: John Bellamy and Ralph Smith, 9 November 1642).

6 Extract from James II's account quoted in Peter Young, *Edgehill 1642: The Campaign and the Battle* (Kineton: Roundwood Press 1967), pp.276–277.

Cavalry skirmish, by Jan Marszten de Jonge. (Rijksmuseum, Amsterdam)

> King's horse and that they came more roundly to them with all their fire reserved, just when our men charged they all began to turn head and we followed an execution upon them for four miles altogether.[7]

Even the Parliamentarian's account had to admit that Ramsay's wing, 'upon the first charge of the enemy, they wheeled about, abandoned their musketeers, and came running down with the enemy's horse at their heels.' Ramsay records that, 'ours discharged their carbines at a long distance, but thereafter basely runaway, and that in mighty confusion.'[8]

At first Captain John Fiennes' troop was accused of being the first to break, but his brother Nathaniel Fiennes claimed this 'honour' went to Captain Robert Vivers' troop of Colonel Goodwin's Regiment and John Fiennes had tried to rally Vivers' and his own troop.

However, not all Ramsay's wing fled, because Prince Rupert in his diary records:

> Van Girish, Lieutenant to Sir Faithful Fortescue came over to the Prince [Rupert], and told him his captain resolved to yield, and that the signal should be the shooting off his pistol to the ground. The time was so short, the Prince could not send notice of it to the Lord Byron's and Sir William Killigrewe's men.[9]

---

7 BL Harl ms 3783 f.60.

8 John Rushworth, *Historical Collections of Private Passages of State* (London: D. Browne, 1721), vol. 5 1642–1645; BL TT 669 f.6, *The Vindication and Clearing of Sir James Ramsay.*

9 Extract from Prince Rupert's Diary, in Young, *Edgehill*, p.285.

According to Clarendon, Fortescue:

> with his whole troop advanced from the gross of their horse, and discharging all their pistols on the ground, within a little more than carbine shot of his own body, presented himself and his troop to Prince Rupert; and immediately, with his highness charged the enemy. Whether this… and the [enemy] not knowing how many more were of the same mind, each man looking upon hiscompanion with the same apprehension as upon the enemy, or whether the terror of the Prince Rupert and the King's horse, or altogether, with their own evilconsciences, wrought upon them, I know not, but that whole wing having unskillfully discharged their carbines and pistols into the air wheeled about, the king's horse charging in the flank and rear and having thus absolutely routed them.[10]

Despite Fortescue changing sides some Royalist cavalry are known to have fallen upon his troop, not having received word of his intention. However, a twist in Fortescue's treachery is that he is listed as having received a commission to raise a regiment of horse in the Royalist army on 25 September 1642.[11]

What part Waller played is not known apart from having his horse shot under him, 'but I was preserved from any hurt'.[12] Whether Captain Edward Kightley's troop was also in Waller's Regiment by this stage is not certain, but his troop was quartered five miles from Edgehill and so arrived late for the battle. However, on his journey to the battlefield he observed the flight of a blue-coated and grey-coated regiment of foot, which belonged to Colonel Charles Essex's Brigade, and several bodies of cavalry who declared that the King had been victorious. When Kightley turned to his troop he said only 36 remained, the rest along with two troops he had met on the way had also fled and his presence prevented the rest from fleeing. He recalls:

> being in a little field and there was a way through and divers of the enemy did run that way, both horse and foot, I took away about 10 or 12 horse, swords and armour, I could have killed 40 of the enemy, [but] I let them pass disarming them and giving the spoil to my troopers, the armies were both in a confusion, and I could not fall to them without apparent loss of my self and those few which were with me.[13]

The horses, swords and armour were probably discarded by the fleeing cavalry.

The Parliamentarian right wing under Lord Fielding also broke and fled upon the advance of the Royalist cavalry, but apart from Charles Essex's Brigade the rest of the infantry held firm along with two regiments of cavalry which saved the day for the Parliamentarian cause.

---

10 Earl of Clarendon, *History of the Rebellion*, vol. 3, p.278.

11 BL Add ms 18,980 f.20.

12 Waller, *Recollections*, p.109.

13 BL TT E.126/13, Captain Edward Kightley, *A Full and True Relation of the Battle fought between the King's Army and the Earl of Essex in a letter from Captain Edward Kightley* (London: November 1642).

Robert Devereux, Earl of Essex, on horse, by Wenceslaus Hollar. (The Wenceslaus Hollar Collection, University of Toronto Library)

After the battle the Earl of Essex retired to Warwick Castle with his army, leaving the Royalists to advance on London. With the City's trained bands standing in Charles' way Rupert wanted a large party of 3,000 horse and foot to force march to London and in one daring move bring the war to a speedy conclusion. Fearing a Royalist advance on London, Parliament ordered its forces from the surrounding counties to screen the approaches to the city and garrisons such as Farnham Castle in Surrey were ordered to be abandoned.

Fortunately for Parliament Charles' council of war was against Rupert's idea of swiftly marching on London, fearing that his force might sack the city once it arrived. Instead the King's army made its way slowly towards London, Oxford was captured on 29 October and on 4 November, Reading. On 7 November Rupert summoned Windsor Castle to surrender and not having enough time or men to lay siege to the castle Rupert marched away and that night quartered at Egham, which was plundered to the value of £1,921 7s.[14] The following day elements of the Royalist army are known to have been at Guildford, Walton-on-Thames and Leatherhead, and later Byfleet. The inhabitants of the latter town claimed that they had been plundered of £200.[15]Many believed that the same fate awaited London, but much to the city's relief, the day before Essex's army had entered London. On 9 November a small party of about 100 Royalists under the command of Sir John Denham, who was the High Sheriff of Surrey, seized Farnham Castle, which controlled a major route between Hampshire and London.

By now the King was at Colnbrook in Middlesex, where on 11 November he received a delegation from Parliament offering to negotiate terms. This delegation seems to have been happy with Charles' response and a ceasefire seems to have been agreed. However after the delegation had left Charles held a Council of War with Prince Rupert, where plans were made for an attack on the town of Brentford, where two Parliamentarians regiments of foot were quartered.

Early the next morning Rupert attacked the two unsuspecting regiments. Lord Brooke's Regiment of purple coats fled, but Holles' redcoats stood their ground and put up a determined resistance through the streets and orchards of the town, According to the Royalist John Gwyn 'which proved so fatal to Holles, his butchers and dyers that day, that [an] abundance of them were killed and taken prisoner, besides those drowned in their attempt

14 Young, *Edgehill*, p. 137; TNA SP 28/178 Deposition of the Parish of Egham.
15 TNA SP 28/179 and SP 28/178, Dispositions for the parishes in Surrey.

to escape by leaping into the river [Thames].' It was only with the arrival of reinforcements that stabilised the situation.

On 13 November, both armies faced each other at Turnham Green, but a part from a few artillery shots, neither side were willing to engage in battle and towards evening the King withdrew his greatly outnumbered army to Hounslow Heath and then to Kingston. Finally the king reached Oxford which he made his capital for the rest of the war.

With the King's army safely in Oxford towards the end of November the Earl of Essex looked towards the recapture of Farnham Castle, whose garrison had been extracting money and provisions from the surrounding countryside. Sir William Waller, with a force of horse and dragoons include Colonels John Browne's and Anthony Fane's dragoon regiments. The former regiment had been issued with 600 'short muskets' on 26 August 1642.[16] The strength of Fane's and the other regiments in Waller's force is not known.

On 24 November a warrant was issued for powder, bullets and match to be delivered to Captain Button's 150 dragoons which were to march to reinforce the Royalists garrison of Farnham Castle.[17] However, whether Button's dragoons arrived in time is not known, certainly Button's name is not mentioned in the list of prisoners.

The exact date when Waller recaptured Farnham Castle is not known for certain, some sources give 26 or 29 November and others 1 December, but judging from the evidence it appears Waller attacked the castle on 29 November. John Rushworth in his *Historical Recollections* records that Waller:

> came before it with horse and dragoons and summoned it; but having no ordnance, they in the Castle condemned the summons whereupon Sir William Waller presently approached with his horse and dragoons and fastened a petard to the gate of the Castle, which broke the gate to pieces. Yet they could not presently enter by reason they within had placed great piles of wood, which being removed by Waller's soldiers they presently entered further into the Castle, whereupon they within yielded themselves upon quarter.

The Parliamentarian news-sheet *Special Passages* gives a more detailed account of the storming:

> Sir William Waller prosecuted his design with so good success that after he came before Farnham Castle within three hours he forced his approach so near the Castle's gates, that with a petard blew one of them open, and made his entrance, whereupon the Cavaliers threw their arms over the wall, falling down upon their knees crying for quarter … which Sir William Waller did give them, not suffering a soldier to affront them, though extremity (according to the law of arms) they should have been all put to the sword, there being sufficient provocation for it, considering that Colonel Fane, brother to the Earl of Westmoreland (who carried

16 TNA WO 55/1937 no folio, Warrant to the Board of Ordnance signed by Essex on 25 August 1642. Delivery was acknowledged the following day.

17 TNA WO 55/423 part 1 f.47, Warrant to deliver 'a competent portion of powder, bullet and shot to 150 dragoons', 24 November 1642.

> himself very valiantly at the assault, and hath more true noble English blood in his veins than the Earl, or any of his brothers have) was shot through the cheek, and divers others wounded, yet revenge was not suffered to be taken … Sir William Waller let all these Cavaliers that had horses ride on horseback to London, and for such as were on foot, hired carts to bring them to Parliament, being about 80 of them … Sir William Waller and Colonel Fane took in the Castle, Master Denham, the high Sheriff of Surrey, Captain Hudson, Captain Brecknox and diverse other persons of quality, with 100 vulgar persons, and all the arms and ammunition in the Castle, and about 4,000 pounds in money and plate; and the common soldiers had pillage to a good value.[18]

Waller had a narrow escape during the storming, from a 'very near shot', he wrote, 'from one of my own men as he followed me in to a narrow passage after I was entered.'[19] Fane died from his injuries on 9 December and was buried at Kingston upon Thames two days later.

Farnham Castle was the first Royalist stronghold to be stormed in England during the Civil War. However Clarendon is contemptuous about the Royalists at Farnham and he gives Marlborough this honour, writing 'I cannot call Farnham Castle in Surrey one, whither some Gentlemen who were willing to appear for the King had repaired, and were taken with less resistance than was fit … and before it deserved the name of a garrison.'[20]

On 1 December the prisoners were taken up to London, via Windsor, and there the rank and file were given the choice of imprisonment or swearing not to bear arms against Parliament again and then released. However some prisoners did not take up this offer, because on 23 December the House of Commons ordered them to be held at Lambeth House.

Hearing of the events at Farnham, the Marquess of Winchester wrote to the King on 2 December:

> Since by your command your majesty's forces at Basingstoke are drawing off, and the enemy now lying within less than 10 miles of this place, I conceive this case [Basing House] to be in apparent danger and cannot be long kept without some assistance from your Majesty's army; for from this county no relief is to be expected it standing for want of your presence and some authority to command it divided in itself.
>
> If this house be any ways considerable for your majesty's service and advantage, be pleased to take it into your consideration and protection least I be necessitated to leave it to the will of the enemy, I reserve more particulars to the relation of this bearer in case your majesty will vouchsafe to speak with him. My duty and affection to your Majesty's Service occasions this address.[21]

---

18 BL TT E.129/5 *Special Passages and Certain information from Several Places*, 29 Nov to 6 Dec 1642 (London, Humphrey Blunden, 1642).

19 Waller, *Recollections*, p.109.

20 Clarendon, *History of the Rebellion* (Clarendon Press, 1826), vol. 3 book vi, p.342.

21 Hampshire Record Office 48M80/F1 Letter from the Marquess of Winchester at Basing to King Charles I about the danger to Basing in the Civil War, 2 December 1642.

Basing House would become a thorn in Parliament's side for the next three years and any convoy travelling through Hampshire from Surrey would need to be escorted by troops from Farnham or Godalming.

Meanwhile for the next few weeks Waller remained at Farnham, lodging at The Bush, and his major, Horatio Cary at The George. Major Nathaniel Whetham, of Colonel Browne's Regiment of Dragoons, which had taken part in the storming, was appointed governor of the castle and Waller and Colonel Sir Richard Onslow of Surrey issued warrants on 17 December summoning each member of the Farnham Company of the Surrey trained bands, 'or an able man in their place', as a substitute, to act as a garrison.

By now it was clear that the war would not be over by Christmas. With this on her mind, Joan Elliot wrote to her brother Sir Symonds D'Ewes on 7 December, from her house near Godalming:

> We are full of misery and fears, having many soldiers near about us who come often to us and puts us in fear. We had yesterday threescore of Parliament's troopers with their commanders, we were fain to give them meat and drink and money to content them, I thank God they did us no clear harm but it will be a great burden for us to bare. Our neighbours have left their houses and are gone and many have been plundered and these fearing the worst for their going. God give me heart and resolution to stay where he had placed me among my poor children and household and I doubt not but God's blessed protection will still be over us and keep us as he hath hitherto done if not I know he will give me strength answerable to the burden he pleaseth to lay upon us. I heartily beg of God a happy peace in this distracted kingdom for Christ's sake.[22]

On 11 December, her husband, Sir William Elliot echoed his wife's fears to D'Ewes:

> I hold it altogether inconvenient for me to be absent from my house or country, being never free from soldiers of one side or other. And have been visited by them, although sustained hitherto little damage by them … I beseech God set an end to these miseries under which most of the southern and northern counties of this Kingdom do much suffer, and must do much more to the ruin of the whole, if a blessed peace or a present fight give not a determination thereunto.[23]

With his affairs at Farnham almost complete Waller looked towards the recapture of Winchester, which had recently declared for the King. The Royalist governor, Sir William Ogle, had few troops at his disposal, and despite being reinforced by Lord Grandison with four troops of horse and 600 dragoons, this force was not strong enough to defend the city.

Fortunately for Waller, who also lacked sufficient troops, when Colonel Browne's Regiment of Dragoon broke into the city the Royalists did not put up much of a fight but withdrew to the castle. Ogle and Grandison were able to retire, because according to the laws of war since they had stormed the

22 BL Harl ms 382 f.18 Joan Elliot to her brother Sir Symonds D'Ewes, 7 December 1642.

23 BL Harl ms 383 f.207 Sir William Elliot toSir Symonds D'Ewes, 11 December 1642.

city Waller's men began to demand their right to plunder Winchester, which Waller reluctantly agreed to, despite the Mayor offering £1,000 not to do so.

On 16 December news of Winchester's surrender was brought to the Committee for the Safety of the Kingdom in London, which resolved that the churches in London and Westminster and the suburbs should hold a service of thanksgiving on the next Sunday; Theodore Jennings, who brought the news, was to receive £20 for 'his good service'.[24]

From Winchester Waller marched to Chichester, which had been seized by Edward Ford for the Royalist cause on 16 November. From Chichester Ford was able to strike out at other parts of Sussex, with the Parliamentarian forces powerless to resist. Therefore it was not until the middle of December that Waller was able to march into Sussex. On 20 December, Waller and Colonel Herbert Morley, the local Parliamentarian commander, arrived at the city. The siege of Chichester lasted a week, with the city surrendering to Waller, and on 28 December the Royalist commanders were sent to London as prisoners. In less than a month Waller had secured Sussex and Surrey and most of Hampshire.

24 *Journal of the House of Commons,* volume 2, p.892.

2

William the Conqueror

On 11 February 1643 the Earl of Essex and Lord General of the Parliamentarian Army appointed Waller, 'Sergeant Major General of all the forces of the county of Gloucester… Wiltshire, Somerset and Shropshire that are already raised and to be raised for the defence of King, Parliament and kingdom and suppressing of the malignant party there.' Waller also had 'authority to raise five regiments of horse and five of foot in the said counties'.[1]

On Sunday 22 March Waller marched out of Bristol with "competent force" of about 3–4,000 horse and dragoons and 2,000 foot, accompanied by "Sir Edward Hungerford and great store of gentry of those parts." That evening Colonel Burghill fell upon a troop of Royalist horse at Sherston in Wiltshire. According to the Parliamentarian Scout Master General, Sir Samuel Luke, after four sentries were killed the whole troop surrendered, with the loss of just one man of Parliament's side. The following day Waller marched on Malmesbury arriving on 24 March. The town's governor, Sir Herbert Lunsford, hearing of Waller's advance, sent out a party of horse to confront the advancing Parliamentarians. After an initial show of force, the Royalist cavalry withdrew leaving their infantry to defend Malmesbury.

Waller sounded a parley for the town to surrender, but according to Luke the Royalist 'replied with a great deal of scorn and disgrace that they would not do it, and thereupon hung out there above four bloody flags upon the castle.'[2]

Undaunted Waller pressed forward, the Royalist foot making use of the gardens within the town to harass his advance. Soon the lower part of the town was in parliamentarian hands, with the Royalists withdrawing to the upper part of the town which had been fortified. According to Waller:

1 C.H. Firth, and R.S. Rait, *Acts and Ordinances of the Interregnum, 1642–1660* (London: HMSO, 1911), pp.79–80, Ordinance to Appoint Sir William Waller Sergeant Major General of the forces in Gloucester and other adjacent counties and for paying his army, 11 February 1643.

2 Sir Samuel Luke, *Journal of Sir Samuel Luke*, vol. 1 (The Oxfordshire Record Society, 1947), p.43.

Page from Henry Hexham's drill book, showing postures of musketeers. (Author's collection)

We fell on upon the west Port, in which they had cast us a breastwork and planted a piece of Ordnance. The street so narrow at the upper end next the work that not above four could march in breast, this business cost hot water. As we fell on we advanced two drakes, and under that favour our musketeers possessed themselves of some houses near the Port from whence we galled the enemy very much. If our men had come out roundly we had then carried it, but the falling of some cooled the rest. And so the first assault failed, after a fight of near half an hour.

Whilst we were preparing to renew the assault the enemy showed himself near the town with seven or (as some say) 10 troops of horse. Whereupon Sir Arthur Heselrige fell out upon them with eight troops, but upon his approach they retired speedily. In the meantime before his return we gave on again upon the town and had a very hot fight, which after an hour's continuance at the least we were fain to give over for want of ammunition, the main part whereof was unluckily stayed behind by a mischance of the carriage and could not come up till the next morning. I was in such want of powder, and especially ball, that if the enemy had fallen out upon me I could have maintained a very small fight, and I had no notice thereof from the officer until I was reduced to this straight.[3]

Looking towards West Port from the location of the West Wall Gate in Malmesbury. (T. Harris)

3 BL TT E.94/12, *A Letter from Sir William Waller to the Earl of Essex of a great victory he obtained at Malmesbury.*

Extensive pockmarking of various calibres on the wall of Malmesbury Abbey. Evidence of the hard fighting that took place around a town that was very much in the front line during the Civil War. (T. Harris)

With little or no ammunition Waller decided to mask his withdrawal by a bluff, and at 2:00 a.m. to mask the noise of the drawing off of his two drakes he had 'the drums beat and trumpets to sound' as if he was going to launch another assault. Fearing this, the Royalists sounded a parley and surrendered the town. According to Waller 300 Royalist foot and a troop of horse surrendered, Luke states that Colonel Herbert Lunsford and 'many other commanders, but not above 3,000 common soldiers with 14 colours and some 30 troopers' were captured. Although, according to John Rushworth, 'near 300 common soldiers' plus a piece of ordnance and some ammunition were captured. The commanders were sent to Bristol, while the common soldiers were imprisoned in the church.[4]

Sir Edward Hungerford was left to garrison the town with his own regiment of foot and a company of dragoons, plus enough ammunition and 200 muskets to arm the local inhabitants. However, shortly afterwards Hungerford 'for reasons best known to himself' abandoned the town. After capturing Malmesbury Waller looked to capture Cirencester, which was being used as the headquarters of the Royalists in the West, but hearing that Prince Rupert had reinforced the garrison, he, along with a force under the

4 Luke, *Journal*, vol. 1, p.43; Rushworth, *Historical Collections*, vol. 5, 1642–1645.

governor of Gloucester, Edward Massey, turned his attention to the small Royalist army in the Severn Valley. Crossing the Severn in boats Waller marched to Huntley and then Higham, where he surprised a Royalist force and captured about 150 commanders including many gentlemen of Wales and Herefordshire and '1,444 common soldiers well armed'. What happened to these prisoners Waller does not say, but he continues;

> We then marched to Wales, the Welch left their garrisons, they quitted Newman, Rossebridge, Monmouth, Chepstow, we entered those towns, very weary of the Welsh ways over the mountains, and sensible of their wants.[5]

Hearing that the armies of Prince Maurice and Lord Herbert were closing in on his position, Waller could either confront Herbert's Army, which would mean that he would have to march further into Wales away from his base, or retire to Gloucester, 'through Prince Maurice's Army'. He chose the latter and on 10 April he sent away his ordnance and baggage, which was escorted by his infantry, while Waller with his horse and dragoons marched all night towards Chepstow hoping to fall upon Prince Maurice's forces which were quartered at Newnham, Michael Deane and Rosse. However, Waller arrived too late to beat up the Royalist quarters at Newnham. Hearing of Waller's advance the Royalists quartered there fell back to Little Dean, where Waller:

> found their foot in a body, and their horse on a hill upon the other side of the town, their foot came towards us, and having given one volley of shot, they retired, and our dragoons following in order entered the town, so we had full possession of the Prince's quarters; we stood about three hours expecting their charge, the report being they had vowed we should never return.[6]

Waller states that his aim was not to give battle, but 'when they saw us gone, they came down from the hill and fell hotly on our forlorn hope, and some few they killed, and some they took; we conceive their loss was as great, that they lost as many men, and two of very good quality; last night we came to Gloucester.' This was the 11 April, and Waller penned the letter the following day, as a postscript he added, 'we are now marching towards Tewkesbury'.[7]

Prince Maurice, mounted. (The Turton Collection)

5 'A Letter from Sir William Waller to Both Houses of Parliament, 12 April 1643', in John Washbourne, *Bibliotheca Gloucestrensis, a collection of scarce and curious tracts relating to the county and city of Gloucester illustrative of and published during the Civil War* (Gloucester, 1825), p.196.

6 'A Letter from Sir William Waller to Both Houses of Parliament, 12 April 1643'.

7 'A Letter from Sir William Waller to Both Houses of Parliament, 12 April 1643'.

On 13 April while Waller was advancing north up the Severn, they met Prince Maurice at Ripple a village about three and a half miles from Tewkesbury. Waller's force occupied the high ground known as Old Nan's Hill or Ordnance Hill and could see Maurice's army deploying in front of him. Both sides were roughly 2,000 strong, although Waller's force was composed of mainly cavalry and dragoons, with only a company of foot with some artillery pieces. Waller ordered some of his cavalry to charge, but when these were repulsed, he decided to withdraw, ordering his dragoons and musketeers to cover his retreat towards Ripple itself. Seeing that Waller was withdrawing, Prince Maurice ordered part of his force to attack the

Looking along Waller's position's on Old Nan's Hill ridgeline at Ripple. (Photo Charles Singleton)

Parliamentarian dragoons, which were driven back. The dragoons disordered the musketeers, which had lined some hedges at the entrance to a lane that Waller's cavalry was withdrawing down. Meanwhile a second force of Royalist cavalry managed to work their way around Waller's flank. To meet this new threat Sir Arthur Heselrige charged with his cavalry but was repulsed. The Royalists pursued Waller's army along the Tewkesbury Road, until they met a detachment of the garrison from the town marching to Waller's aid. The musketeers from Tewkesbury put up a firefight, which enabled Waller's men to rally and the Royalists gave up the pursuit.

After his defeat Waller withdrew to Gloucester, but he had not finished with South Wales. At the end of April he advanced into Herefordshire and on 25 April, after a brief siege, Hereford surrendered to Waller. Waller agreed that the officers and soldiers should have quarter and that the town was not to be plundered and the 'ladies civilly treated'. The Royalist commanders were sent to Gloucester as prisoners.[8]

8 Rushworth, *Historical Collections*, vol. 5, 1642–1645.

Harquebusiers engaged in the firefight. Johan Jacobi von Wallhausen 'Ritterkuns', 1616. (Michał Paradowski's archive)

In his *Recollections* Waller recorded:

> In my retreat from Chepstow, when Prince Maurice had lined all the passages between that and Gloucester, with a very considerable army, to intercept me: I had no way left, but to transport my foot and train of artillery cross the Severn to Berkeley Castle (from whence they were secured) and with my horse and dragoons to beat through his quarters: upon the march that night through the Forrest of Dean; it happened through the sleepiness of an officer, that the main body was separated a great distance from the fore troop (with which I marched) so that I was fain to make a halt for above half an hour, within little more than a mile from the Princes headquarters, in broad daylight, the alarm taken, and not 120 horse with me. Nevertheless it pleased God in his infinite mercy to direct the rest of my troops to me, and under the conduct of his providence, I made a safe and an honourable retreat to Gloucester, in despite of the enemy who charged me in the rear, but with more loss to him than to me.[9]

On 2 June Robert Cooke, Colonel Burghill and other officers wrote to William Lenthall, the speaker of the House of Commons, warning him that:

> It is true that God's blessing upon Sir William Waller's weak forces hath often raised our admiration and engaged our thankfulness… But at this time Sir Ralph Hopton is marching very strong from Cornwall, Prince Maurice with the Lord Marquess strong and increasing in power are advancing towards him; if they meet the conjunction will in time prove dangerous to you, present to us. Our desires

9 Waller, *Recollections*, pp.109–110.

> are to interfere and with hazard to endeavour a prevention, but our men are not only too few to encounter theirs, but, which is worse, too many to be paid by us, and the want of money hath bred such mutinous dispositions in the soldiers that no arguments will make them stir. If by your advise his Excellency would be pleased to supply us with forces proportionable to that party that is advanced from Oxford, where we little expected spare forces for remote attempts, and that you would be pleased to supply us speedily with a good sum of money, we should hope, by God's assistance, to afford you such an account as may justify your thrift for the Commonwealth in redeeming a heavy rent with a reasonable fine. You may perhaps hear a noise of new regiments raising, and so over value the strength of these parts, but the truth is for want of money neither can the new be completed nor the old encouraged. If we can obtain no supply we must wait upon God, and petition him to list our preservation amongst his wonders; or if we sink under the burden, it must suffice that we have done our duty to our country in troubling you with these necessary though unpleasant lines.[10]

On 9 June Lenthall wrote to Waller, assuring him:

> that although for the present they cannot send you relief proportionable to their desires and your merit, yet they have resolved to send you a further supply with as much speed as the condition of their affairs can admit. And have given an express command to two worth members… to take a more particular care of you in the absence of Sir Arthur Heselrige.[11]

However, despite the Committee of Gloucestershire's pleas and Lenthall's reassurances to Waller, they could not hold back Sir Ralph Hopton, who had been battling through Cornwall and Devon, which he finally managed to secure on 16 May at the battle of Stratton. Stratton allowed Hopton's small Royalist army to enter Somerset and unite with the forces of Prince Maurice and the Marquess of Hertford. According to the concept of honour both Maurice and Hertford should have taken command of the combined armies, since Hopton was a mere knight. True, on paper they were in command of the army, but neither were as capable a general as Hopton and they allowed him to take command in the field. Their combined armies were 2,000 horse, 4,000 foot, 300 dragoons and 14 to 16 guns. Among this number were 3,000 Cornish foot which, according to Hopton, were 'all old soldiers' with a string of successes in battle behind them. Despite drawing detachments from the various garrisons, including Bristol, Waller had a much smaller army with 2,000 foot, 2,500 horse and 500 dragoons. At about this time Horatio Carey, who had been with Waller since Edgehill and had risen to the rank of colonel, deserted to the Royalists.

The Royalists' plan was to occupy Wells, Taunton, Bridgewater etc., and so surround Waller's base at Bath. Taunton fell to the Royalists at the beginning of June without a short being fired; according to Colonel Edward Popham

10 HMC 13th report, Appendix 1, *The Manuscripts of His Grace The Duke of Portland, preserved at Welbeck Abbey* (London: HMSO, 1891), p.712, Robert Cooke, Colonel Burghill and others of the Committee at Gloucestershire to William Lenthall, 2 June 1643.

11 HMC 13th Report, Appendix 1, p.713, William Lenthall to Sir William Waller, 9 June 1643.

Drill postures for pike, from Henry Hexham. (Author's collection)

the townspeople had mutinied against the garrison, and Popham believed the town of Bridgewater had also surrendered.[12]

As the Royalists advanced on Wells, the Parliamentarians fell back towards Glastonbury, where his cavalry faced the pursuing Royalists several times to allow their infantry to withdraw to Chewton Mendip.According to Richard Atkyns, a captain in Prince Maurice's Regiment of Horse:

> We had two very hard days march thither: but before we came to Glastonbury, we had intelligence of some forces newly raised, marching towards their body; whom acommanded party of ours pursued, and did some execution upon... When we came to Wells, intelligence was given us, that Sir William Waller's army was drawn out on that side of Bath; we marched toward them as far as Chewton, which I suppose, is about halfway; the sun was then an hour high, and many of our horse and foot tired with our march; so the foot had orders to quarter at Wells, as the headquarters, and the horse thereabouts.[13]

While the Royalist army settled down to their quarters, the Lord Carnarvon's Regiment of Horse, with or without orders, continued its pursuit. Atkyns continues: 'The Lord Carnarvan with his regiment of horse went to give their whole army an alarm; but came so near them, that for haste, they sent out a fresh regiment of horse. And another of dragoons to fight him.' This appears to have been Waller's own regiment of horse and probably his dragoons. However, Carnarvon's Regiment was:

> much wasted, and his horses tired with the long march, were forced to retreat; and the enemy had the pursuit of them to Chewton, where Prince Maurice was hurt and taken prisoner. We were then a mile in our way towards our quarters when Colonel Brutus Bucke acquainted our regiment with this unwelcome news; which I heard first, having the honour to command the rear division of the regiment.[14]

Without waiting for orders Atkyns decided to assist Carnarvon, and so wheeled about with the rear body of Maurice's Regiment, which according to Atkyns mustered about 100 men. By now it was 'about half an hour before sunset', and Atkyns with Lord Carnarvon and the Lord Arundel of Wardour decided to attack the Parliamentarian cavalry which had formed in two divisions with about 200 dragoons in front of them. However, according to Atkyns a mist suddenly came down and masked the Royalists' charge, which made the dragoons mount their horses after one volley and gallop off. This mist dissipated as quickly as it had descended leaving the Royalist cavalry to charge their Parliamentarian counterparts. The Parliamentarian dragoons on

12 Rev. O. Ogle, and W.H. Bliss, *Calendar of the Clarendon State Papers preserved at the Bodleian Library,* vol. 1 (Oxford: Clarendon Press, 1872), p.241, Colonel Edward Popham at Glastonbury to Colonel Nathaniel Fiennes, 5 June 1643.

13 Richard Atkyns, ed. Peter Young and Norman Tucker, 'The Vindication of Richard Atkyns', in *Military Memoirs, the Civil War, Richard Atkyns and John Gwyn* (London: Longmans, Green and Co. Ltd, 1967), pp.14–15.

14 Atkyns, *Vindication*, pp.14–15.

the wings of their cavalry were unable to fire, 'seeing us so mixed with their men', and also mounted and galloped off leaving their cavalry to its fate.[15]

According to Atkyns, during the cavalry melee 'I gave one Captain [Edward] Kightley quarter twice, and at last he was killed: the Lord Arundel of Wardour also, took a dragoon's colour.' However he continues, 'though this was [a] very great success, yet we were in as great danger as ever; for now were in disorder and had spent our shot; and had not time to charge [i.e. reload] again.' With the left-hand division of the Parliamentarian cavalry broken and with half the Royalist cavalry in pursuit Atkyns now turned his attention on the right-hand division, and with 'not 30 men' he charged three troops of fresh cavalry, which was also routed since they had not yet deployed because of a wagon yard in their way.[16]

However, the Earl of Clarendon gives a different series of the events, the Earl of Carnarvon having routed a party of Waller's cavalry, pursued the fleeing Parliamentarians until they came upon a stronger body of Parliamentarian cavalry and so Carnarvon's regiment was forced to flee 'broken and chased by the enemy: who immediately drew up a large front of horse and dragoons, much stronger than the Prince's party, who had only his own and Carnarvon's Regiments, with some gentlemen volunteers.' Seeing this Prince Maurice deployed his cavalry and charged 'so vigorously, that he utterly broke and routed that part of the front… But almost half the enemy's horse that, being extended larger that his [Maurice's] front were not charged, wheeled about, and charged the Prince in the rear.' Maurice is said to have received 'two shrewd hurts in his head and was beaten off his horse' and captured in the melee that followed. He was only rescued when Carnarvon's regiment, which had rallied by this time, charged the Parliamentarian cavalry's rear and managed to drive them off.[17]

A lull in the fighting followed for several weeks. It was during this lull that Hopton wrote to Waller. Unfortunately, Hopton's letter has not survived so we do not know its contents, but it seems that he wanted to meet his old friend. Waller's reply has survived and is seen as prime example of the tragedy of the Civil War:

> Certainly my affections to you are so unchangeable, that hostility itself cannot violate my friendship to your person, But I must be true to the cause wherein I serve. The old limitation *usque ad aras*[as far as the altar], holds still, and where my conscience is interested, all other obligations are swallowed up. I should most gladly wait on you according to your desire, but that I look upon you as you are engaged in that party beyond a possibility of retreat, and consequently uncapable of being wrought upon by any persuasion. And I know the conference could never be so close between us, but that it would take wind and receive a construction to my dishonour. That great God which is the searcher of my heart knows with what sense I go upon this service, and with what a perfect hatred I detest this war without an enemy; but I look upon it as *Opus Domini* [the work of the Lord], which is enough to silence all passion in

15 Atkyns, *Vindication*, pp.14–15.
16 Atkyns, *Vindication*, pp.14–15.
17 Clarendon, *History of the Rebellion* (Oxford: University Press, 1839), vol. 4, book vii, pp.107–110.

> me. The God of peace in his good time send us peace, and in the meantime fit us to receive it. We are both upon the stage and must act those parts that are assigned us in this tragedy. Let us do it in a way of honour and without personal animosities.

This was not the only gallantry shown. In an undated letter, King Charles states:

> Our will and pleasure is and we do hereby charge and command you and every of you to suffer Mr Malachy Dudeny and Samuel Somester etc being servants of Sir William Waller knight with their horses and a coach and six horses quietly to pass from London into our county of Devon and there attend and wait on the person of Miss Waller daughter of the said Sir William Waller and to bring her from thence to London… with her said servants, coach and horses and other necessaries quietly to pass without any manner of let hindrance or molestation whatsoever and further that you offer them civil and courteous entertainment in all places through which they shall pass in their said journey.[18]

This was probably a pass for safe passage for Margaret Waller, who had been baptised at Exeter Cathedral in February 1633 and so was about 10 years old at this time.[19]

However, the ceasefire soon came to an end, and on 20 June 1643 the *Weekly Intelligencer* reported that:

> Waller's army about Wells is very strong having great store of horse and many pieces of ordnance also there are eight or 10 troops more going to him and that he is like to have a complete and well armed army being joined with Sir Edward Hungerford, Colonel [Alexander] Popham and John Horner, Sir Walter Earle, Colonel [William] Strode and some others and six gallant troops of horse which went to him from London the last week under the command of Sir Arthur Heselrige. Some troops are reported to come to him out of Devonshire, so that the horse and foot, counting the Trained Bands that advance with him, Sir William is conceived to be full 10,000 strong."[20]

On 22 June Waller and Heselrige wrote to William Lenthall:

> We cannot acquaint you with our condition. We have a body of horse by God's Blessing able to do the kingdom good service. The enemy's horse still at Wells, that part of the country is altogether unfit for horses it grieves our soul, We dare not attempt what we desire. We must not hazard your trust like fools neither can we stay here and starve. We have long and often supplicated you for money, find us but a way to live without it or else we humbly beg a present supply if not this horse will certainly disband which thought makes our hearts to bleed.[21]

18 BL Harlms 6804 f.62.
19 Adair, *Roundhead General*, p.31.
20 BL TT E.55/8 *The Weekly Intelligencer,* 13–20 June 1643, p.188.
21 Bodleian Library Tanner ms 62A/123, Sir William Waller and Sir Arthur Heselrige to William Lenthal, Speaker of the House of Commons, 22 June 1643. British Library microfilm reel 24.

> The Marquess and Prince [Maurice] stayed at Wells about 10 or 12 days to refresh their troops, Sir William Waller in the meantime holding his quarter about Bath, whither there came to his assistance Sir Arthur Heselrige with a very strong Regiment of extraordinary armed horse (by the royalists surnamed the Lobsters because of their bright iron shell with which they were all covered).[22]

John Vicars refers to Waller's army as 'a flying army of horse', but he desperately needed infantry. In a letter dated the 24 June Edward Cooke, an officer in Waller's army, wrote to Colonel Nathaniel Fiennes, the governor of Bristol, asking for 'some 500 commanded men' from the garrison to be sent 'with all possible speed', since Waller 'hath not 500' foot. Fiennes was reluctant to weaken Bristol's garrison in case he was attacked, but later claimed that he sent Colonel Alexander Popham's 'new raised' regiment of foot, 'very well armed' and about 1,200 strong. However, there is evidence that Fiennes also sent a detachment of his own regiment to Waller, since in 1649 Christopher Coles appealed to the Wiltshire Quarter Sessions claiming to have been in Captain Thomas Eyre's company of Fiennes' Regiment of Foot at Roundway Down, where his father was killed and he was wounded.[23] Fiennes' trial also found that he had only sent between 700 to 800 to Waller, rather than the 1,200 he had claimed. The Bristol contingent appears to have arrived the day after the battle of Lansdown, but is known to have been at Roundway Down, where Popham's Regiment is said to have 'lost all their arms, (not many of these men returning to Bristol, and those without arms).'[24]

It was not just Bristol that had supplied detachments from their garrisons. Fearing the absence of some of his garrison might lead to a 'second revolt' around Weymouth, Sir Walter Erle of Wareham complained to the speaker of the House of Commons that:

> A command comes from Sir William Waller for me to march towards him with all the strength that I can make; at the same instant, comes another to require me to provide 300 musketeers to be laid abroad my Lord of Warwick's fleet, which is bound for the west, neither of which can any way consist with the safety of this county and those places of importance in it... if either of them be yielded unto I shall... be brought into a far worse condition than ever I was in before... [Nevertheless] I have in the first place given order fortwo troops of horse, such as they are to join with those of Hampshire, and to to march towards Sir William Waller, though with no small hazard, and am now giving order for 200 musketeers to be put aboard the fleet.[25]

---

22 Sir Ralph Hopton, *Bellum Civile, Sir Ralph Hopton's Narrative of his Campaigns in the West, 1642–1644*, ed. C.E.H. Chadwyck Healey (Somerset Record Society, 1902, vol. xviii), p.51.

23 Stuart Peachey and Alan Turton, *The Fall of the West*, volume 7 (Bristol: Stuart Press, 1994) p.737.

24 John Vicars, *England's Worthies under whom all the civil and bloudy wars since anno 1642 to anno 1647 are related,* reprinted (London, Benbow, 1821) p.37; Hopton, *Bellum Civile,* p.89, Edward Cooke to Colonel Nathaniel Fiennes, 24 June 1643; T.B. Howell, *A Complete Collection of State Trials and proceedings for high treason and other crimes and misdemeanors...* vol. 4, 1640–1649 (London: Longman, Hurst..., 1816), pp.257, 292.

25 HMC 13th report, Appendix 1, pp.716–717, Sir Walter Erle to William Lenthall, Wareham, 30 June 1643.

On 25 June Waller wrote to William Lenthall, the speaker of the House of Commons, thanking him for 'these poor troops, which came very seasonably to keep life in us, even when we were in a gasping condition.' Unfortunately, Waller does not say where these reinforcements came from and their strength, but the following day Sir Samuel Luke reported, 'that Sir William Waller's horse and foot were about 8,000 for the present, but he expected three regiments of foot more, one from Borstall, one from Gloucester and another from Portsmouth, and that the enemy's forces are reported to be 15,000.'[26]

According to Sir John Byron, at the battle of Roundway Down, despite these reinforcements, Waller had five infantry regiments mustering about 2,500 men, six cavalry regiments of 2,500 men, a regiment of dragoons and seven brass cannon. As already stated Waller's infantry included Fiennes and Popham. Waller had commissioned Robert Cooke, Thomas Stephen and Sir Horatio Carey to each raise a regiment of foot in Gloucestershire in the spring of 1643, but how far advanced these were is not known. According to secondary sources there may have also been detachments of Tom Essex's and Sir John Meyrick's regiments with Waller. According to the accounts of Colonel William Strode, his weak regiment appears to have been garrisoning Bath and Bristol at the time of the battles of Lansdown and Roundway Down.[27]

At the beginning of July the Royalists were on the offensive again, entering Bradford on Avon on the 2 July; Waller set out to intercept them at Claverton Down, but the following day weight of numbers began to tell on his army and he was forced to withdraw to Bath again. Hopton thought about occupying Lansdown Hill, but decided to wait for Prince Maurice arrive. When the Royalists finally decided to occupy the hill they found Waller already waiting there.

The battle was fought over three hills, Toghill, Freezing Hill and Lansdown. The steepest hill, which Captain Richard Atkyns of Maurice's Regiment of Horse describes as like 'the eaves of a house for steepness', was Lansdown Hill. The Royalist newsbook *Mercurius Aulicus* describes it as 'a place of very great advantage'.[28] Walter Slingsby, who commanded Lord Mohan's Regiment of Foot, describes it as 'a piece of ground almost inaccessible'. To add to this position, Slingsby adds:

> [On] the brow of the hill, he had raised breastworks in which his cannon and great store of small shot was placed; on either flank he was strengthened with a thick wood which stood upon the declining of the hill, in which he had put store of musketeers; on his rear he had a fair plain where stood ranged his reserved of horse and foot; some bodies of horse with musketeers he bestowed upon some other places of the hill, where he thought there was any access; thus fortified stood the Fox [Waller] gazing at us.[29]

---

26 HMC 13th report, Appendix 1, p.714, Sir William Waller to William Lenthall, 25 June 1643; Luke, *Journal*, vol. 2, p.105.

27 TNA SP 28/175/1 unfolio, Accounts of Colonel William Strode of the county of Somerset, 1642–1643.

28 *Mercurius Aulicus*, 8 July 1643.

29 Walter Slingsby, account of Lansdown printed in Hopton's *Bellum Civile,* pp.94–97.

The view towards Freezing Hill and the Royalist advance from the base of Lansdown Hill. (Photo: David Wilton)

Hopton also mentions these breastworks, which were made of 'faggots and earth'. About 'a demi culverin shot' or about 400 paces behind Waller's army was a stone enclosure for sheep. Although Slingsby puts the wall 'within musket shot' or about 80 yards and Atkyns at 'half musket shot' or 40 yards once they had obtained the hill, it is not known where they were standing when they estimated these distances.

Slingsby recalls that:

> our whole Army was ranged in order of battle upon the large corn field near Tughill. In this posture we continued about two hours; nothing passing but loose skirmishes upon Tughill, betwixt a party of our vanguard and a party of horse and dragoons of the enemy sent down the hill for that purpose.

Atkyns recalls that, 'The ground we stood in, was like a straight horn, about six score yards over at the end towards Marshfield, and 20 score over at the end towards their army; on both sides enclosed with a hedge, and woods without that.'[30]

30 Atkyns, *Vindication*, p.17.

Since the Royalists were deployed on a lower hill than the Parliamentarians, they could not see the movements of Waller's army. Therefore according to Atkyns the battle opened with some skirmishing, which lasted, 'four or five hours, we sent parties out of each body to skirmish, where I think we had the better.'[31]

Hopton also mentions these skirmishes:

> About eight that morning being the 5th of July 1643 all drew forth and within a very short time a light skirmish was engaged with dragoons in the hedges on each side; but the chief commanders of the King's Army, considering that the continuing of that kind of fight would be to little effect, but might only waste their ammunition (whereof they had not plenty) drew off and retreated in battle towards their quarter to Marshfield. [32]

Meanwhile Waller, observing the Royalist movements at the top of Lansdown and perceiving that Hopton was beginning to withdraw, decided to launch some of his cavalry in an attack. According to Hopton, Waller 'took the courage to send down great parties of armed horse and dragoons to charge them bothin the rear and flank.'[33] Attacked by cavalry the Royalist army had no choice but to stand and fight. Slingsby continues, 'we faced about again

The area of Waller's initial positions on the brow of Lansdown Hill. (Photo: David Wilton)

31 Atkyns, *Vindication*, pp.17–18.

32 Hopton, *Bellum Civile,* pp.53–54.

33 Hopton, *BellumCivile,* pp.53–54.

and advanced upon them endeavouring to regain our ground where we were before ranged: which we got with much difficulty and hazard, our horse receiving some dangerous foils.'[34] Atkyns puts this movement at about 3:00 p.m. when a party of Parliamentarian cavalry descended the hill:

> commanded by Colonel [Robert] Burghill, Major [Jonas] Vandruske and others; not less than 300, and five or six hundred dragoons on both sides of the hedges, to make way for their advance, and to make good their retreat. And this was boldest thing that I ever saw the enemy do; for a party of less than 1,000 to charge an army of 6,000 horse, foot and cannon in their own ground, at least a mile and a half from their body.[35]

Slingsby also mentions this incident, but suggests that there were far more Parliamentarian cavalry involved:

> The king's Army found that the Rebels would not be drawn to fight but upon extreme advantages; and therefore faced about and marched towards our quarter in order as we had stood which the ground would admit of, being a continuing plain large field all the way to Marshfield; when we had marched near a mile the whole strength of Waller's horse and dragoons descends the hill, and falls upon our rear.[36]

The only Parliamentarian eyewitness account of this stage of the battle was written on 15 July by Edward Harley, who was a captain in Waller's Regiment of Horse, who wrote to his father that both sides faced each other in battle formation, then:

> We fell upon their rear guard and presently began to retreat, which, Sir William perceiving, he sent out a party of horse with musketeers to fall upon them, which they did with very good success, but other parties of our horse being engaged in places of disadvantage were forced to retire to the hill we possessed. The enemy pursued hotly and got that ground where our ordnance was planted, but then our body of horse charged them with as much resolution as could be, and in particular Sir Arthur Heselrige and his regiment received them a push in the thigh with a pike. Our regiment charged twice, and in the second charge my bay horse was killed under me, but I thank God brought me well in this hot service.[37]

Harley was probably with Major Dowett, who according to a Parliamentarian newsbook records:

> Our General Sir William Waller perceiving their army to retreat, immediately commanded Major Dowett to take out a party of 200 horse, and that seconded

34 Slingsby, account in Hopton's *Bellum Civile,* pp.94–97.
35 Atkyns, *Vindication*, p.18.
36 Slingsby, account in Hopton's *Bellum Civile,* pp.94–97.
37 HMC Portland Manuscripts p.112, Edward Harley to Sir Robert Harley at Westminster, 15/25 July 1643.

> by 200 more, commanded by Colonel Carr, both parties advanced towards their army. And charged them so gallantly, that they put all their army to a disorderly retreat, as that their horse took the rear of their foot; but they taking heart again in a full body, with their great artillery caused our party to retire yet orderly, which Sir William perceiving, sent Colonel Burghill with a party to relieve them, and carried all again, which put the enemy to [a] second retreat, but the fight was variously maintained for two hours, at length our foot growing weary, a fresh supply was sent, who being but fresh soldiers, did not make good their ground, which constrained our parties to retreat, after Colonel Burghill had received a shot through his right arm, as his sword was even at the throat of the Lord Carnarvon.

Slingsby also records that the Parliamentarian cavalry did not have it all their own way:

> had not our foot been excellent we had certainly suffered there: The Rebels horse not enduring our charges of horse and volleys of small shot that fell upon them from our approaching bodies of foot, they retired themselves out of that field; but left all their dragoons upon the walls and hedges upon the far end of the field near Tughill from whence our foot beat them suddenly. The enemy's horse being now pressed into the lane that leads over Tughill to Lansdown, were observed to be in some disorder by reason of the narrow and ill passage. Prince Maurice therefore takes all our horse and wings then on both sides [of] the lane within the hedges with small shot, and so smartly fell upon them, that some run in great disorder; but it seems they had (like provident soldiers) placed their best horse in the rear who being compelled, turns about and fights desperately, and there gives our horse another foil with the death of Major Lower, Major James and many others; but our horse being still assisted by the foot, at last beat them down Tughill, where in the bottom they were cruelly galled by our foot that then drew up thick upon Tughill.[38]

Waller is said to have charged several times that day but 'escaped a shower of shot'.[39] Hopton's army returned to its original position, where Waller's artillery once more opened fire on the Royalists below. However, Hopton's Cornish infantry were willing to storm Lansdown, which that morning had seemed so impregnable to the Royalists.

> Now did our foot believe no men their equals, and were so apt to undertake anything, that the hill upon which the Rebels stoodwell fortified little without musket shot (from whence they racked us with their cannon) could not deter them; for they desired to fall on and cried let us fetch those cannon.[40]

38 Slingsby, account in Hopton's *Bellum Civile*, pp.94–97.
39 Waller, *Recollections*, p.110.
40 Slingsby, account in Hopton's *Bellum Civile*, pp.94–97.

Finally, according to Slingsby:

> Order was presently given to attempt the hill with horse and foot: great parties of musketeers was sent out of either of our wings to fall into those woods which flanked the enemy, and in which they had lodged store of small shot for their defence, the horse were to pass up the highway, but were at first repulsed; Sir BevilGrenville then stood on the head of his regiment upon Tughill, who advanced presently putting all his shot upon his left hand within a wall, and carried with him horse on his right hand, the ground being best there for horse, and he himself lead up his pikes in the middle: he gained with much gallantry the brow of the hill receiving all their small shot and cannon from their breastwork, and three charges of horse, two of which he stood: but in the third fell with him many of his men: yethad his appearing upon the ground so disordered the enemy, his own musketeers firing fast upon their horse, that they could not stay upon the ground longer; the rebels' foot took example by their horse and quit their breastworks retiring behind a long stone wall that runs across the down; our foot leaps into their breastworks; our horse draws up upon their ground; our two wings that were sent to fall into the two woods had done their business and were upon the hill as soon as the rest.[41]

Hopton adds to this scene:

> And then the whole army in the best order they could in that broad way that leads to Lansdown advanced towards the enemy, sending out as they went strong parties of musketeers on each hand to second one another, to endeavour under the cover of the enclosed grounds to gain the flank of the enemy on the top of the hill, which they at last did, but the pike and the horse with the rest of the musketeers that advanced up the broad way, as the space would bear, had much to do, by reason of the disadvantage of the ground, the enemy's foot and batteries being under cover of their breastworks and their horse ready to charge upon the very brow of the hill; where the king's forces were five times charged and beaten back with disorder. There was Sir Bevil Grenville slain the head of his pikes and Major Lower in the head of a party of horse, and Sir Nicholas Slanning's horse killed under him with a great shot, and the whole body of horse so discomforted that of 2,000 there did not stand above 600. Yet at last the recovered the hill, and the enemy drew back about demi culverin shot, within a stone wall, but there stood in reasonable good order, and each part played upon the other with their ordnance, but neither advanced being both soundly battered.[42]

The Parliamentarian newsbook states that the Royalists were eager to revenge themselves for the loss of their officers:

> The enemy (enraged by the wounds to their choice commanders, from so small a party of ours) charged up to our ground, which ground after a hard dispute was yielded unto them, partly by force, partly voluntarily, upon good advice that

41 Slingsby, account in Hopton's *Bellum Civile,* pp.94–97.
42 Hopton, *Bellum Civile,* pp.53–54.

considering our horse in number exceeded theirs as much as their foot did ours, we might have sufficient room to fight on.

Finally after much effort the Royalists obtained the top of the hill. According to Slingsby:

> The enemy (observing our front to enlarge it self upon the hill, and our cannon appearing there likewise) began to suspect himself, and drew his whole strength behind that wall, which he lined well with musketeers, and in several places broke down breaches very broad that his horse might charge if their were occasion, which breaches were guarded by his cannon and bodies of pikes.
>
> Thus stood the two armies taking breath looking upon each other, our cannon on both sides playing without ceasing till it was dark, legs and arms flying apace, the two armies being within musket shot: After it was dark there was great silence on both sides, at which time our right wing of shot got much nearer their army lodging themselves amongst the many little pits betwixt the wall and the wood from whence we galled them cruelly.

The Royalist newsbook, *Mercurius Aulicus* records:

> We assaulted again and again, three several times and the fourth time with unimaginable difficulty we possessed the top of it [Lansdown], which Sir BevillGrenville maintained with his stand of Cornish pikes against all the power of horse, foot and cannon, to the wonder and amazement of both friends and enemies, where this brave gentleman was most honourably, though unfortunately slain in front of his men, with his Sergeant Major and captain lieutenant dead at his feet, ending his life with as much honour as mortal flesh is capable of.[43]

The Parliamentarian newsbook continues:

> Both armies being on the plain, [the] charges grew so hot on both sides, as the like was never seen in England; yea some old soldiers did say, '*that the furious fights in France were but a play in comparison of this*.' Not one regiment of ours but charged them horse and foot four or five several time; especially Sir Arthur Heselrige, who charged most bravely, and was himself so far engaged, that had he not gallantly bestirred himself, and killed the man that encountered with him, he had been taken prisoner: in which conflict he received a wound in the thigh at push of pike, but blessed be God no danger in it, being the next day able to walk abroad. And general Sir William Waller (although the chief care of ordering the battle lay upon him) in his own person charged four times upon them.

Mercurius Aulicus continues that after gaining the hill, 'we rallied our horse and drew up our cannon and by that time it grew dark, notwithstanding shot of all sorts played on each other till midnight.'[44] Such was the fierceness of the bombardment the Mayor of Bristol recalled, both sides 'shot plentifully

---

43 *Mercurius Aulicus*, 8 July 1643.

44 *Mercurius Aulicus*, 8 July 1643.

'Wallers Wall', the final defence line of the Parliamentarians at Lansdown. (Photo: David Wilton)

at each from three in the afternoon till 11 of the clock at night which we in Bristol heard and saw them give fire.'[45] Slingsby also mentioned that the battle ended at 11:00 p.m., when:

> we received a very great volley of small shot but not mixed with cannon by which some of us judged that he was retreating, and gave this at his expiring; but the general apprehension through our army was that the enemy had intention to try a push in the night for their ground, which they had so dishonourably lost; for we were then seated like a heavy stone upon the very brow of the hill, which with one lusty charge might well have been rolled to the bottom.
>
> It was not long before we knew certainly that they were gone, at their departure they left all their light matches upon the wall and whole bodies of pikes standing standing upright in order within the wall as if men had held them; we were glad they were gone for if they had not I know who had within an hour; but indeed had our horse been as good as the enemy's the rebels had never gone off the field unruined.

Hopton on the other hand puts it at 1:00 a.m., when:

> all things grew quiet, where Prince Maurice and Sir Ralph Hopton remaining in the heads of the troops all that night, about one of the clock heard an advancing of horse and foot, but without drum or trumpet and they presently received a smart volley from the enemy's musketeers, which was answered with the like,

45 BL TT E.59/25, *A letter from the Mayor of Bristol to a Gentleman.*

The stone wall that acted as Waller's second defensive line at Lansdown. (Photo: David Wilton)

> but being very dark no more was done, and all things grew quiet again. So after an hour's silence the chief commanders before mentioned rightly judging that this might be the enemy's parting blow, gave a common soldier a reward to creep softly towards the place where the enemy stood, to bring certain notice whether they were retreated or no, who found them gone.[46]

The Parliamentarian newsbook states that it was the exhaustion of Waller's army that forced it to withdraw:

> Thus the battle being in continued for the space of nine hours at the least, until the enemy's horse left their foot naked; and night being come on, hindered us from completing our victory.
>
> Our Horse being in continual service for three days and without meat and water for 24 hours, and our foot much scattered, it was held fit by a council of war, that we should return to Bath for refreshing our horse and men and rallying our foot, well knowing we might easily recover the hill, and so fall upon the enemy again to prosecute our victory.
>
> Our retreat was so orderly performed, that the enemy durst not follow us, having now learnt by experience, that our giving ground hath been much to their disadvantage. The next morning, whilst we were preparing for a march, we were informed that the enemy was retreated to their old quarters at Marshfield.

46 Hopton, *Bellum Civile,* pp.53–54.

Among the casualties on Waller's side was Major Strachan, a lieutenant and two cornets, while Heselrige had been wounded and Colonel Burghill was shot through his right arm, which would force him to retire from the army. On the Royalist side the most significant officers lost were Sir Bevil Grenville, Lieutenant Colonel Joseph Wall and Major George Lower. Lord Carnarvon and Colonel Sir Humphrey Bennet were wounded.

According to Rushworth's *Historical Collections*, 'the numbers of Common soldiers lost on either side, are very differently and uncertainly related.' Waller claims that:

> Many of their chief officers were slain or hurt, we lost one one sergeant major [Carr] and two cornets and not 20 common soldiers. We had the advantages of the ground… [but the Royalist infantry] beat us from it, though they bought it at a dear rate when our foot left it we maintained it with our horse.[47]

However, the biggest blow to the Royalists would come on the following day. They were already low on gunpowder and they had allowed some Parliamentarian prisoners to smoke their pipes on the ammunition wagon, which:

> took fire, blew up many men and hurt many: especially my Lord Hopton: Major Shelane died the next day and was much lamented: this disaster encouraged the rebels and discouraged us. Our were bad before but now worse, our foot drooped for their Lord whom they loved and that they had not powder left to defend him, for as I remember we had then but nine barrels left.[48]

Captain Atkyns recalls that 'I found his Lordship [Hopton]miserably burnt, his horse singed like parched leather.' Clarendon says of the incident, that Hopton:

> Was by the blast of the powder thrown from his horse, which was killed, and [he was] so hurt, that he was looked upon as dead for many days, though, by the diligence of his servants, with God's blessing, he recovered… but the marks of that ill accident were never worn out, and deprived him of that graceful and lustre in his person and countenance, which he formerly had.[49]

According to the Mayor of Bristol:

> we hear of which was the next morning following blown up by an accident in which were many killed and dangerously hurt whereof Sir Ralph Hopton was one, who was yesterday carried in his bed to a coach a miserable spectacle, his head being as big as three and both eyes blinded besides which he was shot in his arm a day before, It pleased God to put a wonderful courage into the heart of Sir William Waller and Sir Arthur Heselrige the last charging with his regiment

47 BL Tanner ms 62/164–5, Sir William Waller and Sir Arthur Heselrige to Sir William Lenthall, 12 July 1643.

48 Slingsby's account in Hopton, *Bellum Civile*, pp.94–97.

49 Clarendon, *History of the Rebellion* (Oxford: University Press, 1839), vol. 4, book vii, pp.107–110.

Sir Ralph Hopton. Waller had served with him as a young officer in Bohemia over 20 years prior to the Civil War.

the whole body of the enemy which came up, the horse being lined with pike and musketeers which he broke through and did much execution on them, the battle not ending till 11 o'clock at night, The one retreating to Bath the other to Marshfield.[50]

During this time Waller and Heselrige complained to William Lenthall, 'for the last fortnight we have had scarce leisure to eat and sleep.'[51]

An anonymous letter, probably written by an anonymous colonel of one of Waller's cavalry regiments records that on Sunday the enemy:

retreated to the Devizes, we pursued and fought with him [Hopton] and killed many of his horse, and especially foot: but it being late we durst not enter the town, but still kept the field in a great near Rood. The next morning, being Monday, we drew up to Bagnall hill with our whole body. That night we sent out many parties and drew down to Roundway; we brought in many prisoners, beat the Lord Crawford, took eight colours and some officers.

Thursday night we had resolved on a general assault: but this resolution was scarce taken, but news came that the enemy from Oxford was within two miles, with 2000 horse, which made us draw up to Bagnall Hill, without drum or trumpet. Where we found the enemy in sight, march towards us; we longed to charge them with our horse, which we did with some disadvantage, and were put to a retreat disorderly: But rallied again with the help of our reserve. The enemy came on, and we charged them the second time, and then all our horse were routed, their reserve standing firm. We fled, they followed, yet our foot, being scarce considerable, stood one hour and a half, and forced their horse to retreat divers time: but their foot coming up from the Devizes, made ours leave their arms and fly. We have lost only fifty horse and the most two hundred command soldiers slain and taken prisoners; about five hundred arms. No man of note killed or hurt, only Sir Arthur Heselrige who received a wound in his army and a hurt in his ear, but not dangerous: he fought very bravely. We now we killed many of their best men, but not known to us by name, because we lost the field: We retreated all to this city and hope to make good Bath also.

As this was a great loss to us, so likely to all the west, unless the Lord General suddenly help; however, we acknowledge God's over ruling power in our great deliverance.[52]

On 10 July the Royalists arrived at Devizes, where they held a council of war. It was decided that the horse should slip through Waller's lines that night and

50 BL TT E59/25, *A letter from the Mayor of Bristol to a Gentleman.*

51 Bodleian Library Tanner ms 62A/164, Sir William Waller and Sir Arthur Heselrige to William Lenthal, Speaker of the House of Commons, 12 July 1643.

52 Washbourne, *Bibliotheca Gloucestrensis,* p.202. 'A true relation of the fight…

gallop to Oxford with all speed to raise a relieving force. However, not all the Royalist cavalry appears to have escaped, because anonymous letter, recalls, 'That night Prince Maurice and the Marquis [of Hertford], with most of their horse stole away for Oxford; we did light upon their rear with a small party and took 17 or 18 prisoners.'[53]

The following day:

> We fell upon the town, which they well defended: in the afternoon [they] desired a parley and two hours cessation which on good reason was granted them: but they notconforming to our demands, we fell on again that night, though coldly. The next day Wednesday, we continued our assault, beat them from all their out works and guards: but that day and night being extreme[ly] wet, hindered us much.[54]

Waller made his quarters in a farmhouse from where he ordered his cook to have his supper ready for when he returned after he had viewed his troops. However, when he returned he saw the cook had just started to prepare his meal, so 'in a sudden impatience' Waller resolved not to eat at all, and review his cavalry on Roundway Down, but according to Waller, 'I had not gone above a musket shot', when a party of Royalists raided the farmhouse in an attempt to 'despatch me, and retired in the darkness of night, with safety enough.'[55] Waller put this incident down to Divine Providence, like another incident a few days later:

> I rode with a small party about the quarters, particularly to see how the dragoons were laid. On the further side of the town; and being [*sic*: read beginning] to return back, it pleased God to put it suddenly into my mind, to go by another way than that I came, which some of the party, and some of mine own servants (who stayed behind) not observing, but taking the former way, they were all taken by the enemy, I came back safely.[56]

Meanwhile the Royalist cavalry had covered the 44 miles to Oxford that night, and arrived the next morning. Because of the Queen landing at Bridlington, Charles had taken much of his army to meet her, so Hopton's exhausted cavalry found only Lord Wilmot's and Sir John Byron's cavalry brigades in Oxford. Nevertheless the Royalists acted quickly and on 12 July these brigades, along with the cavalry of Hopton's army under the Earl of Crawford marched out of Oxford, commanded by Lord Wilmot. After rendezvousing with some stragglers of the Western Horse at Marlborough, Wilmot proceeded to Devizes. With only 1,800 horse and two light guns, he appeared near the town on 13 July. A messenger was sent to Hopton to advise him of their approach and that he should draw out his forces when they arrived to attack Waller's army. However, the messenger was intercepted and Parliamentarian patrols informed Waller of the Royalist approach, which

53 Washbourne, *Bibliotheca Gloucestrensis,* p.202. 'A true relation of the fight…

54 Washbourne, *Bibliotheca Gloucestrensis,* p.202. 'A true relation of the fight…

55 Waller, *Recollections*, p.111.

56 Waller, *Recollections*, p.111

according to Waller came as a surprise to him since he believed that Essex was blockading Oxford to prevent any such eventuality. He later claimed that this was a deliberate act on Essex's part since he was jealous of Waller's reputation and many wanted Waller to replace Essex as the Lord General of the Parliamentarian armies. Either way on hearing the news of Wilmot's approach, Waller:

> drew off his horse, foot and cannon to an open plain piece of ground, upon the top of a steep hill from the town, and about a mile's distance from thence, called Roundway Down, where the enemy was to pass and there he put his men in order.[57]

Unfortunately this 'open plain piece of Ground' has not been identified. Byron records, 'we shot off our ordnance from a high hill that overlooks the town', which may be a reference to Roughbridge Hill, which overlooks Roundway Down, whereas 'Waller appeared with his whole army upon an opposite hill within less then two miles of us.' This hill appears to have been Roundway Hill.[58]

When Wilmot's force arrived, much to his surprise instead of finding Hopton's force he found Waller's army ready to intercept him. Seeing his way blocked and with no help from Devizes Wilmot called a council of war, where it was decided that they should fight without Hopton's force. According to Richard Atkyns, Waller drew up his foot 'in the middle between two wings of horse and the cannon before his foot'. This is confirmed by Clarendon who states that Waller 'had placed all his horse in several small bodies at some distance … from [each] other, and all between them his foot and cannon.' Heselrige's Regiment of Cuirassiers 'stood nearest to them, who were men upon whom Waller principally depended … and if they could rout them it was probable it might had a good effect upon their whole army.'[59]

Wilmot drew his own and Sir John Byron's brigade abreast, with Crawford's brigade in reserve, and 'not be employed till it should please God to renew their courage with our success.'[60] Wilmot sent out a forlorn hope to meet the one Waller had sent forward. According to Sir John Byron, the Parliamentarian forlorn hope was 'gallantly encountered by Sergeant Major Paul Smith (who led our Forlorn Hope, consisting of 300 commanded men) and forced them to turn their backs.' Atkyns records:

> we took advantage of [the Parliamentarians' disorder] and immediately charged the whole body; the charge was so sudden that I had hardly time to put on my arms, we advanced a full trot three deep, and kept in order; the enemy kept their station, and their right wing of horse being cuirassiers, were I'm sure five, if not

---

57 Clarendon, *History of the Rebellion*, vol. IV, p.608.

58 English Heritage Battlefield Report: *Roundway Down, 1643* (English Heritage, 1995).

59 Atkyns, *Vindication*, p.23; Clarendon, *History of the Rebellion* (Oxford: University Press, 1839), vol 4, book vii, pp.124–126.

60 Byron, *Relation*.

> six deep, in so close order, that Punchinello himself had he been there, could not have gotten in to them.[61]

Seeing the advancing Royalist cavalry, Heselrige 'rashly led on' his cuirassiers:

> leaving the foot, galloped up the hill and charged the king's forces very disadvantageously, and so were presently put to a disorderly retreat. Yet with the help of their reserve, they rallied and stood a second charge; but then were totally routed.[62]

This is confirmed by Sir John Byron, who states that:

> Sir Arthur Heselrige seconded these [the Parliamentarian forlorn hope] with his formidable Regiment of Lobsters, I mean his cuirassiers who the lieutenant general intermined with his brigade, and forced them to retreat, not so, but that they rallied themselves again and charged the second time, but with worse success. For then my Brigade being drawn up to second my Lord Wilmot, they all ran away that could, and from that time Sir Arthur Heselrige appeared no more in the battle.[63]

According to Clarendon 'all' the Royalists cavalry fell upon Heselrige's Regiment, but this seems unlikely, since there were other bodies of Parliamentarian cavalry in the field.

Clarendon continues: '[Heselrige's Cuirassiers] stood well, and longer than was expected, could not bear that shock; and when they were broken, they fell upon their own next body of horse, and disordered them.'[64]

Edward Walsingham in his biography of Sir John Digby, who commanded a regiment of horse in Wilmot's brigade also mentions this encounter. Digby:

> Commanded a strong body of horse, where with he fell upon Sir Arthur Heselrige's cuirassiers with such resolution and dexterity that many being killed upon the place he put the rest to a shameful rout in which encounter Sir Arthur himself was grievously wounded, but soon after these cuirassiers rallying again at a distance upon a second charge made by Sir John were forced to trust more to their horses heels then their own hands, yet may made more hast then good speed, for in their swift horse race riding upon the spur down the then slippery hills some broke their own necks, or their horses or both.[65]

But it was Atkyns who had the 'honour' of engaging Heselrige, who was in his cuirassier armour. Heselrige:

61 Atkyns, *Vindication*, p.23; Clarendon, *History of the Rebellion* (Oxford: University Press, 1839), vol 4, book vii, pp.124–126.

62 Rushworth, *Historical Collections*.

63 Byron, *Relation*.

64 Clarendon, *History of the Rebellion*, vol. IV, p.609.

65 Edward Walsingham, *Hector Britannicus or Sir John Digby*, in Camden Miscellany vol. XII (London, 1910), p.85.

> discharged his carbine first, but at a distance not to hurt us, and afterwards [fired] one of his pistols, before I came up to him, and [he] missed with both [pistols]: I then immediately struck into him and touched him before I discharged mine; and I am sure I hit him, for he staggered, and presently wheeled off.

At this point Atkyns did not realise that it was Heselrige, but then hearing that it was, he decided to engage him once more:

> I came up to him, and discharged the other pistol at him and I am sure I shot his head, for I touched it before I gave fire, and it amazed him at that present, but he was too well armed all over for a pistol bullet to do him any hurt, having a coat of mail over his arms and a headpiece (I am confident) musket proof, his sword had two edges and a ridge in the middle, and mine [was] a strong tuck; after I had slackened my pace a little, he was gone 20 yards from me riding three quarters speed, and down the side of the hill…about six score paces more I came up to him again… and struck him a good while [with my sword] and tried him from head to saddle and could not penetrate him nor do him any hurt.[66]

Soon Atkyns was joined by his cornet, a Mr Holmes, who 'felt' or touched Heselrige before he discharge his pistol, but it was 'but a flea biting to him'. Finally both Atkyns and Holmes resorted to killing Heselrige's horse, which was unarmoured. With his horse's loss of blood and the offer of quarter Heselrige finally stopped. While Heselrige was fumbling to untie his sword to present it to Atkyns, they were charged by some Parliamentarian troopers who had rallied on seeing Heselrige a prisoner. Atkyns was slightly wounded by a pistol shot in the shoulder and Heselrige managed to escape.[67]

Despite Atkyns' claim, Heselrige did have a number of wounds insomuch that prayers were said for his recovery. However, this encounter may have had a lasting effect on Heselrige because up to this point accounts record his bravery in battle, but from this point we read little about him engaging in battle, and even being accused by Denzil Holles of cowardice at the battle of Cheriton, when he was found crying under a hedge and told to leave the field.[68]

With Heselrige's Regiment of Horse routed, it was Sir John Byron's brigade's turn to attack while Wilmot's brigade reformed:

> Waller drew his whole army down the hill, and advanced with his own brigade of horse, with two pieces of cannon before it, and two great bodies of foot on the left flank of it, these it fell to my share to charge with my brigade, my Lord Wilmot in the meantime rallying his men together to second me if occasion should be. And I marched towards them up the hill, their cannon played upon me at a very near distance, but with very small loss, killing but two in Colonel Sandys' Regiment; The musketeers all this while played upon our flank and hurt and killed some;

66 Atkyns, *Vindication*, pp.23–24.

67 Atkyns, *Vindication*, p.25.

68 John Adair, *Cheriton 1644: the Campaign and the Battle* (Kineton, Roundwood Press, 1973), p.175.

> and another regiment of their horse was watching an opportunity to charge us either in the rear or in the flank, but were hindered by Lord Crawford. By this time we were come very near to Waller's Brigade and the command I gave my men was, that not a man should discharge a pistol till the enemy had spent all his shot, which was punctually observed, so that first they gave us a volley of their carbine, then of their pistols, and then we fell in with them, and gave them ours in the teeth, yet they would not quit their ground but stood pushing for it a pretty space, till it pleased God, (I think) to put new spirit into our tired horse as well as into our men, so that though it were up the hill, and that a steep one, we overbore them and with that violence, that we forced them to fall foul upon other reserves of horse that stood behind to second them, and so swept their whole body of horse out of the field.[69]

Unfortunately, Captain Edward Harley of Waller's Regiment does not record his regiment's part in the fighting that day, except, 'there was a great body of the enemy, which we found afterwards to be between forty and fifty colours of horse besides dragoons, but at the very first charge all our horse run away.' Although in a postscript herecalls, ' I lost ten horses and two men in the fight last week [at Lansdown] and last time [at Roundway Down] I have lost five or six more so that my troop is now very weak.'[70]

The Royalist cavalry pursued the fleeing Parliamentarians 'near three miles over the Downs in Bristol way till they came to a precipice, where their fear made them so valiant that they galloped down as if it had been plain ground, and many of them brake both their own and their horses necks.'[71] Major Walter Slingsby, who was in Devizes during the battle, records:

> We could see the enemy's whole body of horse face about and run with speed, and our horse in close body firing in their rear till they had chased them down the hill in a steep place, where never horse went down nor up before.[72]

Clarendon records that the Parliamentarian infantry were broken by their own cavalry and likewise fled, but this is not so. According to John Rushworth, 'Waller's foot made a better resistance', and Harley records, 'we left our foot, who behaved themselves very bravely as long as they were able to defend themselves, and shifted for themselves.'[73]

Sir John Byron, who was at this point rallying his brigade, records:

> My Lord Wilmot charged their foot with the horse he had with him, but could not break them, and in the charge Dudley Smith was slain and Lieutenant Colonel Weston, hurt and many others, but when they saw my horse rallied together again

69 Byron, *Relation.*

70 HMC Portland Manuscripts vol., 1 p. 113, Edward Harley to Sir Robert Harley at Westminster, 15 July 1643. For details see Appendix 3.

71 Byron, *Relation.*

72 Slingsby's account in Hopton, *Bellum Civile,* p.98.

73 Rushworth, *Historical Recollections*; HMC Portland Manuscripts, vol. 1, p. 113, Edward Harley to Sir Robert Harley, 15 July 1643.

'Oliver's Castle', scene of the disastrous flight of the Parliamentarian Horse. (Photo: David Wilton)

> before them, and the lieutenant general continuing still in the rear of them, and that the Cornish Foot began to sally out of the town.[74]

Walsingham continues:

> Sir John [Digby] observing the main body of [Waller's] foot to stand on a neighbouring hill in Battalia resolved to give them also a full charge, wherefore ranking in their files and marshalling his men, he commanded that when by making a circuit they had gained they had gained the hill, and were come at a competent distance, they should suddenly ride in with full speed upon them and disorder their ranks, but it seemeth, they mistaking his command wheeled on the contrary hand to his directions, notwithstanding which error, he accompanied but with one man confidently marched up close unto them and almost round about them; (though in the mean space many fierce volleys though in vain and without hurt played upon them) and returned to the Body of horse which stood in the bottom and gazed with admiration of his resolute and venturous attempt.
>
> The foot now seeing themselves abandoned by their army of horse which was long since fled out of the field, and animated with the confident boldness of Sir John who they saw making ready for a charge, throwing down their muskets, swords, bandoliers and coats made themselves as light as their could to run for their lives. The King's horse in part giving them as it were law, (like eager greyhounds let out of the slip) broke forth into speedy pursuance of them.[75]

Byron suggests in his account of the battle that Waller's infantry at first made an orderly retreat:

> They thought it not fit to stay any longer, they began first gently to march off, their officers marching before them, amongst which (as I have been told since) Sir William Waller himself was and Popham. With that I advanced toward them with those troops I had rallied, and shot at them with the cannon I had formerly taken, their officers thought it not fit to stay any longer, but such as had horses rode away as fast as they could, and too fast for us to overtake them, and the rest blew up their powder, and threw down their arms and betook to themselves to their heels. Our horse fell in amongst them and killed 600 of them, and hurt many more and took 800 prisoners and all their colours and this was the success of their great conqueror.[76]

Slingsby also suggests that Waller's infantry made an orderly withdrawal, even though they must have known that it would have been useless:

> Waller went in so much haste that he left all his body of foot and cannon standing upon the very crown of the hill, who for a while made a gallant resistance against our horse, defending themselves in hopes their general would be so mindful of them, as to return into the field and fetch off his foot and cannon; but perceiving

74 Byron, *Relation*.
75 Walsingham, *Hector Britannicus*, pp.85–86.
76 Byron, *Relation*.

> he stayed too long, and that our Cornish Regiments was coming apace upon them, they thought it not so safe to stay for their encounter, and therefore began to move towards the next enclosures hoping to make their retreat; but drawing over the downs, seeing several bodies of our horse pressing hard upon them on all sides they began to fall in pieces, and melt into such disorder that they suffered miserably; there were about 1,800 in number of which above 600 was then slain, the rest all wounded and taken with their colours and arms, and nine brass pieces of cannon.[77]

According to Byron the Royalists took 28 ensigns and eight cavalry cornets, plus the seven pieces of ordnance. Whereas Rushworth states that, 'The king's forces took four pieces of ordnance, abundance of arms and many prisoners. Sir William Waller, Heselrige (who was wounded), Colonel Popham, Colonel Strode and other commanders escaped to Bristol.' While Harley records, 'We have not lost many men, considering what a miserable rout we were in. All our cannon, baggage and ammunition are lost and very many arms.'[78] It has been estimated that Waller's losses were about 600 killed and 800 men and all his guns and baggage were captured. Even so, on 19 July Waller was reported to have had 2,000 horse and the following day, it was reported that he had 'marched by Eversham this day with 17 colours (all horse) towards Warwick.'[79]

On the other hand Rushworth records that, 'within [a] few days [of the battle] Sir William Waller repaired to London; where notwithstanding the disaster, he was highly caressed and endeavours set on foot to raise him a new army.'[80]

Many reasons have been given as to why Waller lost the battle of Roundway Down so decisively: the tactics used, the superiority of the Royalist cavalry and the exhaustion of Waller's cavalry. These reasons have their pros and cons, but as Edward Harley puts it:

> We must needs look upon this as the hand of God almighty against us for twas he only that made us fly. We had very much confidence, and I trust the Lord has only brought this upon us to make us look more to him, who I am confident when we are weakest will show himself a glorious God over the enemy of his Truth. So this time nothing hath been gained by us, with multitudes, and I beseech the Lord give us faith to live by that and then I doubt not but our broken bones shall prevail over the enemy's mighty strength.[81]

With the destruction of Waller's army, Royalist attention now turned to Bristol, England's second city, the garrison of which Waller had weakened just before the battle of Lansdown to reinforce his field army. On 23 July

77 Slingsby's account in Hopton, *Bellum Civile,* p.98.

78 Byron, *Relation*; Rushworth, *Historical Collections*, vol. 5, 1642–1645; HMC Portland Manuscripts vol. 1, p. 113, Edward Harley to Sir Robert Harley, 15 July 1643.

79 BL Add ms 18980, letters to Prince Rupert, ff.86, 87.

80 Rushworth, *Historical Collections*, vol. 5, 1642–1645.

81 HMC Portland Manuscripts, vol. 1, p. 113, Edward Harley to Sir Robert Harley at Westminster, 15 July 1643. For details see Appendix.

Bristol was besieged by the Western Royalists and elements of the King's Oxford army, commanded by Prince Rupert. On 26 July Bristol was stormed and after the curtain wall had been breached Colonel Nathaniel Fiennes, the city's governor, surrendered. However Hopton's army had suffered in the assault, and after a year's hard fighting it had ceased to be an effective fighting force. After the fall of Bristol, only Plymouth and Gloucester and a few other towns still kept the Parliamentariancause alive in the West. After the fall of Bristol, the Royalists now looked towards Gloucester, which they besieged on 10 August.

3

The Autumn Campaign

After Roundway Down Waller returned to London with some officers, where much to his surprise he received a hero's welcome. However, the Londoners' cheers hid the fact that with his defeat and the subsequent fall of Bristol the Royalists now controlled the west of England apart from a few garrisons. Every effort was to be made to relieve Gloucester, which was now besieged by Charles' Oxford Army and the Royalist armies of the West.

Fearing a Royalist advance the day after Bristol fell, the Lords and Commons published *An Ordinance for the better securing the peace of the County of Surrey,* which declared:

> Whereas the County of Surrey is in great danger speedily to be invaded by Forces raised against Authority of Parliament, and because timely remedy cannot beprovided, if a long and tedious debate should happen about preventing thismischief. It is this day ordered by the Lords and Commons in Parliament … [that there] shall be Committees for disposing the Affairs of the said county, and appoint Officers for the same, Fortify Towns or other places within the said County and with the said forces to fight with, kill and slay, any that shall invade that County without authority of Parliament, associate amongst themselves or with other counties for their mutual defence, imprison and punish offenders against any order and or Ordinance of Parliament, and to assess and levy money, according to the several Ordinances of Parliament; and appoint Collectors and Treasurers to receive the same, and to issue out the same for the uses aforesaid.[1]

It was proposed by Parliament that Waller should raise a new army and salvage the situation in the West. However, the situation had changed from the year before when volunteers flocked to the colours. Gone were the days that regiments of foot mustered over a 1,000 men, from the summer of 1643 a colonel with 500 men was considered to have a strong regiment. Both sides had to resort to 'impressment' or conscription. On 11 September the Venetian Secretary, Gerolamo Agostini, reported that,

1 BL TT E.65/22, *An Ordinance of the Lords and Commons assembled in Parliament for the better securing and settling the Peace of the County of Surrey.*

> Waller is collecting his men with great energy. To complete the number fixed and also to reduce the cost, they have had to send several companies of the trained bands. Those who do not want to go undertake to maintain a man in their place. As these are not paid it causes great inconvenience and may be of little good.[2]

The following day the House of Commons ordered that 500 men be impressed for Waller's army. The *Parliament Scout* reported:

> Pressing being now practised everywhere, but in the best manner in the Associated Counties [of the Southern Association] for there they take them that can be best spared, whereas before many housekeepers went and lost their lives which is found there a great impoverishment to the counties, besides the miseries brought upon the wife and children.[3]

A week later the Venetian Secretary reported that Waller's regiments:

> had more officers than soldiers so far. In the difficulty of obtaining volunteers and the unsatisfactory service to be expected from the pressed men, they have sent for all the river boatmen, who are extremely numerous and tried to persuade a part of them to take [up] arms; but they did not favour the occupation and so the results are like to be scanty.[4]

A petition from Sussex also complained that, 'Our men are daily impressed, which causeth them to fly to other secure counties by reason thereof we shall be unable to manure our lands and defend the frontiers of our county.'[5] At first the 'masterless men' who were a burden on the parish were impressed, but as the war progressed more and more men had to be used to meet the parish's quota of recruits.

The situation was not helped by the Earl of Essex, whom some people wanted replaced in favour of Sir William Waller, since all he had done that spring was capture Reading, while Waller was seen as a more aggressive officer earning the nicknames of 'the Night Owl' since he favoured night marches to surprise the enemy, and 'William the Conqueror' due to his many victories. However, Roundway Down had changed this, in fact Sir John Denham who had been the Royalist governor of Farnham Castle wrote a poem:'Poor Sir William the Con, so fast did he run that he left half his name behind.' Essex was in no rush to send his rival for command of the Parliamentarian army another commission to raise a new army, despite news being brought to London of the surrender of Bristol and that now Gloucester was besieged.

---

2 Letter from Gerolamo Agostini, Venetian Secretary in England to the Doge and Senate, 11 September 1643, *Calendar of State Papers relating to English Affairs in the Archives of Venice, 1643–1646* (London: His Majesty's Stationery Office, 1926) [CSP Ven] vol. 27, p.267.

3 BL TT E.67/34, *The Parliament Scout*.

4 *CSP Ven* vol. 27 p.267, Letter from Gerolamo Agostini, Venetian Secretary in England to the Doge and Senate, 18 September 1643.

5 BL Tanner ms 60B/250, *The Humble petition of all the inhabitants in Chichester and Arundel Rapes of the general grievances which we presented by the not engaged as well as engaged party*, undated.

When Essex finally sent the commission to Parliament he had left the name blank and he told Anthony Nicholl that he wanted a veto on who Waller commissioned as colonel, which the House of Commons was against. Finally on 29 August 1643 Waller received his commission to raise a new army, and he began to raise new regiments.

Waller had his own regiment of horse and dragoons, plus those of Colonel Robert Burghill and Heselrige for a nucleus for his cavalry. Burghill, however, had retired from the army following the wound he had received at Lansdown and his regiment passed to Jonas Vandruske, a Dutchman who had been his major in the West. Following its defeat at Roundway Down Heselrige's regiment had abandoned its cuirassier armour in favour of the arms of the harquebusier.

Waller had always been short of infantry and he appears to have left his meagre regiment of foot in the West to reinforce the garrisons still loyal to Parliament. An exception may have been Colonel Robert Cooke's Regiment which may have been taken over by Colonel Edward Cooke. Two colonels who appear to have had no connection with Waller's Western Brigade were Christopher Potley and James Wemyss, who were each to raise a regiment of foot.[6] Potley was appointed Waller's major general of foot, while Wemyss, as the master gunner of England, was well suited to command Waller's artillery, so his regiment was armed with 'firelocks' or flintlocks so that it could guard the guns. Waller and Heselrige also set about raising their own regiments of foot; at least some of Heselrige officers had come from Lord Brooke's Regiment, Brooke being killed in March 1643 at the siege of Lichfield.

When issuing the commissions on 29 August Waller did not forget his former colleagues, Sergeant Major General William Carr was to raise a regiment of horse and one of foot and Francis Dowett who was promoted colonel of a regiment of horse. However, their regiments made slow headway and were disbanded shortly afterwards. Edward Cooke's regiment was reduced into Heselrige's Regiment of Foot in May 1644.

Another regiment of foot commissioned by Waller at this time was commanded by Edward Harley, but was sent to reinforce Plymouth and so did not serve with Waller. Other regiments of foot that Waller could call upon were Colonel Samuel Jones' Regiment, which garrisoned Farnham Castle, and Sir William Springate's Regiment from Kent, which along with two companies of 'Farnham Greencoats' had reinforced Essex's army on his march to relieve Gloucester. Another Kentish regiment being raised was Sir Ralph Weldon's Regiment of Foot, along with Sir Michael Livesey's Regiment of Horse. A regiment of London horse under Colonel Richard Turner was also allotted to serve with Waller. From Sussex came Anthony Stapley's Regiment of Foot and Colonel Herbert Morley's Regiments of Horse and Foot, and Hampshire-supplied Colonel Richard Norton's Regiment of Horse. Waller could also call upon the county trained bands and auxiliaries if necessary.[7]

6 John Adair in his biography of Waller and his book on the battle of Cheriton refers to Andrew Potley, but all the warrants etc., give his first name as Christopher.

7 Laurence Spring, *Waller's army, The Regiments of Sir William Waller's Southern Association* (Farnham: The Pike and Shot Society, 2007), pp.36–38, 40–41, 53, 61–69, 71–76, 106–111, 118–120, 125–129, 139–142, 153–160.

On 2 September William Elliot wrote to Sir Symonds D'Ewes:

> We are hear paying our twentieth parts and raising horses for the exhibition of Sir William Waller, I should be glad to hear something towards an end of our civil distraction, which if God saw fit I wish might be without any more effusion of Christian blood and that some happy and profitable accommodation might give hopes thereof. We or I praise God in health although not without fears.[8]

The majority of Waller's regiments were gathering at the rendezvous at Windsor, with orders to assist Essex's Army if needs be. Fortunately Essex not only relieved Gloucester but won the First Battle of Newbury on 20 September. This success put a stop to the murmurings of his enemies, who wanted to replace him, and now he demanded that Waller return his commission insofar that if he did not Essex would resign his. On 9 October after being assured that he would receive another commission, albeit with less favourable terms, Waller gave up his commission. However, Essex refused to grant Waller a new one, even when the House of Commons granted an ordinance on 4 November uniting the counties of Surrey, Sussex, Kent and Hampshire for their mutual defence and naming Waller as sergeant major general of all men raised in these counties. Still Essex refused to grant Waller his commission, so that on 1 January 1644 the House of Commons recorded that Essex be 'desired forthwith to grant a commission' to Waller. Finally Essex did, but not before he had written an open letter to the House of Commons, which was published on 2 January 1644, declaring his loyalty to the cause 'so long as he hath one drop of blood.'[9]

Fortunately for Parliament months of hard fighting had greatly reduced the Royalist army in the West and detachments were needed to block up the remaining garrisons and recruits were being drawn off to reinforce Charles' Oxford Army which was besieging Gloucester. Coupled to this Sir Ralph Hopton, their commander, had to recuperate from the burns he had received at the battle of Lansdown, so any advance eastward during the summer was unlikely.

However, in September Hopton was ordered to raise a new army 'for the clearing of Dorsetshire, Wiltshire and Hampshire, and so point forward as far as he could towards London.'[10] This has given rise to the theory that Charles wanted a three pronged attack on London and so end the war, but Charles was never in a position to launch such a strategy since it would mean that the Earl of Newcastle, who commanded the King's army in the north, would have to fight his way south from the northern counties of England. With the Scots marching into England on Parliament's side at the beginning of 1644 this was out of the question, but even so Charles would need to capture Hampshire

8 BL Harl ms 382 f.119, William Elliot to Sir Symonds D'Ewes, 2 September 1643.

9 Quoted in Firth and Rait, *Acts and Ordinances of the Interregnum*, pp.333–339; *Journal of the House of Commons, volume 3 1643–1644* (London: HMSO, 1802), pp.355–356; Earl of Essex, *A letter from his Excellency Robert Earl of Essex to the Honourable House of commons concerning the sending of a commission forthwith to Sir William Waller* (London, 2 Jan 1644).

10 Hopton, *Bellum Civile*, p.61,

and Surrey, or Berkshire and Middlesex if he was to make another advance on London.

Hopton set about raising his new army, which on paper mustered only 1,580 horse and about 2,000 foot. His efforts were hindered by Sir William Ogle seizing Winchester for the Royalist cause once more, so Hopton was forced to send badly needed troops to his aid.[11]

Nevertheless, Ogle's actions made the inhabitants of western Surrey uneasy. On 24 October Sir William Elliot of Godalming wrote to Sir Symonds D'Ewes:

> I cannot but communicate to you the great fears and distractions we now are in, the King's forces are near us and they have fired Wokingham and Twiford within 15 miles of us and do threaten within a week to fire Guildford and Godalming, they having it in there [*sic*] commission as they give out from there council of war on that side, I pray advise us what to doe, I know my wife will not be by me persuaded to remove. And I know a house to hold my company in London will not be easily had. And either I must run the hazard of staying or my undoing by removing.[12]

After returning from his successful campaign Essex decided to send his army into winter quarters, since winter usually put an end to the fighting, but for Waller his campaign was just beginning. On 3 October, according to the pamphlet *Certain Information*, Waller with a force 6,000 strong, consisting of 50 troops of horse and four regiments of foot, marched out of Windsor for Farnham, which would become his headquarters until April 1645. However these figures are grossly exaggerated because at the beginning of November Waller only had 16 troops of horse and the foot regiments were by no means at full strength.[13]

To bring his army up to strength a brigade of London Trained Bands, under the command of Sir James Harrington, was mustering at Windsor to reinforce Waller's army. Elias Archer, a lieutenant in the Yellow Auxiliaries of the Tower Hamlets, whose regiment formed part of the brigade, records the march to Farnham:

> Sabbath day October 29, the whole brigade was drawn out into the fields, intending to march away that day, but (being late) we returned to our quarters.
>
> Monday, October 30, We marched to a green about half a mile from Windsor, where we made [a] halt and Rallied our men, each regiment drawing into a Regimental form, where likewise our Train of Artillery and Wagons of war came to us, and sowe marched towards *Farnham* through Windsor Forest where in the

11 Adair, *Cheriton 1644*, pp.29–30; BL Harl ms 6804 ff.137, 224.

12 BL Harl ms 382 f.120, Sir William Elliot of Godalming to Sir Symonds D'Ewes, 24 October 1643.

13 BL TT E.75/3, *Certain Informations from several parts of the kingdom,* 30 Oct–6 Nov 1643 (London: William Ingler, 1643); Surrey History Centre G52/6/2 (1), *A True Relation of the Marchings of the Red Trained Bands of Westminster, the Green Auxiliaries of London and the Yellow Auxiliaries of the Tower Hamlets, under the command of Sir William Waller from Munday the 16 October to Wednesday 20 December 1643* (London, 1643).

> afternoon wemet some of Waller's Troops of horse, his own regiment of foot, and one company of Blew-coats with snaphance muskets, which guard the train of Artillery only, allthese marched with us.[14]
>
> When we came to Bagshot we made [a] halt again in the closing of the evening, and refreshed ourselves about an hour, and then marched forwards and about one or two a clock on Tuesday morning we came into Farnham, where we rested all that night.
>
> Wednesday the first, all our foot Forces (except the Green Regiment [of Auxiliaries] which were quartered two miles from Farnham) were rallied in Farnham Park, where there was added to our former advancing Forces, four companies of soldiers belonging to Farnham Castle so that then in the park were 29 Colours of foot companies, besides horse and Dragoons; this day a Clerk of a Company of Sir William's own Regiment of foot, was (by a Council of war) condemned to dye, for a mutiny by him, and some others raised in the field, and on Thursday November 2 he was hanged on a tree in the Park to the example of the Whole Army.[15]

While the London Brigade were marching to join Waller Sir William Elliot had been led to believe by Parliamentarian propaganda, that if he paid his taxes then there would be no need for troops to resort to free quarter. However he soon found this was not the case; 'we have soldiers continually billeted amongst us,' he wrote on 31 October, 'which is strange considering the payments we undergo that they should be upon free quarter.'[16]

On 28 October a party of 100 horse from Winchester, under the command of Sir Humphrey Bennet clashed with elements of Waller's army at Andover. Though a small affair, Waller began to look to recapture Winchester, so held a muster at Bentley Green on 3 November and then marched to Alton. However by now winter was beginning to set in and the 'extremity of wet and snow' prevented the army marching the next day. On 5 November news was brought to Waller that Hopton's army had arrived at Winchester. Hopton had received strong reinforcements at Andover, comprising the brigades of Lord Gerard and the Earl of Crawford, and was later joined by Sir Jacob Astley with 900 foot and three regiments of horse.[17]

Waller altered his course and marched to besiege Basing House, a few miles from Basingstoke, where he arrived on 6 November. Basing House is described as:

> The seat and mansion of the Marquis of Winchester, stands on a rising ground having its form circular, encompassed with a brick rampart lined with earth and a very deep trench, but dry. The lofty gatehouse with four turrets looking northwards, on the right whereof without compass of the ditch, a goodly building containing two fair courts, before them is the Grange [barn], severed by a wall and common roads, again divided from the foot of Cowdrey's Down by meads

14 The bluecoats were those of Lieutenant General James Wemyss' regiment.

15 SHC G52/6/2 (1), *A True Relation of the Marchings of the Red Trained Bands of Westminster*.

16 Harl ms 382 f.121, Sir William Elliot to Sir Symonds D'Ewes, 31 October 1643.

17 Hopton, *Bellum Civile*, pp.64–66.

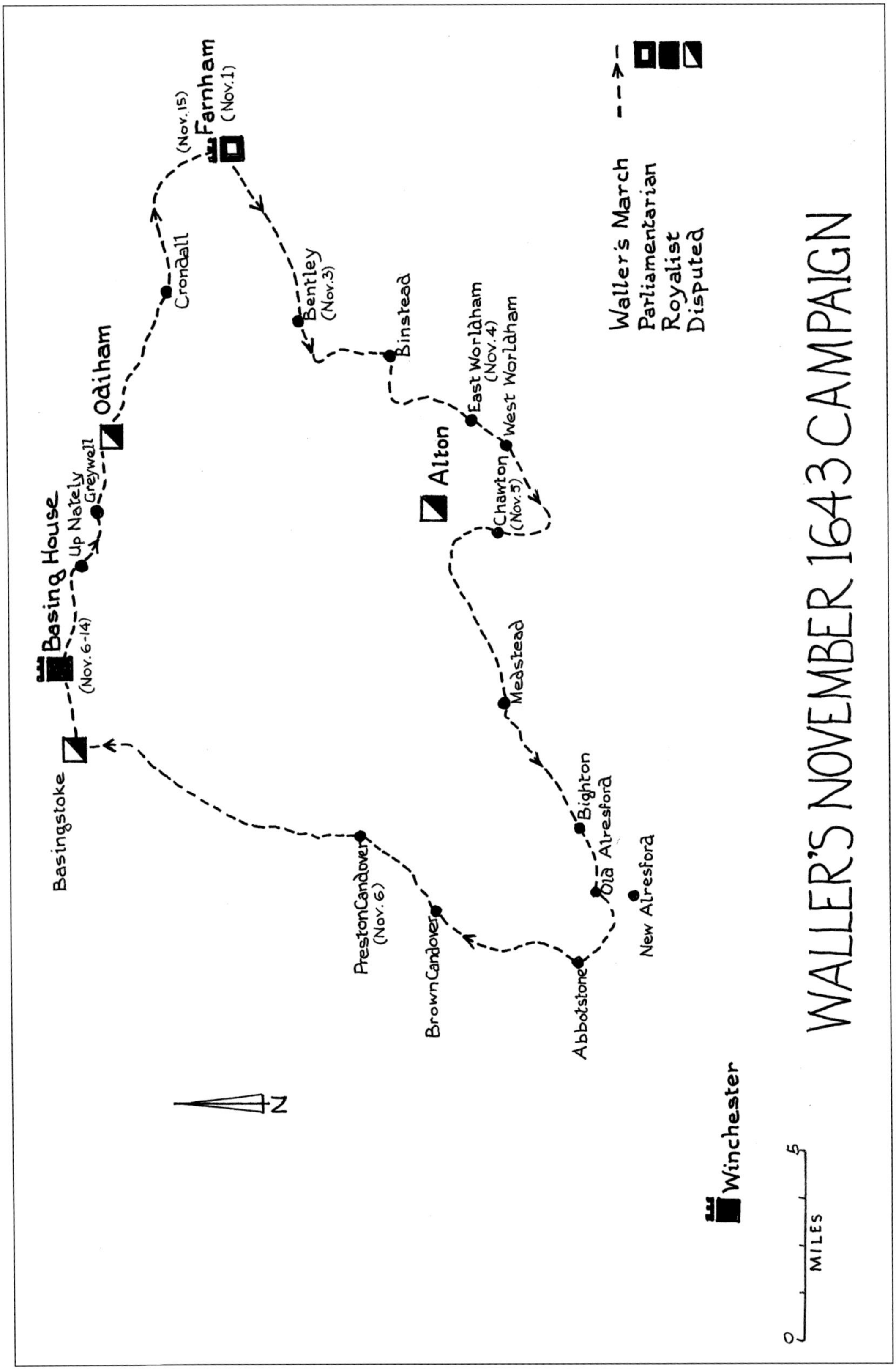

Map 1 Map showing Waller's Autumn Campaign, 1643.

> rivulets and a river running from Basingstoke, adjoining upon the east, the south of the castle hath a park, and toward Basing Town, a little wood, the place seated and built as if for Royalty.[18]

The garrison consisted of two regiments of musketeers, the Marquess of Winchester's and Colonel Marmaduke Rawdon's, and two troops of horse, in all about 500 strong, who were a thorn in the side of the local Parliamentarians. Although these two regiments were on the same side, they hated each other. A detachment of 100 men of Rawdon's Regiment was sent to Basing House under the commanded of Lieutenant Colonel Robert Peake. However, in a petition, probably dated 1644 or early 1645, Rawdon claims that the Marquess had offered Peake the lieutenant colonelcy of his regiment, therefore he along with 50 soldiers of Rawdon's Regiment transferred to the Marquess's Regiment, 'without my knowledge'. When Rawdon, who by now had arrived at Basing with the rest of his regiment, tried to recruit men in Hampshire, 'diverse of which my Lord took from me against my will'. The Marquess accused Rawdon's officers of being 'mutinous and quarrelsome' which he objected to, and claimed that the Marquess' regiment had three times as many women as Rawdon's Regiment and that the Marquess wanted to be rid of Rawdon's regiment altogether.[19]

On 7 November Waller attacked the outbuildings on the north side of the house, but the assault was repulsed with loss. A second attack was made, this time three pieces of ordnance were used as a diversion. The Royalist newsbook*Mercurius Aulicus* records the second attack, the forlorn hope:

The siege of Basing House. Engraving attributed to Hollar. (TheTurton Collection)

18 BL TT E.27/5, *A Description of the Siege of Basing Castle; Kept by the Lord Marquis of Winchester for the service of His Majesty: against the Forces of the Rebels under the command of Colonel Norton* (Oxford: Leonard Lichfield, 1644).

19 Hampshire Record Office, 40M83/1, *The humble Declaration of Sir Marmaduke Rawdon, Colonel*. Their catalogue states *c*.1643, but Rawdon was knighted on 28 December 1643 so it must be after that date.

> fell upon the Grange; Captain Clinson (captain lieutenant to Waller himself) led those up to the Grange, who with small hurt possessed themselves of all the buildings on that side, whence having steady aim at the hole, and fighting from safe places, they much annoyed the Garrison, who were strongly assaulted on the north side of the works, but so bravely quit themselves, that they forced the Rebels back into the Houses, whence they shot thick upon the Garrison, the great guns all the while thundering at the castle and new buildings. The Rebels having got possession of all the adjoining houses, necessitated the Garrison to a speedy remedy, which was to set them all on fire, and at the same time to sally out into the Grange. [This] was undertaken by the two Lieutenant Colonels Peake and Johnson, who bravely issuing forth with some few men, made boldly to the barn in despite of the enemy's shot, and in two or three places fired the corn and retreated in safety ... This bold enterprise seconding the fire, made the Rebels think among so many deaths at hand (as fire, sword and water) how to save themselves by flight, which hastily practised.

This and the coldness of the night caused the London Brigade to mutiny, which forced Waller to retire into Basingstoke for a few days rest.

On 12 November Waller returned to Basing and decided to try and storm the house on two sides, Waller's own regiments of foot and dragoons and a detachment of Colonel Jones' greencoats, plus a petardier were to attack the Basing village side, while the London brigade would attack from the park side. The garrison repulsed these attacks, helped by the women of the garrison who threw down stones and bricks on to the Parliamentarians below. However, most of the casualties suffered by the Westminster Liberty Regiment were self-inflicted, as Lieutenant Archer recalls:

> Being designed to set upon the south west part of the house, through the park... whether the fault were in their chief leader, at that present either through want of courage or discretion I know not, but their Front rank fired before it was possible they could do any execution, and for want of intervals to turn away speedily the second and third ranks, fired upon them so consequently the rear fired upon their own front, and slew and wounded many of their own men, which the enemy perceiving fired a Drake or two among them which did them much injury...it was told [to] me since by a captain in that regiment that they had seventy or eighty men slain and hurt in that disorder.[20]

It was not just the London Brigade that had bad luck that day, the petardier placed his petard on a door, which had been reinforced with earth, and so made no impression when it exploded. If he had attached it to the brick wall then Waller's army would have gained a foothold within the house. With this failure Waller again drew his army into Basingstoke the following day.

By 14 November Hopton had finished organising his army and was marching to relieve Basing House, with about 3,000 foot and dragoons and

---

20 SHC G52/6/2 (1) *A True Relation of the Marchings of the Red Trained Bands of Westminster*.

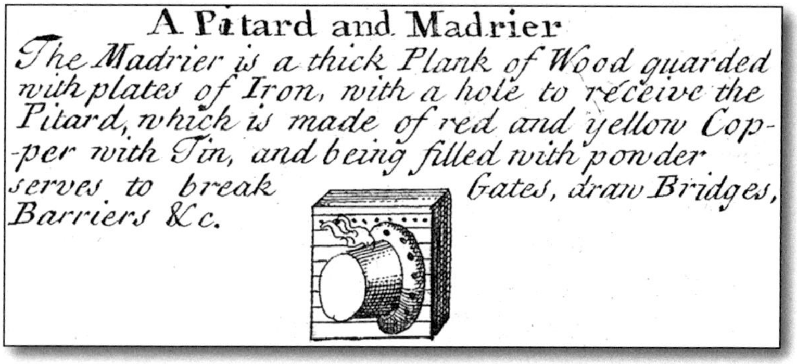

17th century illustration of a Petard. (The Turton Collection)

2,000 horse. On hearing of Hopton's advance Waller held a council of war, which decided to give battle to Hopton's weaker army. However the London Brigade again mutinied with cries of 'Home! Home!' which forced Waller to order his army to retire to Farnham.

As one would expect, estimates of Waller's losses during this siege vary considerably from 300 to just 30 killed and 100 hurt. However the surviving company strengths of both Waller's and Jones' regiments show that because of the bad weather and the fighting at Basing House 16 percent of their companies were either sick or wounded.[21]

Among the letters captured by the Royalists was a letter by Susan Rodway, whose husband Robert was serving in Captain Warren's Regiment of the Westminster Liberty Regiment. It was printed in the Royalist newsbook *Mercurius Aulicus* to encourage the soldiers to desert:

> Most dear and loving husband, my king love remember unto you hoping that you are in good health as I am at the writing hereof. My Little Willie have been sick this fortnight. I pray you to come home if you can come safely. I do marvel that I cannot hear from you as well other neighbours do. I do desire to hear from you as soon as you can. I pray you to send me word when you do thence you shall return. You do not consider I am a lone woman. I though you would never have left me thus long together, So I rest every praying your safe return.

Susan ends the 'ever praying for you till death I depart.' It is usually presumed that Robert Rodway died on the campaign, but in fact Robert, who was a tallow chandler by profession, did not die until November 1669, having not only survived the English Civil War, but also the Great Plague and the Fire of London. Unfortunately he would outlive his children, including 'little Willie' to whom Susan referred to in her letter, whose burial is recorded on 19 October 1646. Susan died about 10 years after her husband.[22]

On 15 November Waller entered Farnham and 'began to fortify the town with breastworks, and the like.'[23] While Hopton's army was still at Basing House some of Waller's men began to 'forage': as Lieutenant Archer records for 21 November 'Some of our soldiers went abroad, to a Park called the Holt, about a mile and a half from Farnham to kill deer and (being a very thick

21 TNA SP 28/135, The account book of Nicholas Cowling.

22 Laurence Spring, 'For God Sake Come Home! Soldiers' Wives, 1620–1660', in Serena Jones (ed.), *Home and Away, The British Experience of War, 1618–1721* (Solihull: Helion, 2018), pp.107–108.

23 SHC G52/6/2(1), *A True Relation of the Marchings…*

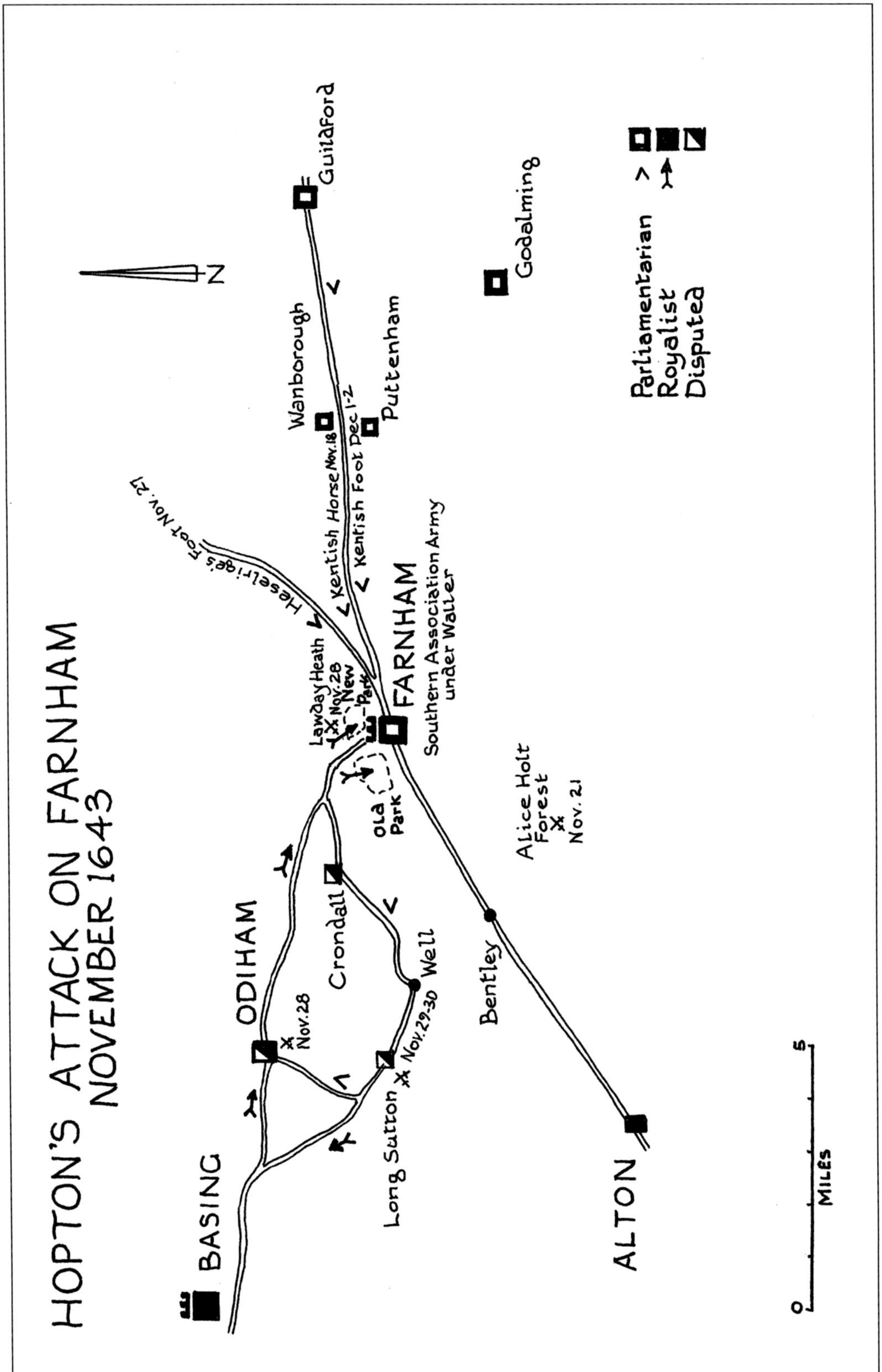

Map 2 Map showing Hopton's advance on Farnham, 1643.

misty day) the enemy's scouts came upon them and took 9 of them prisoners, all Captain Levett's men.'[24]

On 23 November Waller complained to William Lenthall that:

> I crave leave to offer to your consideration the necessitous condition under which we labour. Want of money and want of clothes have produced want of obedience and want of health, I had almost said want of heart in this army; working like a malignant fever upon the spirits of our men, and dulling the edge of our swords, though I am confident the metal is unaltered. I cannot but take notice with humble thankfulness of £5,000 voted for our supply, but I beseech you give me leave without offence to tell you it is impossible for this sum or lessthan double the proportion of this sum to stop the clamorous wants of our soldiers, for the last payment was so small that it would not enable them to buy themselves so many necessaries as they wanted for this winter service and their hopes being fixed upon this supply, if this shall fall short, it would be instead of a satisfaction prove an irritation to them.[25]

William Cawley writing on the same day to William Lenthall confirms Waller's sentiments:

> If speedy course be not taken to supply this ... army with a round sum [of] at least £10,000 for a small sum will rather discontent than satisfy – its much feared by those who know that a sudden ruin of this brigade will inevitably follow. I find Sir William Waller ... very much troubled that he cannot punish the abounding vices and enormities of his soldiers for fear of mutinies and desertions to which for want of pay they are too apt, which not only produces a contempt of their officers, but great discontent also to the country, from whom they are sometimes necessitated to take that for their livelihood which the people can ill spare.[26]

On 25 November the House of Commons voted Waller a further £5,000 together with a similar sum which they had voted on the previous Monday to be immediately sent to Waller.

However, the local population did not just have to fear the unruliness of Waller's soldiers but also the advance of Hopton's army to the Hampshire–Surrey border, as Sir William Elliot records from his house at Godalming:

> God knoweth we are full of fears and distractions, Sir William Waller hath been this sennight [week] returned to Farnham Castle and the King's forces lying at a near distance before it, but by reason of the daily stealing of his forces from him Sir William is not able to give them battle, and the London regiments daily crying home. So that if there be not a present care taken to supply his army it may be loss of our county, we are exceedingly pressed with soldiers and my house is filled

24 SHC G52/6/2(1), *A True Relation of the Marchings...*

25 *HMC 13th Report, Appendix Part I,* p.139, Sir William Waller to William Lenthall, 23 November 1643.

26 *HMC 13th Report, Appendix Part I,* p.139, William Cawley to William Lenthall, 23 November 1643.

> amongst the rest, but I see no remedy where the conditions of those counties are such to have armies lying in them, our eyes must be upon the Lord for a redress of these miseries; I pray you if there be any good news or hope of accommodation, or that the Scots be come in, impart unto me.[27]

The Parliamentarians waited for Hopton's advance, and on 24 November they had an alarm:

> All our forces were drawn out into the Park, where we stood upon our guard all that day, and the night following, and about eleven a clock the next day, news was brought that the enemies forces were all withdrawn to Odiham, five miles from us, whereupon we marched into the Town, and refreshed ourselves for that day and the night following.[28]

Hopton did not in fact arrive at Odiham until 26 November. Some Royalist detachments were stationed at Crondall and Long Sutton 'While these two armies lay at Odiham and Farnham'. Hopton wrote:

> Scarce a day passed without some action. Amongst the rest Van Drust, a principle Commander of horse of Sir William Waller's army, taking notice that Sir Edward Stowell with his regiment, and a troop or two more, quartered at Sutton (a quarter very untenable) and therefore the Lo: Hopton had given Sir Edward Stowell an Officer of his own 30 dragoons, to help strengthen it). The said Van Drustwith a strong party of horse and dragoons attempted that quarter about two hours before day, but he was at the entrance so well entertained by the dragoons, and so handsomely charged by Sir Edward Stowell himself in the midst of that quarter, as he was broken, routed and chased some miles homeward, having left behind him seven or eight of his men dead in the quarter.[29]

While at Odiham Hopton received a strong reinforcement of horse and foot, and so resolved to march on Farnham on 28 November:

> About an hour before day he [Hopton] drew out all his horse and foot (saving reasonable guards which he left upon his quarters and upon the train (for he carried but 2 small pieces with him) and presented himself in battle upon the nearest part of the heath owards Farnham, and drew out 1000 musketeers and some parties of horse to advance towards their quarters to drew them out. But Sir Wm. Waller, resolving not to hazard a battle drew out his foot into the little Park, close under the Castle, and kept his horse close, playing only with his cannon out of the Castle, and resolving, as he did afterwards, very soldier like, to take his advantage upon our retreat, The Lo. Hopton, after some time perceiving that there was nothingcounsellablly to be done in that place retreated, advancing his foot and his two little pieces to the end of the Heath, there to make a stand towards Odiham upon the edge of the enclosures, and made his retreat, as orderly as he could, over

27 BL Harl ms 382 f.123 Sir William Elliot wrote to Sir Symonds D'Ewes, 21 Nov 1643
28 SHC G52/6/2(1), *A True Relation of the Marchings…*
29 Hopton, *Bellum Civile,* pp. 66–67.

> the hill with his horses, his rear being all the way very smartly entertained by the Enemy; And so he [Hopton] retreated without disorder, or any considerable lose back to his quarters.[30]

On 28 November Waller wrote to Speaker Lenthall:

> Yesterday morning I had notice by my scouts, that the enemy showed himself in a party of about 300 horse upon the heath a mile and a half from me. Whereupon I sent out a party to visit them who entertained them with a warm skirmish for near two hours. In this time we discovered their whole body advancing. Whereupon I drew out that small stock I had in the Park under the favour of the Castle. Besides foot I had not above ten troops with me, the rest being quartered in villages more remote, where they can find provisions, came not up till toward evening. The enemy drew up in a full body before us upon the heath, as near as we could judge about 5000 horse and foot, and after a while advanced into the Park to us with their foot and some horse within musket shot, but we gave them such entertainment with our pieces that they thought it their best course to retire to the heath again, where they made a stand, but were quickly driven from thence in disorder by our culverins, whereupon they all retreated. I sent some parties of horse and dragoons after them, who charged them in the rear and beat them off the down into the lane. We took some prisoners and killed some men and divers horses. If my horse had come up time enough I might have done good execution upon them. That night the enemy quitted Crundall and retired further towards Hook. I have sent out parties after them to discover which way they move. The Kentish troops came last night hither from Guildford to quarter with me. There came with them likewise five companies of Sir Arthur Hesselrigge's regiment. But to allay the accession of strength I am now informed that the London Regiments resolve to be gone to-morrow or the next day at the furthest, but I hope they will not. I humbly desire there may be some course taken that they may stay, till some other strength come up to me, otherwise I am left at sixes and sevens, neither able to follow the enemy nor defend myself, and my old friend [Hopton] will quickly take his advantage (of) it to my destruction.[31]

Waller would later write in his *Recollections*:

> At Farnham God appeared wonderfully for me, when the Lord Hopton drew up his whole army within demi-Culverin shot of me, being with the forces of Sir Jacob Astley (who was then joined with him) at least eight thousand horse and foot; and (thorough the mistake or neglect of my adjutant general, and the slackness of my men, in drawing to the rendezvous) I was not able to face him with two thousand. Inthat extremity the Lord took the opportunity to show himself for me, by sending a mist all the morning, that by reason thereof the enemy durst not give on.[32]

30 Hopton, *Bellum Civile,* pp.67–68.

31 HMC Portland ms vol. I pp.159–160, Sir William Waller to William Lenthall, 28 November 1643.

32 Waller, *Experiences*, quoted in Adair's *Cheriton,* p.53.

Realising that Waller would not be drawn into battle Hopton had no choice but to withdraw his army to Odiham. Because of lack of provisions in the surrounding countryside, Waller had to disperse his cavalry over a wide area, so he only could call upon 10 troops on this occasion. However he still managed to pursue Hopton with only six troops of horse.[33]

The countryside around Odiham had also been stripped bare of provisions, with Waller refusing to fight, and winter setting in Hopton held a council of war:

> upon consultation with his Officers, it appearing that those quarters grew bare, and that there was little good to be done upon the enemy, being so sheltered under the walls of Farnham, he removed his own tertio to Alresford, Sir John Berkeley with his horse and foot to Petersfield, and left Sir Jacob Astley's foot, and the Lord Crawford's horse and dragoons at Alton.[34]

However, Hopton decided to make one last move before the snows came and he sent Sir Edward Ford and Colonel Joseph Bamfield to Arundel. On their arrival they believed their force too weak to attack the castle, and so asked for reinforcements. Hopton decided to take personal command of this enterprise and with the brigade which was quartered at Petersfield, marched through the night arriving on the morning of the 2 December. With Hopton's arrival the castle surrendered with little or no resistance and Ford and Bamfield were appointed joint governors, with a garrison of about 700 foot, three regiments of horse and some loose troops of horse. The fall of Arundel Castle opened the doorway for a possible Royalist advance into Sussex and Kent, where Hopton could recruit his army the following spring.[35]

A few days after the surrender of Arundel Castle, Hopton sent Sir Humphrey Bennet's regiment of horse and Sir William Courtney's regiment of foot to Romsey to block up Southampton. However the Royalists did not press home the siege with much enthusiasm and the two Royalist colonels left their posts, leaving their regiments in disorder.[36] On 11 December Colonel Richard Norton, the governor of Southampton, sallied out with a strong party of horse and foot and beat up the Royalists' quarters 'and in effect ruined both regiments'.[37]

On 3 December Waller received news of Arundel Castle's surrender and was determined to retake it, but first he could not leave Crawford at Alton, which is about 10 miles from Farnham. However, news that Waller would soon be marching to retake Arundel Castle, 'bred some discontent in our London Forces', records Archer for 3 December, 'who then every

33 BL TT E 77/14, *A Great Overthrow given to Sir Ralph Hopton's whole army by Sir William Waller near Farnham with only six troops of horse and some foot; the rest of his army being stated in several quarters in other places* (London: Anon., 1643).

34 Hopton, *Bellum Civile*, p.68.

35 Hopton, *Bellum Civile*, pp.68–69.

36 Hopton makes the excuse that Bennet was carrying out his duties as Sheriff of Hampshire and that Courtney, seeing the two regiments in disorder, rode to Winchester to consult with Bennet on the matter.

37 Hopton, *Bellum Civile*, pp.69–70.

The ruins of Arundel Castle, before restoration. (From James Dalloway's *A History of the Western Division of the County of Sussex*)

day expected to be discharged from the service, and the time being so long expired, which was prefixed for our return.'[38]

Despite having received Sir Michael Livesey's Regiment of Horse and Heselrige's and Sir William Springate's foot regiments as a reinforcement, Waller could ill afford to lose the London Brigade.[39] Therefore he used a carrot and stick approach. The stick was an example of discipline, namely the execution of a turncoat, Bartholomew Ellicot, who had been taken prisoner by Waller's army at this time. On 6 December, Ellicot, who Lieutenant Archer said was 'sometimes a Butcher near Temple Barre', was:

> once a Captain in the Parliament service, and lately in the Kings Army, who was theweek before taken prisoner, was hanged in the market place at Farnham, for running away from the Lord Generals Army, and carrying divers sums of money with him, which should have paid soldiers, and endeavouring to betray the town of Aylesbury. He died in a miserable condition, justifying himself in the Acts, and condemning the council of War, which found him worthy of death, stoutly affirming that there is no Popish Army protected by the King, with divers such like expressions, which for brevity I omit.[40]

The carrot came on 12 December, when Waller held a muster in Farnham Park, where he persuaded Harrington's London Brigade to remain with him another week. According to Archer:

---

38 SHCG52/6/2(1), *A True Relation of the Marchings…*

39 Heselrige's regiment wore blue coats and carried blue colours and Springate's regiment had redcoats with white colours.

40 SHC G52/6/2(1), *A True Relation of the Marchings…*

In the morning most of our Forces were again drawn into the Park, where our men were mustered, and we remained all day, expecting to be discharged and march homewards on the morrow, and about an hour and a half before night, Sir William came into the Park to us, and at the head of every Regiment of our London Brigade, he gave us many thanks for our service past, and told us that according to hispromise and our expectations we were to be discharged, & march homewards on the morrow, and said he would not detain us (if we were so bent homewards that we would stay no longer) but withal he told us that yet we could not return with much honours in respect of the bad success we had in our chiefest service, certifying us withal, that at the present there was an opportunity which might much avail the States, and bring honour both to God & our selves, if we would but lend our assistance till the Monday following, engaging himself upon his honour and credit, that we should not longer be detained, which we considering gave our full consent to stay, for which he gave us many thanks, in a very joyful expression advising us presently to prepare for the service because delays are dangerous. Whereupon most of our men went presently into the Town to refresh and prepare themselves for the service (where although they before gave their general consent) many of them stayed behind and went not with their Colours.[41]

An anonymous cavalryman of Waller's army recalls:

Sir William Waller in the afternoon, drew forth his forces into a Battalia in Farnham Park, about the number of five thousand horse and foot, amongst which were the Regiment of Westminster, whose behaviour and valour in this service, is never to be forgotten: The manner of the business was exceeding well carried out, both by Sir William and the rest, for strictness of appearance, and likewise for secrecy, that the enemy, nor no Malignant party, could have opportunity to understand the least of their intentions: They were upon their march by seven of the clock in the night, and in an hours march obtained a Heath between Brundon and Farnham; and there after an hour's stay for the foot, whose march were not so quick as the horse, they all willingly and cheerfully marched together, till near one of the clock in the night, in they way towards Basing; but on a sudden were appointed, to face towards the south, and so towards Alton, passing exactly between the hills, till they obtained within half a mile of the said town, altogether undiscovered by the Enemy; our scouts being so diligent, that not a person stirring in those passages was left at liberty, to have any opportunity to inform the enemy of our proceedings; and being now in sight of the town, about nine of the clock in the morning, we understood by the scouts we took that the Lord Crawford was in the town who had there about five hundred horse; the taking of which scouts, some of them escaping, gave opportunity for the said Lord to shift for himself, who conceived himself and all the rest of his forces lost; yet he speedily drew forth about 300 of his horse eastward, towards Winchester rode, where, unexpectedly, he met with some of our horse, and retreated back again into the town, and fled southward, whilst our foot made the woods ring with a shout: There were three or four of them slain in thigh flight and being in narrow lanes after half a mile pursuit, our men retreated again,

41 SHC G52/6/2(1), *A True Relation of the Marchings*…

having taken about 30 horse, and some prisoners; in the meanwhile the foot were not idle, nor Sir William, whose rare exploits in this service may be registered with the rest of his valiant and honourable actions.

The horse were immediately appointed to make good all passages, so that the enemy could not have the benefit of their accustomed running away, but were taken by our horse, our foot in the meantime behaving themselves like men, with great expedition; beat the enemies of their works of the north side and east parts of the town and possessed themselves thereof, where they displayed their colours in the sight of the enemies, then our men advanced speedily into the market place, and the enemy being all musketeers drew themselves into the works near the church, where they had double trenches and a half moon [earthwork] and made the church and a barn there by their chiefest refuge, here grew then a very hot fight, which was continued neat two hours, by reason of a Malignant, who willingly fired his own barn, and other houses, thereby to offend our men with the smoke, we lost about three men: the fire and smoke abating, our men fell close to their work again, and forced the enemy to retreat into the said church and barn, where they were all taken prisoner. The town being thus taken on all sides, the enemy desired and obtained quarter: Yet being infected with Irish Rebels and their wonted treachery, one of themafter quarter given, fired off his pistol in the said church, against Major Shambrook, but by God's Providence, was not killed therewith, but hurt in the thigh, and great hopes there is of his speedy recovery.

In this fight were taken prisoners 700. in the church, near 100 in the barn; about 100 in the field, with divers Irish men and women: also near 200 horse, 1000 arms, one colonel, one major, one lieutenant colonel, thirteen captains, three coronets, one of which with the Prince's Arms, another the Earl of Stratford's with divers other colours hid in the church; there were slain of the enemy near 40 amongst which was Colonel Richard Bolles: the enemy's word was (Charles), ours (truth and Victory).

The mighty providence of God was seen in this, and as in many other mercies towards us: for in this fight for a certain truth, there were not above five of our men slain, and about six wounded, and about six scorched with powder, by reason of their own negligence: This done, our worthy Major General caused the people of the said town to slight the works: took the prisoners, and tied them two by two with match, and are now in Farnham Church and Castle, where they may hear better Doctrine then they have heard at Oxford or among the Irish rebels.[42]

That night Waller's army slipped out of Farnham, at first heading towards Basing House, but this was just a feint to fool any Royalist spies. After two miles he turned for Alton where his army arrived early in the morning of 13 December. Waller, who knew all of Alton's defences because of his network of spies, planned to attack the town from the north and north-west. Waller is estimated to have had about 3,000 men, while the Royalists had about 900 infantry plus several cavalry regiments. The Royalist cavalry were commanded by the Earl of Crawford and the infantry by Colonel Richard Bolle.

42 *A Narration of the great Victory (through God's Providence) obtained by the Parliament's Forces under Sir William Waller at Alton in Surrey* [*sic*] *13 of this instant December 1643 against the Cavaliers* (London: Edward Husbands, 1643).

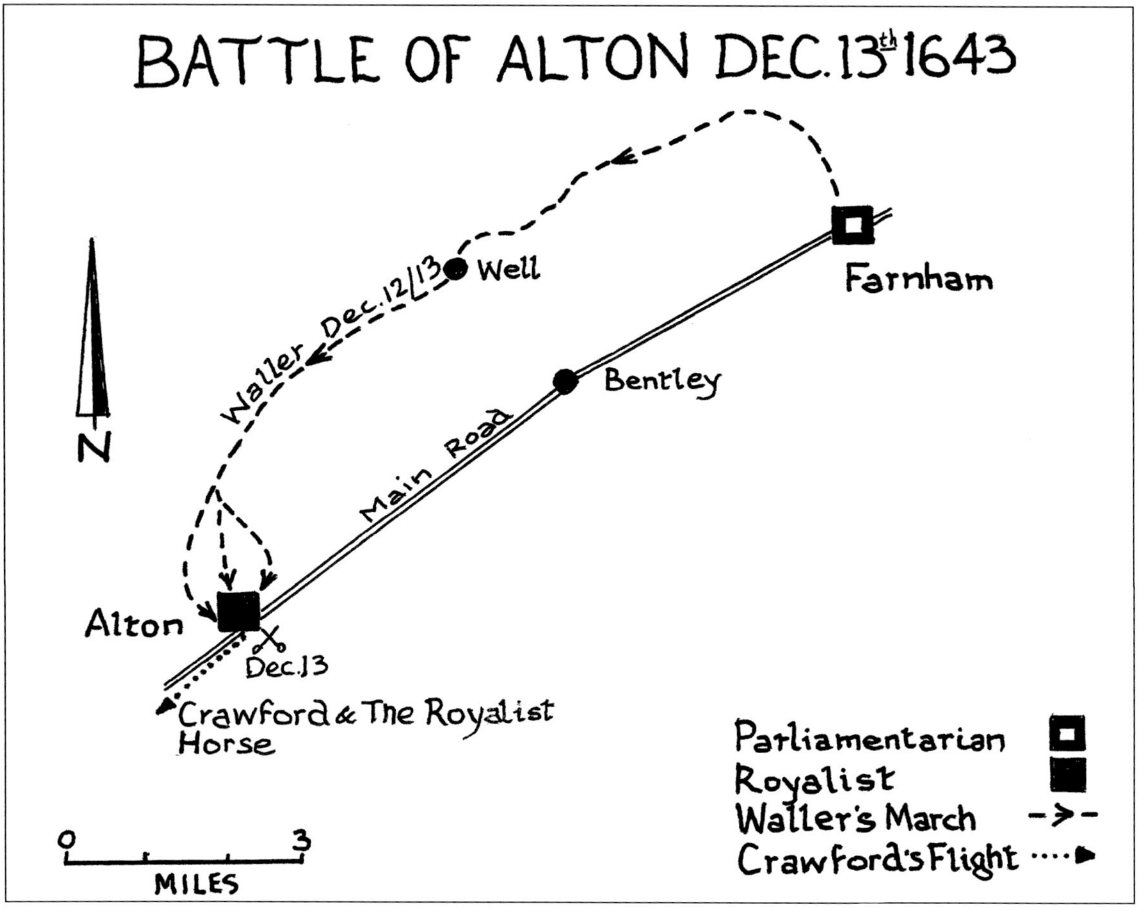

Map 3 Map of Alton campaign, December 1643.

The feint march was a complete success and the Royalists did not know of Waller's approach until he was within sight of the town. On hearing of the Parliamentarian approach, the Earl of Crawford along with the Royalist cavalry tried to escape saying that he could achieve little confined in the town. However Crawford did not get far: coming face to face with the Parliamentarian horse, he turned about and galloped off in the other direction hotly pursued by Waller's cavalry.[43] The Royalist infantry was left to its fate, making a fighting withdrawal through streets of Alton to Amery Farm and then to St Lawrence's Church, which had been fortified in case they should be attacked. Lieutenant Archer recalls:

> Sir William's own regiment of foot, Sir Arthur Heselrige's five companies, and five companies of Kentish men[44] went on upon the north and north west side and gave the first onset by lining the hedges and the like, but could not (as yet)

43 *Lords Journal*, vol. iii p.345, BL TT E.79/3, *Mercurius Civicus, the London Intelligencer*, 14–21 Dec 1643 (London: Thomas Bates, 1643); BL TT E.79/6 *The Parliament Scout communicating intelligence to the kingdom,* 15–22 Dec 1643 (London, John Dillinger, 1643).

44 This was Sir William Springate's Regiment of Foot which wore redcoats and carried white colours.

come to any perfect execution, inrespect that our London regiments were not come in sight of the enemy, and there fore they bent all their force against those three regiments and lined diverse house with musketeers, especially one great brick house near the church was full, out of which windows they fired very fast, and might have done great prejudice to those men, but when our Train of Artillery came towards the foot of the hill, they made certain shot which took place upon that house and so forced them to forsake it, in the meantime our London regiments andfour companies which belong to Farnham Castle[45] came down the hill. Then the Red Regiment[46] and the Greencoats (which greencoats are the four companies of Farnham Castle) set upon a half moon and a breast work, which the Enemy had managed, and from whence they fired very hot and desperately until the Green Auxiliaries marched on the other side of a little river into the town with their colours flying and (being in the wind of the enemy) fired a little thatched house and so blinded them, that this Regiment marched forwards and coming in part behind the work, fired upon them, so that they were forced to forsake the said half moon and breast work, which they had no sooner left but presently the Greencoats and part of the musketeers of the Red, and our Yellow Regiment entered while the rest of our regiment marched into the town with their colours flying.

Now was the Enemy constrained to betake himself and all his forces to the church, churchyard and one great work on the North side of the church; all which they kept near upon two hours very stoutly and (having made scaffolds in the church to fire out of the windows) fired very thick from every place until diverse soldiers of our regiment and the Red Regiment, who were gotten into the Town, fired very thick upon the south east of the churchyard, and so forced them to forsake that part of the wall, leaving their muskets standing upright, the muzzles whereof appeared above the wall as if some of the men had still lay there in ambush and our men seeing nobody appear to use those muskets, concluded that the men were gone, and consulted among themselves to enter two or three files of musketeers, promising Richard Guy, one of my Captain's sergeants…to follow him if he would lead them: whereupon he advanced, and coming within the Churchyard door, and seeing most of the cavaliers firing at our men, from the south and west part of the churchyard, looked behind him for the men which promised to follow him, and there was only one musketeer with him. Nevertheless he flourishing his sword, told them if they come, the churchyard was our own: they Simon Hutchinson, one of Lieutenant Colonel Willoughby's sergeants, forced the musketeers, and brought them up himself. Immediately upon this, one of the sergeants of the Red Regiment… brought in another division of musketeers, who together with those which were before, caused the Enemy's forces to betake themselves towards the church for safeguard, but our men followed them so close with their halberds, swords and musket-stocks that they drove them beyond the church door, and slew about 10 or 12 of them, and forced the rest to a very distracted retreat, which when the others saw who were

45 Colonel Samuel Jones' regiment of foot, which garrisoned Farnham Castle. They wore greencoats and carried white colours.

46 The Westminster Liberty Regiment, which with the Yellow Auxiliaries of the Tower Hamlets and the Green Auxiliaries formed Harrington's London Brigade.

The door of Alton Church, which was damaged when Waller stormed the building in December 1643. (Author's collection)

in the great work on the north side of the churchyard, they left the work and came thinking to help their fellows, and coming in a disorderly manner to the south-west corner of the church, with their pikes in the rear, (who furiously charged on, in as disorderly manner as the rest led them) their front was forced back upon their own pikes, which hurt and wounded many of the men, laying about them stoutly, with halberds, swords and musket-stocks, while some Colonel Bolles their chief commander at the present, who not long before, swore, 'God damn his soul if he did not run his sword through the heart of him, which first called for quarter'.

He being slain, they generally yielded and desired quarter, except some desperate villains which refused quarter, who were slain in the church, and some others of them wounded, who afterwards were granted quarter upon their request.[47]

The Earl of Clarendon records that:

Colonel Bolles, who commanded his own regiment of foot there – consisting of about 500 men which had been drawn out of the garrison of Wallingford– when he found himself encompassed by the enemy's army of horse and foot, saw he could not defend himself or make other resistance than by retiring with his men

47 SHC G52/6/2(1), *A True Relation of the Marchings…*

> into the church, which he hoped to maintain for so many hours that relief might be sent to him. But he had not time to barricado the doors; so that the enemy entered almost as soon, and after a short resistance, in which many were killed, the soldiers, overpowered, threw down their arms and asked [for] quarter. This was likewise offered to the colonel, who refused it, and valiantly defended himself, till, with the death of two or three of the assailants, he was killed in the places; his enemies giving him a testimony of great courage and resolution.[48]

According to popular tradition Colonel Richard Bolle was killed in the church's pulpit, but there is no evidence on the pulpit itself despite it dating from the seventeenth century, and there does not appear to be any mentions in the Churchwarden's accounts of its repair. A possible explanation is that he was killed on the stairs leading to the pulpit. However, the accounts do mention 12s 10d for mending glass, plus 1s 1d for repairing the pulpit window; £3 19s 4d for lime, sand and work to repair the walls and 4s 6d for hooks and gates. The restoration of the church in the nineteenth century further revealed evidence of the fighting with several bullets being removed from the roof timbers. However, the holes made by musket balls can still be seen on the old church door and on the outside of the church. During the early part of the twentieth century some soldiers' graves were also found in the churchyard.[49]

In this fight Waller lost about 100 men, but 867 officers and men. According to one Parliamentarian pamphlet the Royalists were better clothed than Waller's forces, who 'exchanged' their clothes for those worn by the Royalists.[50] After the dead had been buried and the earthworks demolished Waller's army returned to Farnham and as promised he sent the London Brigade home. The loss of the brigade was partly made up by 500 prisoners taken at Alton enlisting in Waller's army. Nevertheless the Venetian Secretary, Gerolamo Agostini, reported:

> Waller's army, assembled at Farnham, is as weak or weaker than ever, so that he has been obliged to come here [London] in person by night. He stayed a few hours and represented the need by word of mouth, obtaining a little money and assurances of succour as well. The latter is to be sent from the army of [the Earl] of Essex which is also languishing from the weakness caused by the withdrawal of the [London] trained bands and by constant desertion.[51]

On 17 December Waller once more marched out of Farnham, this time to recapture Arundel Castle.

---

48 Clarendon, ed. Lockyer, *History of the Great Rebellion*, p.193.

49 Rev. D.L. Couper, *The Story of the Parish Church of St Lawrence, Alton* (Gloucester: The British Publishing Company Ltd, nd), pp.17–18.

50 *Lords Journal*, vol. iii, p.345, BL TT E.79/3, *Mercurius Civicus, the London Intelligencer*, 14–21 Dec 1643 (London, Thomas Bates, 1643); BL TT E.79/6, *The Parliament Scout communicating intelligencer to the kingdom,* 15–22 Dec 1643 (London, John Dillinger, 1643); TT E.78/29, *The Weekly Account*, 13–20 Dec 1643 (London: Bernard Alsop, 1643).

51 Allen B. Hinds (ed.), *Calendar of State Papers relating to English Affairs in the Archives of Venice, 1643–1646* (London: His Majesty's Stationery Office, 1926), vol. 27. Letter by Geolamo Agostini to the Doge and Senate, 18 December 1643.

Photograph of the pulpit of Alton Church, where Colonel Richard Bolle was killed. (Author's collection)

The Siege of Arundel Castle

Despite the loss of the London Brigade, 2,000 Kentish and Sussex men were waiting to join Waller.[52] An undated letter from John Coulton to his friend Henry Jeake recalls the situation at this time:

> I went to my colours and after some time seeking them I found them at Arundel with all our regiment upon the guard it being our turn to be the out guard on the common we remained on Berry Hill all that night and the next day. About 6 o'clock we sent out a party of horse myself being one and Thomas Carew another to discover Hopton, where we found him at Petersfield seven miles beyond Midhurst: we facing his scouts and safely returned (close by their quarters all along) all of us very safe our God be praised we gave intelligence to our general: myself lead on the party the return of us was the next day about 10 o'clock ourselves

52 BL TT E.79/6 *The Parliament Scout communicating intelligencer to the kingdom,* 15–22 Dec 1643 (London, John Dillinger, 1643) These included at least four regiments of Kent Trained Bands. The Sussex contingent was composed of Colonels Herbert Morley and Anthony Stapley's foot regiments.

> and horse had no meat but we a piece of bread and cheese and our horses while we eat it had hay… News came that in Hampshire Colonel Norton had taken 800 prisoners, 140 horses and killed 100 of Hopton's men. Good news and true news a little before Sir William [Waller] took 845 men, killed 120, 300 horse and brought them into Farnham Castle from Alton. All these of Hopton's 4000 men as is said he had no more. The enemy attempted Bramber Bridge but our brave Carleton and Everden with his dragoons and our colonel's horse welcomed them with drakes and muskets sending some eight or nine to Hell (I fear) and one trooper to Arundel Castle prisoner and one of Captain Everend's dragoons to Heaven. All this while the enemy held the castle and a party seized Wistow House within a mile of Bramber Bridge but at last Sir William coming and took Arundel town with 140 prisoners to boot. Whereof 60 bear arms for the Parliament the rest are sent to London, our Winston cavaliers left the house and fled for their lives and in that march at Findon left three carts laden with plunder, the which we with a party of 12 horse we fetched home and refreshed our weary soldiers. These things being by the Lord's hand done my colonel advanced to Arundel leaving at Shoreham Captain Temple; at Bramber, Captain Fuller and Captain Everden and after we sent to our quarters only one regiment of horse a night guardeth the army, Trained bands came in, Hampshire sent in soldiers and brave Captain Dyke with his men and 700 dragoons and four troops of horse all out of Kent, Colonel Behre came with 12 troops from His Excellency [the Earl of Essex] all which remain with us. Two regiments are on [the] march from Londontowards us of the Trained Bands and two regiments of auxiliaries.

Waller's army arrived at Arundel on the evening of 19 December and at 8:00 a.m. the next morning launched a two pronged attack on the town, from the north-west and south-west.

According to the secretary of Colonel John Birch one of these attacks made by 1,400 foot drawn from the regiments of Waller and Heselrige, which were divided into three divisions and commanded by Birch.[53]

> On the left had marched the aforesaid lieutenant colonel[54] with about 200 musketeers; on the right hand your own Major Cotsforth and two hundred musketeers; in the body yourself 40 paces back, with the rest, pikes and muskets.
>
> Thus marching on, the enemy letting fly very thick, you not liking your major's pace who was marching before you n the right hand, but indeed more softly then you used to do in such a shoure, you commanded the captains where you were to come speedily, and ran up to the major's party then about 40 paces short of the Enemy's line; where they being almost at a stand your example drew them instantly on to enter that line, unto which yourself first entered, though it was intricate to set over that steep line; but one assisting another, instantly there was near 200 entered; in which instant of time, before the rest could enter, (and the great fish pond being between our army and the place where you entered, so that the enemy saw you could not be quickly be relieved). out came they with about 100 gentlemen reformadoes on horseback besides foot and other troops of horse,

53 At this time Birch was lieutenant colonel of Heselrige's Regiment of Foot.

54 Ramsay, lieutenant-colonel of Waller's Regiment of Foot.

and gave your disordered foot at that very instant of entry such a charge, that they laid many flat upon the ground, as well as yourself.

The rest went back over the line with great speed; and I think I may say truly not one man stayed within the line, except those that were slain, wounded or prisoners, but yourself; who leaning on the line with one hand, and your halberd in the other, the enemy's horse could not fall upon you but to their great loss. Bestowing some few pistols on you; but God would not have you then hit; and indeed you had never escaped so, had it not been for those musketeers, who lying near you on the top of the line kept off the horse at present, and made some few to fall; so that they were forced to draw further off, and there stand in which place neither could they indeed long continue; for the rest of the musketeers following the example of those by you, got on top of the line and from thence fired so hot on the enemy's horse, that they were glad to withdraw.

Thus God gave you possession of the enemy's ground the second time; which affected, your great care was to make way for some honest captains of horse and their train, which voluntarily came up to your assistance, which being done immediately whilst you were putting those horse and foot in order, whose number were both about eighteen hundred, the enemy looked upon them contemptibly; and there upon drew forth to fall on you near the town wall, where you were between the enemy's two lines. And their horse and foot doing their utmost…At this instant the enemy spending their shot at too great a distance, your order was to horse and foot instantly to assault the enemy; yourself with cheerful speech assuring they would not stand, which proved accordingly. For the enemy feeling the force of the shot poured on them with three ranks at a time after [a] short time gave ground, and, yourself entered the town with them, scarce knowing friend from foe; the enemy as such as they could be taking themselves to the castle; into which place your command was to enter with them. At which instant Sir William Waller's lieutenant colonel…was shot dead, and yourself not gone above 20 paces further received that wonder of God's mercy, the shot in your belly.[55]

A pamphlet written by Daniel Border he records:

The town being cleared of the enemy and won by our men, the Cavaliers played out of the castle with musket shot, but could command but very little of the town, for the greatest annoyance they did us by shooting from thence was on the bridge, where one of our men was shot in the thigh and Captain Butler escaped very narrowly, for he was shot through the holster as he rode over…

In the taking of the town (which is by nature situated in a place of great advantage and was fortified by the enemy), I may not forget the undaunted courage of our men, and especially the blue coats, who run up [to] the enemy's works, and beat them off with the butt ends of their muskets, and indeed to speak the truth, those men which we took at Alton that joined with us did very good service.[56]

55 Webb, J. & T.W. (eds.), *Military memoirs of Colonel John Birch, written by Roe, his secretary* (Camden Society New series vol. vii, 1873), pp.6–8.

56 Daniel Border, 'A Wicked plot against the person of Sir William Waller', printed in James Dallaway, *A History of the Western Division of the County of Sussex*, vol. 2 part 1 (London: Bensley and Son, 1819), p.103.

In a letter to William Lenthall, Waller also records the bravery of the former Royalists soldiers he had captured at Alton, 'upon which service his new soldiers taken at Alton did good execution.'

Waller writing about the days actions states:

> After we had taken a view, and found out a place where we might flank their line with our Ordnance, we fell upon the north side of their works, which we did so scour a weedy hill in the Park on the west side of the pond with our pieces, that we made them too hot for them; which gave such courage to our men, that with the same breath they assaulted a retrenchment which they had newly cast up, and which was very strong; it was drawn from the town gate, down the aforesaid pond near the Mill; at the same time we fell on upon a narrow passage by the Mill, where they had likewise a double work, and very strong; In a short time, by the good hand of God, we forced both, and entered the town with our horse and foot, notwithstanding a brave sally made by their horse; we beat them into the castle, and entered the first gate with them; the second they made good, and barricaded.[57]

The town had fallen and with it most of the castle's provisions, which had foolishly been stored in the town. The castle was too strong to storm so Waller decided to lay siege to it.

On the night of 21 December two sakers were planted in the church's steeple with some musketeers, who were able to fire into the castle. To add to the garrison's misery, two days later the course of the pond was changed which drained the castle's wells.

The castle's condition had grown steadily worse since John Coulton wrote to his friend Henry Jeake:

> Our men plied them still in the castle with alarms so that they had no sleep all the while they held the castle we often attempted it to fear them but no good it did them, but hardened them the soldiers moved to yield us the castle, but was denied. Ford put it one day to a vote, whether his solders would yield or no. They answered no, only six they threw them over the walls and they came to us, who we used courteously and now they bear arms [for Parliament] and by them we knew their strength they had no bread only each soldier had two spoonfuls of soden wheat a day, beef they had nought.[58]

On 28 December the garrison made a sally and took an engineer prisoner. On the same day a Parliamentarian musketeer tried to assassinate Waller, but the ball missed and killed a colonel who was walking next to him. The colonel may have been Mark Dixwell of the Kent Trained Bands and is known to have been killed at the siege. Although the pamphlet, *A wicked plot against the person of Sir William Waller,* records, 'it pleased God that his musket went not off, so that his wicked design was prevented and himself

57 Bodleian Library, Tanner ms 62 f.497.

58 East Sussex Record Office 475/37, John Coulton, clerk under Captain William Morley to Henry Jeake, 8 January 1644.

deservedly hanged.' According to Sir Samuel Luke, the musketeer, 'who being apprehended and questioned for it replied that he was sorry for nothing but that he had not killed Sir William Waller.'[59]

Meanwhile on hearing of Arundel's difficulties Hopton mustered his army again and advanced into Sussex. On 29 December he was reported to be at West Dean, just eight miles from Arundel.[60] The following day Hopton's army marched to within three miles of the town, and hetakes up the story:

> Captain Cox adventured to come out of the Castle, to the Lord Hopton, who thereupon called a council of war of the chief officers, to whom this captain gave an accompt of the state of the place, which was that the commanders had sent him to let the Lord Hopton know, that they were al very well resolved, and that they had made computation of their provisions, and found they should have no want for 14 days. The Lord Hopton asked him if he had seen their store especially their wheat, to which the captain answered that he had the day before seen a heap of wheat in a room, which as he described was computed not to be less that 40 quarters, Hereupon, with the advice of the council of war, the Lord Hopton resolved to draw back to Westbourne, and the parts thereabouts upon design, first to refresh the Army in those good quarters (the King's horse that came with the Lord Wilmot being not very patient of the hard quarter of the hill country of Sussex). In the second place to make use of those 14 days, by all possible ways to recruit his foot[61]...And that in the meantime they might not seem to lie altogether idle in their quarters, the Lord Hopton did upon his retreat send with his quartermasters over and above their ordinary guards, all his dragoons before to invest Warblington House, which, being possessed by the enemy had done much hurt in those quarters; And the Lord Hopton was resolved to take this opportunity to get it.
>
> This party advancing according to orders, got intelligence, about two miles before they came to Westbourne, that Colonel Norton (The Governor of Southampton) was then with a strong party of horse passed through Westbourne, it seemed with purpose to draw upon the rear of Lord Hopton, whom he thought still advancing towards Arundel. The Lord Hopton immediately consulted with Lord Wilmot, and the Lord Wentworth concerning the advantage of this opportunity, and forthwith sending order to the commander of the dragoons to make good the pass at Warblington (which was their only retreat) drew off one brigade of horse, where with they advanced with speed towards the way between Westbourne and Chichester, having sent Major Browne with the forlorn of 120 horse before, to face Colonel Norton upon that way, all which fell out so happily as within a short time after the enemy was come up to face the forlorn hope, the whole brigade was come up likewise, and Sir Edward Stowell was sent with a good strong party to charge them, which was quickly executed, and the enemy

59 Border, 'A Wicked plot against the person of Sir William Waller', p.103.

60 BL TT E.81/10, *A full relation of the later proceedings, victory and good success (through God's Providence obtain by the Parliament's forces under Sir William Waller of the taking of the town and castle of Arundel in Sussex, 20 Dec [1643] to 6 Jan [1644]* (London: John Field, 8 Jan 1644).

61 Hopton's army was very weak with just 2,000 horse, including 1,000 horse from Oxford under Lord Wilmot, and only 1,200 foot.

routed, and many taken and killed upon the place, some escaped to Chichester, but Colonel Norton, with not above 50 horse of 5 or 600, that he brought out, endeavoured to return by Warblington. Two parties of horse one of 24 or 25 of the Lord Hopton's guards, commanded by Major Maxwell as a forlorn hope, and another of 80 horse commanded by Colonel Horatio Carey, were sent after Norton, hoping between these parties, and the dragoons at Warblington, to make sure of him, and what he had left; But Horatio Carey failed of his duty with his party, and the commander of the dragoons upon what unfortunate apprehension I know not, for he was an old soldier and in many other occasion before and since maintained a very clear and good reputation, but then the first discovery of Colonel Norton with his frightened party, he unfortunately quitted the pass, and retreat, and thereby gave Norton the opportunity to charge and route him, where he had the execution of many of his men, the officers hardly escaping. But in the very heat of this execution, Major Maxwell with his little party fell in upon Norton so sharply, as he recovered all that was alive of the dragoons and brought in 24 prisoners of Norton's men, himself hardly escaping. This action being thus past with mixed success, the Lord Hopton settled his quarters for the present at Stanstead and Westbourne, and the parishes adjoining and presently drew down foot about Warblington house, which was gotten in yet within a few days he had rendered the composition.[62]

The castle's condition had grown steadily worse since Captain Cox's report to Hopton, as John Coulton recalls:

At last Sir William fired some grenades which feared them much and brought them to a parley last Friday, January 5 and on Saturday they yielded themselves and [the] castle to Sir William's mercy. There were prisoners in the castle sick and well 1,400 men, six chief commanders; Colonel Ford, Sir Edward Bishop withtheir starved ladies, Colonel Brameton and four more colonels more whose names I know not and Sir William Gearing all which are in prison according to their rank. We are providing gallows for Ford and Bishop what will become of G I know not we have fortified Arundel as strong as ever you saw.[63]

Waller demanded the following conditions of surrender:

1st I require the castle of Arundel to be delivered into my hands by tomorrow morning by 10 o'clock.

2nd That all the colonels of horse and foot, and all the horse, arms, ammunition and military provision whatever, be then delivered unto me entire, and unspoiled.

3rd That all the commanders, officers and gentlemen have fair quarter and civil usage.

4th That all the soldiers have quarter for their lives.

62 Hopton, *Bellum Civile,* pp.74–75.

63 East Sussex Record Office 475/37, John Coulton, clerk under Captain William Morley to Henry Jeake, 8 January 1644.

5th That for security of performance, Sir Edward Bishop and Sir Edward Ford be immediately delivered into my hands.

In his explanation of these terms Waller stated:

1st By fair quarter I understand, giving life to those that yield, with imprisonment of their persons, but civil usage, which is sufficient security, they shall not be plundered.
2nd Concerning the place where they shall be sent I will not determine, but will be left to my own freedom, without further capitulation.
3rd The ministers are included in the articles, and are prisoners as well as the soldiers.[64]

On 5 January 1644 the castle sounded a parley. Colonel Joseph Bamfield, Major Bovill of Lord Bellasis' Regiment of Horse and another captain, were sent to treat with Waller's representatives, Lieutenant General Wemyss, Major Anderson and a Kentish captain. At first the Royalists refused to accept the articles of surrender, but early the next morning the castle surrendered. Seventeen foot colours, two horse colours and 1,000 men were captured, not including the 160 prisoners which were captured on 20 December.[65]As the Royalist garrison marched out without the honours of war, an eyewitness wrote, 'I never saw so many weak and feeble creatures together in my life, for almost all the common soldiers were half starved, and many of them hardly able to set one foot before another.'[66]

With the fall of Arundel Castle, the Kent Trained Bands went home and Colonel Stapley's Sussex regiment returned to Chichester. Colonel Herbert Morley was appointed the governor of the castle. With this success and the winter snows now falling, Waller's army finally went into winter quarters. While Wilmot's brigade of horse was recalled to Oxford leaving Hopton with a greatly weakened army to quarter around Warblington.

However, when the wife of Sir William Springate visited her husband, who was dying of typhus, she remembered, 'We came to Arundel we met a most dismal sight: the town being depopulated, all the windows broken with the great guns, and the soldiers making stables of all the shops and lower rooms: these being no light in the town but what came from the light of the stables.'[67]

64 Dallaway, *A History of the Western Division of the County of Sussex*, vol. 2 part 1 (London; Bensley and Son, 1819), p.106.

65 BL TT E.81/10, *A full relation of the later proceedings, victory and good success (through God's Providence*; TT E.252/16, *A Perfect Diurnall*, 8–15 Jan 1644 (London: Samual Pecke, Jan 1644).

66 Dallaway, *A History of the Western Division of the County of Sussex*, vol. 2, part 1 (London: Bensley and Son, 1819), p.104.

67 Charles Thomas-Stanford, *Sussex in the Great Civil War and the Interregnum* (London: Chiswick Press, 1910), p.116.

4

The Cheriton Campaign

After the surrender of Arundel Castle, Waller had planned to march against Sir Ralph Hopton, but the weather finally forced him into Winter Quarters. This allowed Hopton to recruit his army, as well as recruiting in Sussex and Hampshire he also appears to have received reinforcements from Bristol, which included his own regiment of foot, and from Oxford and Reading.

Meanwhile, to undermine Waller's Southern Association on 16 February Charles issued a Proclamation appealing to his 'loving subjects', not to raise forces without his Majesty's consent or to enter into the Association because by doing so they were committing high treason. The Proclamation offered the counties within the Association a pardon in return for helping the King's cause, the Parliamentarians being 'Anabaptists, Brownists and Atheists.'[1]What effect it had or how widely it was circulated is not known, but it may have been used as an excuse by Sir Richard Grenville, who had recently landed in Ireland to change sides. Grenville had been appointed Waller's lieutenant general of horse, but on 2 March he ordered all his loyal troopers to march to Bagshot in Surrey, where he joined them early the following morning when he declared his intention to change sides. Eight men refused and returned to the regiment, but the rest, including his captain lieutenant, quartermaster, one trumpeter and between 14–35 men, arrived at Oxford on 8 March. He also took £600, a coach and six horses and news of a plot to betray Basing House. That day he penned a letter to William Lenthall, the Speaker of the Commons, informing him that it had never been his intention to serve Parliament.[2] In all future references to Grenville, the Parliamentariannewsbooks referred to him as 'Skellum Grenville'.[3]

1 *His Majesty's Proclaimation forbidding all His Loving Subjects of the Counties of Kent, Surrey, Sussex, and Hampshire, to raise any Forces without his Majesty's consent, or to enter into any Association or Protestation for the assistance of the Rebellion against his Majesty.*

2 Clarendon believes that Grenville had meant to serve the King ever since he left Ireland in August 1643. However his biographer Amos Miller believes this may not be so. Certainly Grenville's companion, Algernon Sidney, who came over with hime, served Parliament loyally as the commander of the Earl of Manchester's Regiment of Horse, until the formation of the New Model Army.

3 Amos C. Miller, *Sir Richard Grenville of the Civil War* (London and Chichester: Phillimore & Co Ltd, 1979), pp.67–71.

With the defection of their colonel the regiment fell into disarray. On 18 March Grenville who was now besieging Plymouth for the King, wrote to the burgesses of the town:

> I being by commission lieutenant general of horse to Sir William Waller had an ordinance of Parliament for raising 500 horse for my regiment at the charges of Kent, Sussex, Surrey and Hampshire, who in three months time had not raised four troops, and my own, when I left them, having two months pay due them, I could getbut one month, for which extraordinary means were used, being a favour none elsecould obtain.[4]

The regiment would have disbanded if it had not been for Major Robert Thorpe, who set about putting it in order again. Colonel Edward Cooke, who had served Waller well in the West, was appointed their new commander and would again serve Waller well until April 1645 when it was disbanded on the formation of the New Model Army.

On 17 March Captain Edward Harley, who had taken over his brother Robert's troop in Waller's Regiment of Horse, records, 'We removed our quarters from beyond Arundel to the Manhood near Chichester. Tuesday, the 19th the heath near Chichester was appointed for the rendezvous for our three regiments of horse.' These regiments were almost certainly Waller's, Heselrige's and Vandruske's Regiment, which had served with Waller in the West. Harley continues:

> From thence that might we marched to Havant. Tuesday the 26th, the general rendezvous for our horse was in the field by East Meon. We had in the field, twenty two troops of my Lord General, eleven of Sir William Waller's regiment, seven troops of Sir Arthur [Heselrige]'s; six of Colonel [Jonas] Vandruske's, five of the Kentish [Sir Michael Livesey's], four troops of Sir Richard Grenville, alias Colonel Cook's lieutenant colonel [Robert Thorpe], four troops of Colonel [George] Thompson, four troops of Colonel [Richard] Norton's.[5]

The 22 troops of the Lord General comprised Sir William Balfour's, John Dalbier's, John Middleton's and John Meldrum's horse regiments, which had been sent to reinforce Waller's army early in March.

The following day, 27 March, Harley records that it was the infantry of Waller's army to rendezvous at a heath near East Meon:

> The strength of them consisted in these regiments, the general's [Waller's], Colonel [Christopher] Potley's, Sir Arthur Heselrige's, the Kentish red Regiment [Colonel Ralph Weldon's], Colonel [Samuel] Jones of Farnham Castle his regiment, and the wooden city brigade under their true colonel, Colonel [Richard] Browne. We

4 HMC 15th Report, Appendix, viii, p.71.

5 HMC 13th Report, Appendix 1, p.107, Captain Robert Harley to his brother Edward, 12 April 1643 [*sic*]. This is clearly a misprint for 1644.

> had only Sir William Waller's and Colonel [Adam] Cunningham's regiments of dragoons; this day we began our march.[6]

It is unlikely that the whole of Jones' regiment were with Waller since this would have left Farnham Castle undefended, so there was probably just four or five companies with Waller at this time. The 'wooden city' or London brigade was formed from the White and Yellow Regiments of the London Trained Bands and on paper mustered 2,214 officers and men. However the regiment had been sent to Waller in December 1643 to reinforce his army at the siege of Arundel and had wintered at Midhurst, so many were probably eager to return to their homes, if they had not already done so.[7]

Harley records that 'of our foot Colonel Browne had the vanguard, Sir William Waller brought up the rear with his three regiment of horse. Here we changed our posture of marching with the regiment. We never marched now but four troops together. The enemy faced us this day with about three thousand horse.'[8]

An eyewitness in the London Brigade confirms Harley account that the Royalists faced Waller's army near East Meon on 27 March:

> So that we were provided to entertain them and drew our men into a body near the town, which done, Orders came to march away, which accordingly we did, in the Forlorn Hope, expecting the Enemy every hour to fall upon us, so that we were forced to stand a mile or more from the town in extreme danger, until Sir William Waller's forces came up from East Meon to join us.[9]

For Harley the tension of facing the enemy was broken, when he saw:

> the Londoners run to see what manner of things cows were. Some of them would say they had all of them horns, and would do great mischief with them, then comes one of the wisest of them crieth 'speak softly'. To end the confusion of their opinions they piled up a council of war, and agreed it was nothing but some kind of looking glass, and so marched away.

With this distraction over the Parliamentarians turned their attention to the business in hand and there was some light skirmishing. However, Hopton sensed a ruse by Waller, as he recalls:

> The armies a while faced one another and the Generals [Forth and Hopton] commanded Sir John Smith (then Major General of the horse) with a good party

---

6 HMC 13th Report, Captain Robert Harley to his brother Edward.

7 BL Harlms 986 ff.11, 15 The White Regiment had 600 musketeers, 520 pikemen and 70 officers while the Yellow Regiment had 506 musketeers, 448 pikemen and 70 officers,

8 HMC 13th Report, Captain Robert Harley to his brother Edward.

9 BL TT E.40/1, *A fuller relation of the great victory obtained (through God's Providence) on Friday 28* [*sic*] *March 1644 by the Parliament's forces under the command of Sir William Waller, Sir William Balfour and Major General Richard Browne, against the forces commanded by the Earl of Forth, the Lord Hopton, Commissary Wilmot…* (London: Laurence Blaiklock, 1644).

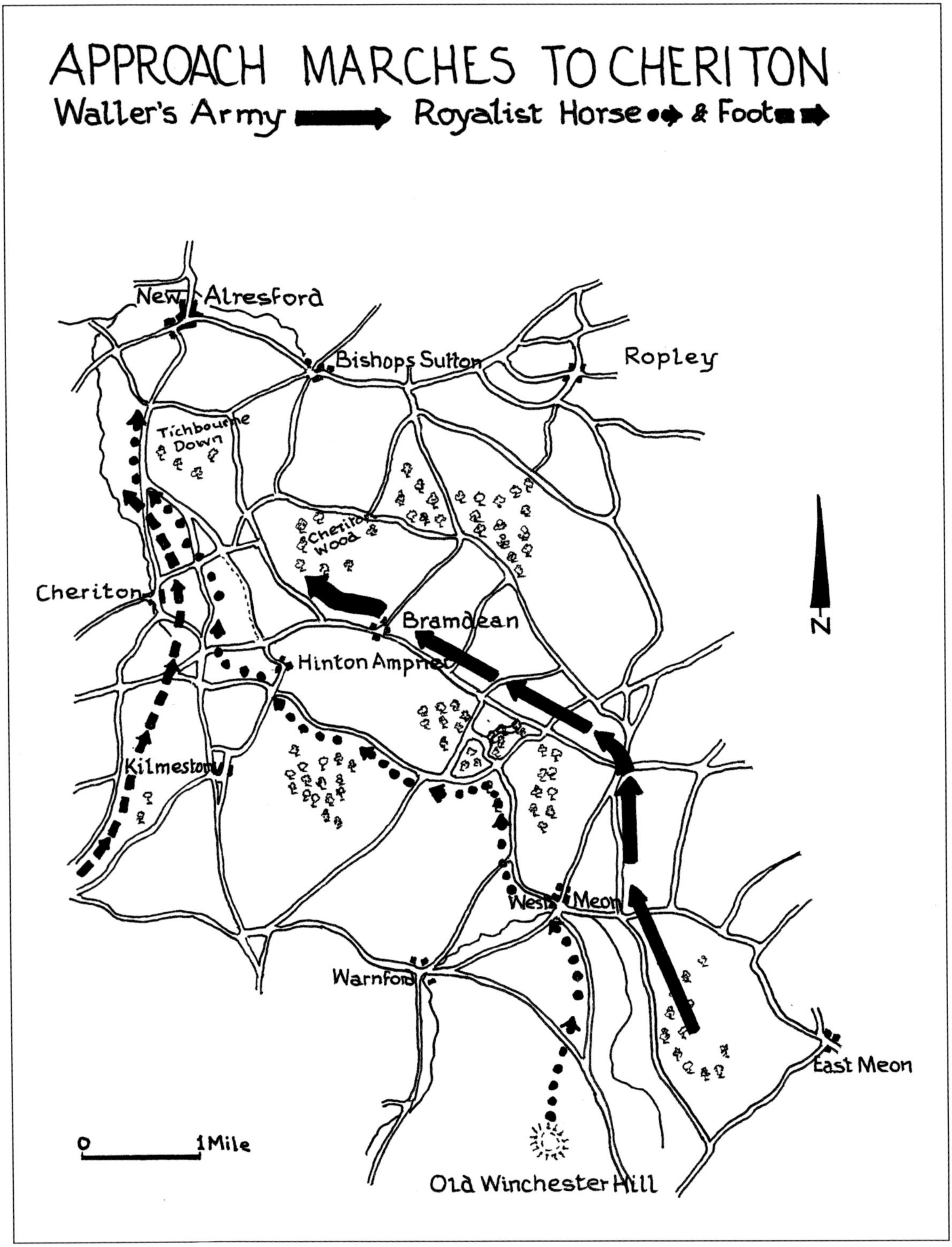

Map 4 Map showing Waller's and Hopton's movements up to the battle of Cheriton, March 1643.

> of horse to advance towards the enemy, to seek to draw him from his advantage to engage from the Woods, and near the plain. But that taking no effect, and the Lord Hopton knowing that country very well and that there was a close way through the woods and lanes from the place where the enemy stood in battle nearer to Alresford then the place where the army then stood, suspected that the enemy's design might be to send Sir William Balfour with his horse and dragoons to possess Alresford; which being a reasonable strong quarter, and within 5 miles of Winchester would have given them great advantage; There was therefore, by the advice of Lord Hopton a party sent to discover that way, which brought word of their march, as was suspected.[10]

With this news Hopton ordered his army to retire to Alresford, 'with as good speed, as could stand with good order'. Hopton sent Sir Edward Stowell's brigade of horse, and his own regiments of horse and dragoons ahead to overtake Balfour's brigade. Both brigades could clearly see each other since they were marching through lanes not a mile apart. Stowell's brigade won the race to Alresford, which:

> Possessed Alresford in time, and the enemy by that check made a halt, and took their quarters about Cheriton. Our army came late to Alresford, they drew not into the town but stood in arms that night on a rising ground joining to the town

The battlefield at Cheriton, looking towards Cheriton Wood across East Down and the Parliamentarian positions. (Photo: Nicola Turton)

10 Hopton, *Bellum Civile*, pp.79–80.

> fronting towards the enemy, only the Earl of Brentford [Forth], his disposition and pain still continuing was (though very hardly) persuaded to take lodging in the town.[11]

Hopton's army quartered on Tichbourne Down, while Waller occupied Lamborough Fields with outposts on East Down. On 28 March Hopton records, 'We disputed that ground that day with little parties, and loose skirmishes, but towards the evening we got the top of the hill [East Down].' Hopton placed a guard of 1,000 musketeers and 500 horse on East Down, under the command of Colonel George Lisle to observe Waller's movements.

> That night Sir George Lisle being very watchful upon the enemy's motions, and giving of them several alarms, and being so near as he heard them span and drive their wagons, conceived they had been drawing off, and so advertised the Lord Hopton, who presently sent intelligence to the Earl of Brentford, and he forthwith directed his orders to command Sir John Smith to draw out a party of 1,000 horse to be ready to wait upon the rear of the enemy, which was presently prepared.[12]

The day dawned on 29 March and the trumpets sounded the reveille: 'to some it was a trusty awaking from the cold sleep, to others it stroke more terror than the earth had done before', wrote Captain Harley, but, 'in the morning when I went to view the army, I saw such a cheerfulness in everyone's countenance, that it promised either victory or a willingness rather to die then lose the field.'[13]

But what field? Unlike Waller's previous battlefields, the site of the battlefield of Cheriton is open to debate. The 'traditional' battlefield with the Parliamentarians drawing up on East Down, while the Royalists drew up on Tichborne Down. However 'Adair's battlefield' has the Royalists drawing up on East Down, while Waller drew his army up on the slope by Hinton Ampner. Both sites have their supporters and critics, but space does not permit to list each argument, it suffice to say that the battle began on the 'Adair's battlefield' during the morning and spread to the 'traditional site' later in the day.

The only certainty of both sites is Cheriton Wood. Harley refers to it, 'there was on the right hand of us – as we now faced – a wood which we did conceive might be of great advantage to us.' Unfortunately, contemporary maps do not usually show woods and the first time Cheriton Wood is shown is a map in the nineteenth century when the wood was almost the same as it is today.

The Hinton Ampner ridge, which runs parallel with what is now the A272 and where Waller's army encamped on the night before the battle, is now largely covered with trees and houses. However the valley between Hinton Ampner and East Down has changed little. Although there are probably fewer hedges today than when the battle was fought.

---

11 Hopton, *Bellum Civile*, pp.79–80.

12 Hopton, *Bellum Civile*, pp.80–81.

13 HMC 13th Report, Captain Robert Harley to his brother Edward.

Battlefield of Cheriton looking towards the Royalists' ridge. (Author's collection)

Battlefield of Cheriton looking towards the Parliamentarian ridge. (Author's collection)

There were hedges on East Down, which forced the Royalist cavalry to filter down a single lane before they could come to grips with their Parliamentarian counterparts. John Adair believes this lane to be Bramdean Lane, which runs along the side of Cheriton Wood towards Waller's lines. However it could also have been Broad Lane, which also runs towards the Parliamentarian ridge.

To the rear of East Down is the much gentler slopes leading to Tichbourne Down, where the Royalists encamped and formed up on the morning of the battle. Further north is the town of Alresford, where Forth had his quarters.

East Down, between the Royalist and Parliamentarian encampments. The precise location of the two sides' deployments, and how the battle developed, is disputed. (Photo: Serena Jones)

Unfortunately there is no plan of the order of battle for either side known to have survived, so we know the exact location of only a few regiments. According to Captain Harley, early in the morning Waller sent a party of 1,000 musketeers belonging to the White Regiment of the London Trained Bands and Colonel Christopher Potley's Regiment of Foot, under the command of Lieutenant Colonel Leighton, to occupy Cheriton Wood. However, Elias Archer who was serving with the London Brigade and therefore was in a better position to observe events records that, 'a forlorn hope was drawn out of our brigade, four files out of every a company, led on by Captain Thompson.' This would mean just 448 men were drawn out of both regiments of the London Brigade. Archer does not mention Potley's Regiment being with the forlorn hope.[14]

Waller's dragoons and a large detachment of musketeers commanded by Major General James Carr, were ordered to occupy Hinton Marsh on Waller's left. Balfour records,'I caused all our horse to draw out in a little heath before our quarters, and the foot to be drawn up in battle in a large spacious field within our quarters in a Heath.' This would have been on the

14 HMC 13th Report, Captain Robert Harley to his brother Edward; BL TT E.40/1, *A fuller relation*… The figure of 448 is based on a file of 8 men x 4 x 14 there being seven companies in each of the White and Yellow Regiments of the London Trained Bands.

Hinton Ampner ridge. The foot in the main body must have been composed of those of Waller, Heselrige, Jones' and Weldon's and the remainder of the Yellow and White Regiments of the London Trained Bands. Since Heselrige's regiment was ordered to reoccupy Cheriton Wood it must have been on the right, with Waller's Regiment of Foot.

The horse must have been at first drawn up on Lamborough Fields, but were drawn down 'into a heath which stood betwixt the two hills', shortly after the battle began and were 'ranged in nine fair bodies'. The artillery were higher up the slope on Lamborough Fields next to or behind the main body of infantry, protected by Wemyss' firelocks.[15]

The Royalist army in some ways is easier to deploy, it advanced from Tichbourne Down to East Down on the morning of 29 March, as Hopton records, 'the foot and horse the Earl of Brentford brought with him on the right wing, with his [Hopton's] own foot and horse drew to the left, which was over against that woody ground [Cheriton Wood] that the enemy newly possessed.' Sir George Lisle's force was already on East Down to watch Waller's movements. As already stated the main body of horse was probably drawn up somewhere in the centre near Bramdean or Broad Lane.

Unfortunately, there is no exact returns for either army. According to Sir Samuel Luke, who was Parliament's Scoutmaster General, on 23 March Hopton's army mustered about '14,000 horse and foot' and on 26 March Hopton was 'about 10 or 12,000 strong'. Whereas the Earl of Clarendon states that,'the king's Army consisted of about 5,000 foot and 3,000 horse; Waller exceeded in horse, but was upon the matter equal in foot.'[16]

On discovering that Waller had occupied Cheriton Wood, the Royalists advanced to the reverse slope of East Down and Colonel Matthew Appleyard was ordered to draw out 1,000 musketeers and to divide them into four bodies. According to Hopton, Appleyard then advanced into the wood:

> But the bodies of our men no sooner appeared on the top of the hill, but the enemy showed how well they were prepared for us, and gave fire very thick and sharp, which our men very gallantly received and returned; But the Lord Hopton foreseeing that our party could not long hold out upon so great disadvantage, and observing an opportunity to cast men into the wood upon the flank of the Enemy, he drew off Lieutenant Colonel Edward Hopton [of Apsley's Regiment] with one division of the commanded musketeers, and commanded them to run with all possible speed into the wood upon the Enemy's flank, where there was likewise a cross hedge to cover them, which they had no sooner done, and given one volley from thence but the enemy fell in disorder and began to run. Colonel Appleyard with his party pursued them, and had the execution of part of them through the wood, and possessed himself of all their ground of advantage, and took a horse colour and some prisoners, but none of their cannon, for they being light guns were drawn off.[17]

---

15 HMC 13th Report, Captain Robert Harley to his brother Edward.

16 Luke, *Journal of Sir Samuel Luke*, vol. II., pp.266, 268, 270; Clarendon, ed. Lockyer, *History of the Great Rebellion,* p.195.

17 Hopton, *Bellum Civile,* pp.81–82.

A Parliamentarian newsbook gives the following account of this action:

> On Friday morning Sir Ralph sent out a party about 8 of the clock after which Colonel Browne's Regiment were drawn out who got into a wood near to the hill where the enemy appeared, and there appeared in the same wood an Irish regiment of redcoats like unto ours, which at first were taken to be friends but when we draw near together, they fired on us and so we were forced to retreat the enemy thereby possessing themselves of the wood.[18]

'Colonel Browne' did not command a regiment at Chertiton, instead as a major general he commanded the London Brigade. The reference to 'redcoats like unto ours' is interesting because neither the Trained Bands nor Potley's are known to have worn red, but it may be referring to Weldon's Kentish regiment which is known to have worn redcoats, although it did not occupy Cheriton Wood. Some sources state the 'Irish redcoats' were Lord Inchiquin's Regiment of Foot, which had landed at Weymouth in January 1644, but they are known to have been near Lyme a few days before the battle, so could not have arrived in time. Therefore they are almost certainly Sir Allen Apsley's Regiment, which according to Hopton help retake the wood.

As Leighton's force retreated they were fired upon by the Royalist artillery and Waller sent Heselrige's Regiment of Foot to secure his right wing. Even so Slingsby records that he 'could discern several companies of thirty, of forty and more in some running over the fields in their rear of their army.'

According to Elias archer, the Royalists 'planted their Drakes on the further side of the wood, which they discharged upon our men so thick, that the place was not tenable, though the greatest part of our musketeers, and some others, were drawn up to them, so that they were forced to retreat in one hour's space, which gave great encouragement to the enemy.'[19] Captain Harley has nothing but contempt for the Londoners in the wood:

> The citizens in the wood, were in the wood but they found the way how to get out, no sooner they did see that the bullets would come otherwise than they would have them but made a foul retreat…with a fair pair of heels, which did so discourage the rest, that they all left their charge with a shameful retreat. Our three hundred horse which were to second our foot as soon as the enemy offered to charge came away in the same confusion.[20]

To be fair to the Londoners at the beginning of the battle both sides used the same field word, *God with us*. After the confusion had been realised this was changed to *God and the cause* by the Royalists, and by the Parliamentarians to *Jesus help us* and later to *Glory be to God*.

At this success Hopton sent Sir John Paulet and Colonel Hays to report to Lord Forth and to find out his opinion of falling upon Waller's right with

18 BL TT E.40/22, *A continuation of certain special and remarkable passages in favour to the Parliament* (London: Samuel Peck, 28 April 1644).

19 BL TT E.40/1, *A fuller relation …*

20 HMC 13th Report, Captain Robert Harley to his brother Edward.

1,000 horse and 1,000 musketeers. However Forth advised against it, and added 'that having now possessed all the ground of advantage on our side, his opinion was that we should not hazard any further attempt, for that he conceived the enemy would now be forced, either to charge us upon their disadvantage, or to retire.' Hopton was satisfied with this advice and after securing his wing he rode over to consult with Forth himself. However:

> Being near the midway upon the brow of the hill he saw troops of the right wing too far advanced, and hotly engaged with the enemy in the foot of the hill, and so hard pressed, as when he came to the Lord Brentford he found him much troubled with it, for, it seems the engagement was by the forwardness of some particular officers, without order.[21]

While Hopton was riding over to consult Forth:

> being near the midway upon the brow of the hill he saw troops of the right wing too far advanced, and hotly engaged with the Enemy in the foot of the hill, and so hard pressed, as when he came to the Lord Brentford, he found him much troubled with it, for, it seems the engagement was by the forwardness of some particular officers, without order.[22]

Edward Walsingham, who was in Sir John Smith's troop, also recalls that it was through rashness that a detachment attacked the Parliamentarians:

> The fight begins where our valiant foot beat the Rebels out of the woods and bravely even bestowed a hopeful victory upon us, until some out of rash gallantry engage both themselves and the fortune of a glorious day, inasmuch that the horse must needs be commanded up, though upon a great disadvantage.[23]

On the other hand the account of Slingsby, who was major general of foot of Hopton's army that day, differs from Hopton's and Walsingham's, claiming that the detachment was ordered to fall on. After reciting the action at Cheriton Wood he goes on:

> This encouraged us so much that we made hast to finish the business (for had we but stood still and make signs of falling on, they had probably melted away without fighting a stroke more), but we were ordered to fall on from both wings, which was the only cause of their standing to fight; for then the enemy finds most of our strength drawn off the hill into the bottom, where Sir Henry Bard, leading on his regiment further then he had orders for, and indeed with more youthful courage then soldier like discretion, was observed by the enemy to be a great space before the rest, and out of his ground, who incontinently thrusts Sir Arthur Heselrige's

21 Hopton, *Bellum Civile*, pp.79–80, 82.

22 Hopton, *Bellum Civile,* p.82.

23 BL TT E.53/10, Edward Walsingham, *Britannicae Virtutis Imago or the effigies of true fortunate expressed to the life in the famous actions of that incomparable knight, Major general Smith who is here represented, June 1644* (Oxford: Henry Hall, 1644).

> regiment of horse well armed betwixt him and home, and their in the view of our whole army (much to our discouragement) kills and takes every man.[24]

Harley corroborates Slingsby's account of a general Royalist attack. He records the Royalists launched a two pronged attack against Waller's left wing, one column heading for Hinton Marsh, the second against the musketeers lining the hedges.

> The enemy being now possessed of the woods…thinking all were his own if he could but possess himself of the village and those hedges we had lined; for that intent he sent down a party of fifteen hundred commanded men to possess themselves of those places. We likewise sent down twelve hundred commanded men to second our own men. These did hold their places very near a heath; then the enemy got ground and fired the village. It was no sooner on fire but the wind turned. Our men, seeing the advantage upon set them to a disordered retreat; our horse seeing it, sent a party of a hundred horse under the command of Captain Butler [of Heselrige's Regiment of Horse] to charge them, and another under the command of Colonel Norton to second them. Captain Fleming [of Waller's horse] commanded another party. They all performed their charges so well that through God's blessing they routed them all, slew about a hundred and fifty and took a hundred and twenty prisoners with divers commanders of quality. we received not much loss, only Captain Fleming hurt in the arm with a captain's leading staff. I do not hear of any other considerable loss or hurt.[25]

Meanwhile the Royalists were also launching attacks on Waller's right wing, one Parliamentarian pamphlet implies that the Royalists had pursued Leighton's force too far;

> We were forced to retreat, the enemy thereby possessing themselves of the wood. Then were a party of the enemy deeply engaged to whose aid those in the wood were forced to come and we having likewise a party of horse drawn out, viz. four men out of every troop they came up and charged the enemy very valiantly and as they came out of the wood, routed them and did beat them all back to their main body after which not withstanding several other parties were continually sent out to second one another.[26]

The destruction of Bard's regiment prompted the Royalists generals to commit their cavalry:

> Then my Lord John Stuart (seeing our foot like to be oppressed with fresh horse) sends down the Queen's regiment of horse, which was most French who descended the hill in this ground with seeming resolution, but retreated after an unhandsome charge. Then we drew down most of the horse and endeavoured to draw up upon that plain ground before our foot, in which our Enemy's horse stood ranged in nine fair bodies, but having one lane's end only to pass into it, they came upon great disadvantages for by that time one body was in the ground

---

24 Slingsby's accountinHopton, *Bellum Civile,* pp.101–102.

25 Captain Robert Harley HMC, *Portland Mss*vol.3 pp.106–110.

26 BL TT E.40/22, *A continuation of certain special and remarkable passages…*

> and drawn up (before another could second it), it was over charged with number; yet I am confident our horse did perform more gallant charges that day then hath been in any one battle.[27]

According to Hopton, it was Sir Edward Stowell's brigade which was ordered to engage the Parliamentarian cavalry first:

> Lord Brentford thereupon ordered his to draw out 1,000 horse, and to command them to advance to the enemy's horse that were in the common at the foot of the hill, and to charge them. He thereupon drew out Sir Edward Stowell for that service with his own brigade, which then consisted of 1,000 horse, who performed it with very great gallantry, but after a sharp and close charge that continued near half an hour, his body of horse was broken and routed, and himself charging home to their cannon was taken prisoner with five wounds upon him. And while the Lord Hopton was ordering this charge, the rest of our horse, all saving Sir Humphrey Bennet's regiment, that stood in reserve on the top of the hill were wholly engaged. In this unfortunate charge we lost many of our best officers; And the Lord John Stuart, brother to the Duke of Richmond, who commanded the Lord Hopton's horse, and Sir John Smith who was his major general of horse, he, with much ado, got off alive, but both mortally wounded.[28]

The Earl of Clarendon dismisses the Royalist cavalry efforts that day: 'The king's horse never behaved themselves so ill as that day. For the main body of them after they had sustained one fierce charge, wheeled about to an unreasonable distance, and left their principal officers to shift for themselves.'[29] However this is extremely harsh, as according to Captain Harley, 'The fight betwixt the horse continued near four hours, their horse being at length discouraged, doing no good with their desperate and bold charges.' Being a cavalry officer who must have been in the thick of the fighting Harley does not go into much detail about the cavalry melee. However, did he have anything to boast about? According to Elias Archer:

> the enemy, who presently came on with their main body of horse, very powerfully and were met courageously, yet being of the greater number (for our whole body was not then together) forced ours to a disorderly retreat, at which time the day was doubtful, if not desperate ... our horse doing little for the space of an hour after their retreat, only some parties encountering with each other, at which time our Noble Major General Browne...drew off 100 men from the hedges, and in his own person led them on to charge the horse, which they did most gladly and courageously and forced the enemy's horse to wheel about, whereupon our body of horse came on again, and very manfully, at which time they charged twice through the enemy's body and put them to a rout, so that they were forced to retreat to the top of the hill, where they had first appeared.[30]

27 Slingsby's account in Hopton, *Bellum Civile*, p.102.

28 Hopton, *Bellum Civile*, p.82.

29 Clarendon, ed. Lockyer, *History of the Great Rebellion*, p.195.

30 BL TT E.40/1, *A fuller relation*... unnumbered page.

If Archer is right and the Parliamentarian horse did retreat, then it may have been at this time that the Royalist cavalry charged reached as far as Waller's artillery. Hopton records that Sir Edward Stowell:

> performed it [the charge] with very great gallantry, but after a sharp and close charge that continued near half an hour, his body of horse was broken and routed, and himself charging home to their cannon was taken prisoner with five wounds upon him. And while the Lord Hopton was ordering this charge, the rest of our horse, all, saving Sir Humphrey Bennet's Regiment, that stood in reserve on the top of the hill were wholly engaged.

Stowell was not the only one to charge Waller's guns, as Edward Walsingham, a member of Smith's troop recalls:

> In a distracted manner they are of necessity to charge a solid body of the Rebels horse, lying under the protection both of cannon and hedges lined with musketeers; their cannon (when he [Sir John Smith] is come within pistol shot with intention to charge in) flies off so freely that amazes his horse, the fire even flashing in his face causes him to rear and turn sideways upon the enemy who seeing all his rider's power employed to keep his saddle, and recover his horse let fly at him as thick as hail and in this interim comes one from among them clad like a lobster [Cuirassier] who with his carbine gives him his third and mortal wound in his belly onthe left side beneath his armour; with this wound he falls and with him the fortunes of the day; and courage of our horse, for no sooner was he down, but daunted with so disastrous an accident they in disorder retreat, scarce any but his [Smith's] own troop remaining on that wing, who resolved to die rather then loose so brave a leader advanced to fetch him off, even to the enemy's nose, and in despite of them gallantly brought him off, his horse and arms, whilst one of the company, a reformadoe lieutenant, in a brave revenge rides up to the armed monster and shoots him in the eye, sending him to answer for his detested act, in so base a manner wounding to death a gentleman.[31]

Sir John Smith died of his wounds the following day. Also to be killed in this cavalry action was Lord John Stuart. It was not just the Royalist generals who took part in the cavalry melee, as Waller himself records that:

> The enemy having by a charge given upon some troops of mine shut me off from my own men, I having then but three in company with me, but it pleased God they were repulsed again, and thereby a way opened for my retreat…I reckon it a mercy that upon a sudden occasion that day, charging without my headpiece, and being known to the enemy (as I afterwards understood from some of them), I came off safe and unhurt.[32]

Now with Smith and Stuart no longer to lead the Royalist cavalry, and it taking fire from the 100 musketeers from the hedges, it began to give ground:

31 BL TT E.53/10 Walsingham, *Britannicae Virtutis Imago …*

32 Waller, *Recollections*.

> By this time the whole horse were in disorder, and the Lord Hopton had much ado to get to the number of 300 horse to stand with him at the entrance into the Common, where all the Enemy's horse stood in bodies before him; The greater part of that little number of horse that stayed with him were of the Queen's Regiment, where Monsr. de Plurie their chief commander doing his duty like a very worthy person in the head of them had his leg shot off to the ankle with a great shot, whereof he shortly after died, and the Lord Hopton's horse received a musket shot in the shoulder; Yet it pleased God that they made that stand good, until, with the advice and assistance of the Earl of Brentford, the rest of the horse and foot were retreated and had recovered the top of the hill, where they had at first drawn up in the morning.[33]

With the cavalry melee continuing in the centre, on the flanks the tide swayed backwards and forwards until the mid afternoon, the time is not clear.[34] Waller then committed more of his infantry:

> two thousand musketeers were drawn out of your [Birch's[35]] request; one thousand whereof on the left wing commanded by Colonel Rea[36] who did very gallantly, the rest by your self on the right wing, all the rest of the army being to second them. These two great parties went on with such success, that in one hour the enemy's army was between them, all our horse and foot coming on in front of them. The first thing that I could perceive, they pulled off their colours, thrust them in their breeches, threw down their arms and fled confused.[37]

Slingsby records Rea's attack:

> The Enemy's left wing advances up to the end of the hill where our right should have been in readiness to resist them, but after some struggling to repulse them, in which Colonel Appleyard was shot, we were compelled to draw off in such disorder as we were forced back to the ground where we had hutted ... and their drew up in some order.

Slingsby's account appears to put Appleyard on the Royalist right wing, whereas in the morning of the battle he had captured Cheriton Wood, which is on their left. This suggests that a detachment of Hopton's army was sent to reinforce Forth's army at some point during the day.

As well as having to engage Waller's regiments of foot, the Royalists on the right wing had to fight off charge after charge from the Parliamentarian cavalry. After firing in volleys, the Royalists fell on with pikes and clubbed muskets; John Jones, a Parliamentarian captain, recalls the heavy fighting on this wing. The Royalists:

---

33 Hopton, *Bellum Civile,* p.83.

34 Birch states 4:00 p.m., whereas Archer believes it was nearer 2:00 p.m.

35 John Birch, lieutenant-colonel of Heselrige's Regiment of Foot.

36 Probably Lieutenant-Colonel Rea of Colonel Edward Harley's Regiment of Foot, which does not appear to have been present at the battle.

37 Webb, J.& T.W.(eds.), *Military Memoirs of Colonel John Birch*, p.11.

> came down with fury on the right wing along the hedges, which we had lined, but could hardly keep it; they fell on with so much courage and resolution, until the Kentish Horse [under Sir Michael Livesey] took a troop or two of them at one charge, and our horse fell on their foot, and drove them from the hedges then they fell down with a great body of horse and foot in those fields, and out foot seconded with 400 musketeers, sent to them, who within three hours fight drove them from the hedges.[38]

Slingsby adds:

> with a strong body of horse charges our foot on the left wing, on that part which my Lord Brentford was pleased to make your servants charge, there the Enemy horse was repulsed with loss. They immediately tried the second charge in which Captain Herbert of my Lord Hopton's regiment was slain, with a fresh body and were again repulsed, and so again the third time, the foot keeping their ground in a close body, not firing till within two pikes length, and then three ranks at a time, after turning up the butt end of their muskets, charging their pikes and standing close, preserved themselves, and slew many of the enemy.[39]

The Parliamentarians fought their way up the slope of East Down, so Hopton had no choice bt to pull his army back to Tichbourne Down. Buy now the Royalists knew that the battle was lost:

> By this time the disorder was so general, and the Enemy pressed in that part so hard (especially with their musket shot) that it was with great difficulty that we got off all our cannon; and making our rear as good as we could with some of the best of our horse and dragoons we recovered our first ground upon the ridge of the hill by Alresford town, with all our army, cannon and carriages; from whence we showed so good a countenance towards the Enemy, that they gave us some respite, unwilling (as it seemed) to hazard their whole armyupon us. And thereby the two Generals had some short time to consult, and the Lord Hopton (who best knew the country) advised by no means to retire to Winchester, it being an indefensible ill provided place, and utterly unsafe for an army in that condition. But that Colonel Fielding (who then commanded the Ordnance) should presently march off with the train and carriages towards Winchester, but being a mile on his way should turn upon the right hand towards Basing. The foot (with only a little party of 100 horse to abide in the rear,) to take the lower way through Alresford towards Basing, which after a mile entered into the lanes and woods, and that the horse should make their retreat by the way of the Downs; All this was executed accordingly.[40]

Captain Harley also recalls the final stages of the battle. The Royalists:

> Made a fair retreat to the top of the hill were their foot were. Colonel James Carr and Major Strachan had so plied their business on the left of our army that they

38 BL TT E.40/12, *A continuation of certain special and remarkable passages…*

39 Slingsby's account in Hopton, *Bellum Civile*, pp.101–102.

40 Hopton, *Bellum Civile,* pp.83–84.

> forced the enemy to draw off their ordnance, and quickly engaged all the enemy's foot on them, but seeing their horse to retreat would no longer abide the charge of our foot and dragoons, but made a speedy retreat to a hill a little beyond the place were we did fight. When we had possessed with our horse the hill which the enemy had, we were at a stand whether we should advance on the enemy. It was once by some ordered that we should return to our stations which we had before; and I believe we should not have pursued if Colonel Wemyss had not showed himself very violent for it. To him under God doth belong much of our victory. Through his persuasion it was ordered we should again fall on them and give them a general charge. This delay of ours gave them leave to draw off all their cannon and most of their carriages, but no sooner was our cannon come up and played on them awhile but they prevented our charge commanding every one to shift for themselves, and so they proved their horses to be better than ours.

Meanwhile Birch recalls that:

> Others hot in pursuit had not followed them [the Royalists] above 100 paces into their own ground [East Down] before one, whom I shall not name, overtook you, commanded you to stand; but for what end I never yet could tell, except it was to give the enemy leave to run away, and carry away their cannon, sure I am you stood there three quarters of an hour, until the enemy was far enough. The reason is too deep for me to give; only this I am sure of; had the enemy's commander in chief been there, he could not have commanded anything more advantageous to them.[41]

Harley also records that the Parliamentarians were ordered not to pursue:

> When we had possessed with our horse the hill which the enemy had, we were at a stand whether we should advance on the enemy. It was once by some ordered that we should returnto our stations which we had before; and I believe we should not have pursued if Colonel Weymss had not showed himself very violent for it. To him next under God doth belong much of our victory. Through his persuasion it was ordered we should again fall on them and give them a general charge. This delay of ours gave them leave to draw off all their cannon and most of their carriages, but no sooner was our cannon come up and played upon them awhile but they prevented our charge in commanding everyone to shift for himself, and so they proved their horses to be better than ours.[42]

Who the officer was that stopped the pursuit, unfortunately history does not record, but it was probably Waller himself. John Adair is probably right when he writes, 'the hesitation of the Roundheads once they had gained East Down– more soldierly caution to allow a regroup than a sinister plot to allow old friends to escape without being utterly ruined.'[43] However, it does show that Waller had some disciplined cavalry under his command, that they

---

41 Webb, J. & T.W. (eds.), *Military memoirs of Colonel John Birch,* p.11.

42 Captain Robert Harley, HMC *Portland Mss* vol. 3, pp.100–103.

43 Adair, *Cheriton,* p.136.

could be controlled in the presence of a retreating enemy, unlike cavalry of other armies of the time. This discipline is usually associated with Cromwell's regiment of horse and the cavalry of the New Model Army.

To cover their retreat the Royalists left 1,000 musketeers in Alresford to fight a rearguard action:

> And the Earl of Brentford did, with admirable conduct and gallantry, send off the horse, remaining himself with his page last upon the ground, and then got off himself hardly pursued by the enemy's horse until he got over the next pass, where he faced again. And at the same time the Lord Hopton drew out his 1000 foot out of the town, and with the foot recoveredBasing about one of the clock that night without further resistance. But the Earl of Brentford was forced to face about at every pass for the first 2 or 3 miles, and many of his horse broke from him; yet, it pleased God that all both horse and foot, cannon and carriages came safe to Basing that night.[44]

At General Weymss' insistence, once the Parliamentarian cavalry had reformed they were unleashed again, this time for the bloody business of the pursuit.

> Now when it was too late we followed them on the spur unto Winchester's walls we took diverse carriages and store of ammunition. The enemy in his flight set Alresford on fire, and for their reward we coming into the town before they well knew of it, we gave none of them any quarter. Very many Irish men were slain here. Our whole body of horse halted three miles short of Winchester; our parties went to Winchester's gates.[45]

Colonel Richard Neville's Regiment of Horse, described by Hopton as 'a little party of 100 horse to abide in the rear', was attached to the retreating Royalist infantry, although according to Elias Archer they offered little protection:

> our horse pursued them two miles at least, until the Enemy's horse overtook their own foot, who cried out (as the country people say) '*Face them!, Face them! once more face them*' which they did, but to small purpose; our horse came up, and at the first charge they were all routed and fled, our horse pursued them until they over took the foot, routed them likewise, and dispersed them several ways, some fled to Basing, some to Alton and some to Winchester, and by the way they cried out '*the kingdoms lost, the kingdoms lost*' etc. and when they left Alresford where they had long quartered, they set the town on fire at both ends, which doubtless had burnt to the ground, but that our men came in and put it out, there was only four or five houses burnt.[46]

The lane, Sutton Scrubbs, where the Parliamentarians caught up with the fleeing Royalists is said to have run with blood.

---

44 Hopton, *Bellum Civile,* pp.84–85.

45 Webb, J & T.W. (eds.), *Military memoirs of Colonel John Birch,* p.11.

46 TT E.40/1, *A fuller relation …*

As the sun began to set on 29 March 1644, the sun silhouetting the smouldering villages of Hinton Marsh and Alresford. The exact number of dead is unknown, Harley believes 'in all we did not lose sixty men. The enemy, I am confident, had slain three hundred men besides horse'. Archer gives the number of Parliamentarian dead as just 40. The Royalist newsbook *Mercurius Aulicus* denies the Parliamentarian pamphlet figures of 1,000, 600 and 400 Royalist dead, but does not give its own estimate. It does admit that:

> we lost very gallant men, especially the most Noble and Valiant Lord John Stuart, the renowned knight, Sir John Smith...two brave gentlemen, Colonel Sandys and Colonel Manning, and the valiant Lieutenant Colonel Scot [of Manning's horse]... and some wounded (though but few) wounded, as that brave soldier Colonel Appleyard... Captain Henry Pearson, a gallant deserving gentlemen, with some few others whose names we yet know not.

The Parliamentarians came off lighter, Colonels John Meldrum and George Thompson, Major Boswell [or Bosworth] of Colonel John Middleton's Regiment of Horse, Captain Fleming and Captain Lieutenant Milton of the London Trained Bands were all wounded. And no field officers were reported killed. According to *Mercurius Aulicus* Waller lost three colours, but unfortunately does not describe them or say which regiments they belonged to. Nor could Waller claim to have captured any colours.

On 30 March elements of Waller's army faced Winchester, and the next day Waller's and Heselrige's Regiments of Horse and Waller's Regiment of Dragoons beat up the Royalists quarters at Newbury. On 5 April Christchurch fell, and the following day the fortified manor house at Bishop's Waltham. On 9 April Winchester was stormed by Waller, but the castle held out. Elements of Waller's army were even reported to be on the outskirts of Salisbury. However the London Brigade were eager to return home and began to mutiny, with their old cries of '*Home! Home!*' The Committee of Both Kingdoms tried to make the London Brigade stay by paying them £1,000, but to no avail and without the support of his London Brigade Waller was forced to return to Farnham.

On 17 April, the same day Waller arrived back at Farnham, a party of Waller's army beat up the Royalists quarters at Sunning, near Reading, which was the last success of the campaign. It was not the first time, neither would it be the last, time that the London Brigade would let Waller down, but his army was too weak to take the field without the support of the London Trained Bands.

5

The Oxford Campaign

Though Waller was back in Farnham, the Battle of Cheriton had some far-reaching implications, it resulted in Hopton's army being reduced into the King's Oxford Army, which removed the threat of a Royalist advance on London through Surrey or Sussex for several months. It also made a Parliamentarian offensive possible. As Sir Edward Walker, the King's Secretary of War, wrote, Cheriton 'broke all measures and altered the whole scheme of the King's counsels. For whereas before he hoped to have entered the field early, and to have acted an offensive part, he now discerned he was wholly to be upon the defensive part; and that was like to be a very hard part too.'[1]

The Committee of Both Kingdoms planned that the armies of Waller and Essex should besiege the Royalist capital, Oxford and destroy the king's main army. The Committee also planned that the Earl of Manchester's Eastern Association would also take part in the forthcoming campaign, but due to the surrender of Sir John Meldrum's Army at Newark on 21 March, it was feared that there would be a Royalist advance into the Eastern Association counties, so Manchester's army had to be withdrawn from the offensive. However, the campaign did not bode well for the Parliamentarian cause because both still Essex and Waller hated each other.

On arriving back at Farnham Waller found a new London brigade waiting for him, under the command of Sir James Harrington, to replace Browne's. The brigade was made up of the Tower Hamlets Regiment, the Southwark Auxiliaries and the Westminster Auxiliaries. On paper the Tower Hamlets Regiment should have mustered 1,304 officers and men, but in April 1644 it mustered just 880 officers and men.[2] Unfortunately, the muster rolls of the other two regiments have not survived, but both on paper were about 1,000 strong, so may have been just 600–700 strong when they joined Waller, so the strength of the brigade may have been about 2,080–2,280 officers and men compared to its overall paper strength of the 3,304.

Waller's other infantry regiments appear to have been the same as had fought at Cheriton, while he had received an additional cavalry regiment

1 Clarendon, ed. Lockyer, *History of the Great Rebellion,* p.195.

2 Spring, *Waller's army,* p.137.

from Kent, which appears to have been reduced into Sir Michael Livesey's Regiment. This by no means offset the loss of Balfour's Brigade which had been recalled by Essex on 18 April, since he needed it for his own forthcoming campaign.

For a month Waller's army refreshed itself in its quarters in and around Farnham. On 28 April John Wight wrote to Sir Poynings More of Loseley Manor:

> Sir William Waller, with his army hath been at Farnham near 3 weeks. Since which time ever we seldom miss one day without warrants for provisions, hay etc. or one thing or the other, besides some quartering we have had, but Compton and Puttenham ever since with two or three troops a piece, that they know not how to subsist any longer, I cannot get a pony rent from any of Compton and Farncombe or Godalming.[3]

Waller did try to instil discipline in his army: the court martial papers show charges brought against soldiers for military matters rather than crimes against civilians. On 22 April John Boreman, a soldier in Waller's regiment of dragoons, was court-martialled for 'making of a mutiny in the Company at Mitcham, and then running away with several others.' Boreman was sentence to be hanged. At the same court martial the Provost Marshal General was ordered that if he found 'any private soldier drunk, that he shall have power to inflict the punishment of putting on a pair of handcuffs, and with a chain to draw the party up until he stand on tiptoe with a can or jug about his neck near the main Guard, and there to stand according to discretion.'[4]

Unfortunately, evidently these measures had no effect, as on 11 May John Wight again wrote to Sir Poynings More, informing him that:

> The unruliness of the soldiers at Compton doth so exceed that they threaten to break into the house daily, shot you coneys [rabbits] and have twice attempted to cut the head of the great pond in the park. Nicholas complained to their lieutenant, who took them off at that time but as he said…'no-one could order them except the State would allow them their pay.' It is a miserable condition that this poor Division is in to pay weekly for their provisions… and yet [we] are daily in danger of pillaging.[5]

Finally, much to the relief of the inhabitants of west Surrey and east Hampshire, on 17 May Waller finally marched out of Farnham for Bagshot at the head of a 9–10,000-strong army with 24 pieces of ordnance, many leather guns and about 60 wagons with provisions and ammunition. According to Richard Coe, a soldier in the Tower Hamlets Regiment, 'Our City Brigade and the Kentish Regiment were quartered in the park, where was plenty of mutton, veal, and lamb, some venison and good water, but neither bread

3 SHC LM Cor 5/34, John Wight to Sir Poynings More, 28 April 1644.

4 'Court Martial Papers of Sir William Waller's Army', printed in Adair, *Cheriton*, pp.200–201.

5 SHC LM Cor 5/36 John Wight to Sir Poynings More 11 May 1644

nor beer… but what we brought with us which was very little, there we lay Saturday night and Sunday.'[6]

Waller's army quartered at Bagshot from 18 until 20 May while he rode over to Henley-on-Thames to consult with Essex on the forthcoming campaign. Despite their hatred for each other the campaign got off to a good start, as on 17 May the King abandoned Reading, which was occupied by Essex on 23 May.

Waller in the meantime appears to have marched to Basing House, and quartered at Basingstoke until 24 May when they set off towards Abingdon, although the City brigade camped at Aldermaston that evening, where they remained until 26 May when they advanced to Compton. It was here that Richard Coe records a soldier in Captain Grove's Company was 'shot by accident and sent for [*sic*] London, in the afternoon another of our Regiment had the like mischance.' Unfortunately, Coe does not record whether these two soldiers were accidentally shot while training or for some other reason. Murder cannot be ruled out because a few days later the court martial of Waller's army records that the officers of Potley's and Weldon's Regiment were to inquire into the death of John Jenkins, a soldier in Potley's Regiment on 30 May. Unfortunately the outcome of the enquiry is not known. At another court martial a Sergeant West of Waller's own regiment of foot was accused of abusing "in some scandalous and reproachful language" soldiers of the Tower Hamlets Regiment. What West had against the Tower Hamlets Regiment is not recorded, but he was ordered to apologise to the whole regiment.[7]

While at Compton the City Brigade could see some of the colours of Essex's Army marching towards Abingdon. On 25 May the Royalists garrison had been given orders to abandon Abingdon, which was one of the satellite towns which surrounded Oxford. Essex seized Abingdon the following day. That day Coe records:

> Our forces could not march to Abingdon that night, there being no quarter to entertain two such armies; therefore Sunday night, and Monday night we lay wide of Abingdon and on Tuesday hearing my Lord's [Essex's] Army to be marched away, we followed in the rear andwent through Abingdon after my Lord's Army, (by the way we saw two of my Lord's men hanged for violence and plundering. It was written so on their breasts, and that night we lay at Newnham Wood, where we burnt (it being rainy weather) I believe £50 worth of wood if not more.[8]

The campaign was going well for the Parliamentarians and even Clarendon had to admit that:

---

6 BL TT E.2/20 Richard Coe, *An exact diarie. Or the Brief Relation of the Progress of Sir William Waller since the joining of the London Auxiliaries with his forces which was the twelfth of May until their return homeward on Thursday the 11 of July following … by Richard Coe under Captain Gore of the Tower Hamlets Regiment.* (London: Humphrey Tucker, 19 Jul 1644).

7 BL TT E.2/20 Richard Coe, *An exactdiarie*; the court martial papers of Waller's army printed in Adair, *Cheriton,* pp.206–207, 31 May and 7 June 1644.

8 BL TTE.2/20 Richard Coe, *An exact diarie …*

The infantry of Waller's Armies 1.
(Illustration by Mark Allen © Helion & Company 2019)
See Colour Plate Commentaries for further information.

The infantry of Waller's Armies 2.

(Illustration by Mark Allen © Helion & Company 2019)

See Colour Plate Commentaries for further information.

Officers, Ensigns and Musicians.
(Illustration by Mark Allen © Helion & Company 2019)
See Colour Plate Commentaries for further information.

Cavalry and Dragoons of Waller's Armies.
(Illustration by Mark Allen © Helion & Company 2019)
See Colour Plate Commentaries for further information.

Cavalry Standards.
(Illustration by Mark Allen © Helion & Company 2019)
See Colour Plate Commentaries for further information.

Cavalry Standards.

(Illustration by Mark Allen © Helion & Company 2019)

See Colour Plate Commentaries for further information.

Infantry Colours.
(Illustration by Mark Allen © Helion & Company 2019)
See Colour Plate Commentaries for further information.

Infantry Colours.
(Illustration by Mark Allen © Helion & Company 2019)
See Colour Plate Commentaries for further information.

> Without striking a blow, the [Essex and Waller] got the possession of Reading and Abingdon, and were masters of all Berkshire, and forced the king to draw his whole army of horse and foot on the north side of Oxford, where they were to feed on his own quarters, and to consider how to keep Oxford itself from being besieged and himself being enclosed in it.[9]

At Oxford everything was in turmoil and the King could not call upon reinforcements from his armies in the north or west. Therefore Charles decided to remain at Oxford until Waller and Essex made their move. Fortunately, the king 'was very happy that the two armies lay so long quiet near each other, without pressing the advantages they had, or improving the confusion and distraction which the king's forces wee at that time too much inclined to do.'[10]

Charles placed various outposts along the crossings over the rivers Cherwell and Isis which are on the east and west sides of Oxford. Waller sent a party of his dragoons to capture the bridge at Newbridge, but they were driven back. However, on 28 May Essex had better luck and managed to transport his army over the Thames at Stanford Ferry, just three and a half miles from Oxford, and marched the following day to Islip. For the next five days Essex tried to force a passage across the Cherwell, but was repulsed. Meanwhile on 31 May Waller retraced his steps to Abingdon, which his men plundered.[11]

On 1 June Waller's army succeeded in capturing the bridge at Newbridge, which was guarded by about 100 musketeers. According to Sir Edward Walker these musketeers were captured, with their ammunition spent and a detachment of Waller's army having crossed the river in boats.[12]

Richard Coe corroborates Walker's account, by stating that two files of each company were drawn out of the Tower Hamlets and Weldon's regiments for a forlorn hope which was commanded by Captain Gore, who led them on with:

> [Such] willingness and courage... notwithstanding the enemy had cut part of the bridge and made it unpassable, yet our commanders with a boat or two, called punts and some planks fell on sobravely that they made them forsake the bridge, took 30 persons upon quarter and 40 more among which were divers Irish, and a woman who was whipped and turned away.[13]

Usually women treated in such a way were prostitutes. Elements of Waller's army quartered at Newbridge for three nights to repair the bridge, while a detachment crossed to the Oxford bank on 2 June. Hearing that Waller had also crossed the Thames, the King, who was then at Woodstock, recalled his

---

9 Clarendon, ed. Lockyer, *History of the Great Rebellion*, pp.203–204.

10 Clarendon, ed. Lockyer, *History of the Great Rebellion*, p.204.

11 Brigadier Peter Young and Margaret Toynbee, *Cropredy Bridge 1644: The Campaign and the Battle* (Kineton: Roundwood Press, 1970), pp.30, 32.

12 Sir Edward Walker, *Historical Discourses upon several occasions* (London: Samuel Keble, 1705), p.18.

13 BL TT E.2/20, Richard Coe, *An exactdiarie...*

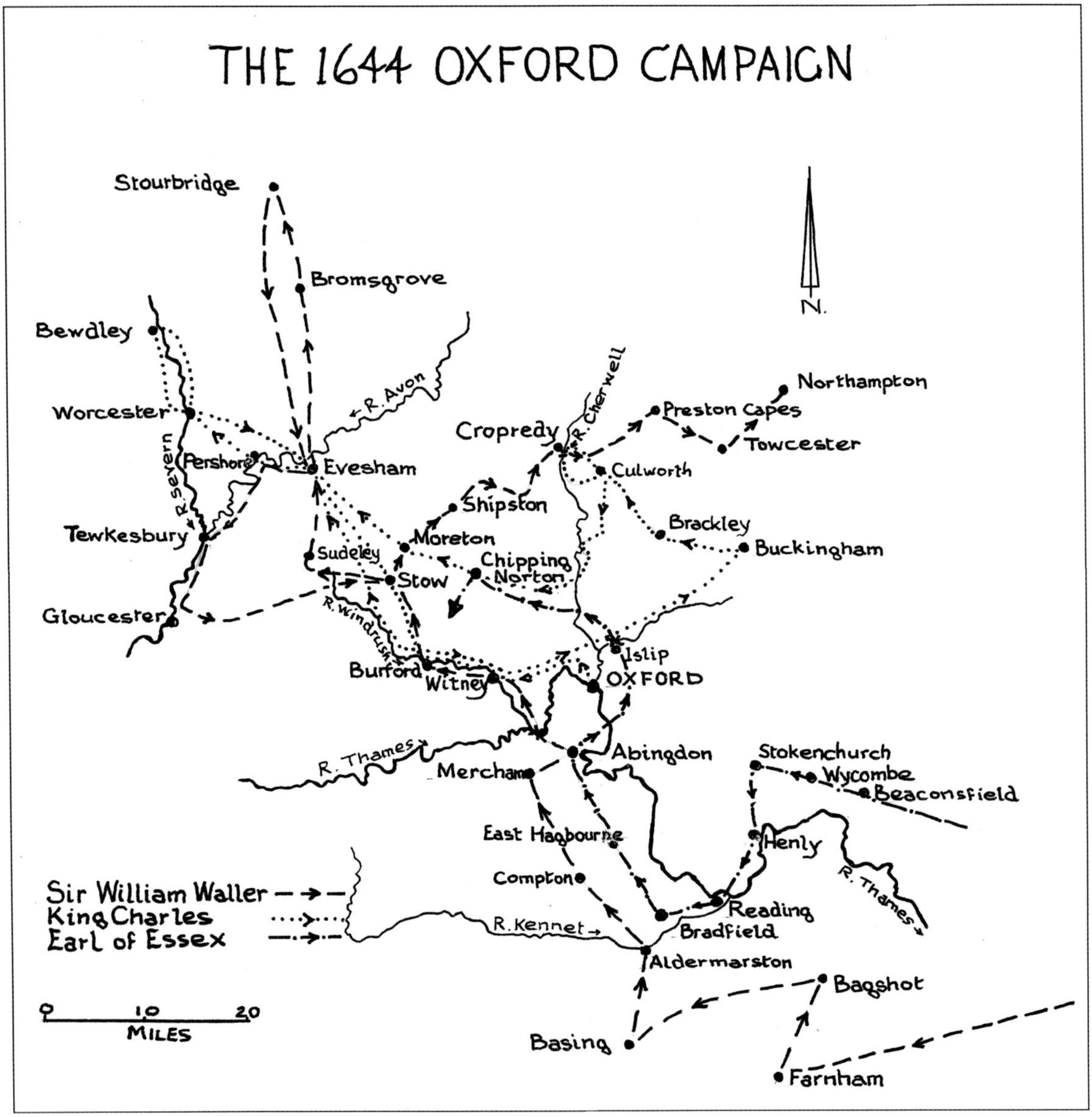

Map 5 Map showing the movements of the armies during the Oxford campaign, 1644.

men guarding the river crossings and returned to Oxford. On 3 June with the panic in his army over, Charles called a Royalist council of war where it was decided that he should leave Oxford that night with 5,000 horse and 2,500 musketeers. To cover their departure from Oxford a detachment made a thrust towards Waller, who was still at Abingdon, to 'amuse the Rebels'. This detachment of Royalists returned to Oxford that evening.[14]

On hearing of the King's escape the armies of Waller and Essex set off in pursuit, Waller's army marching via Witney and Fifield. Richard Coe recalls, 'We marched all day and night, and came a little before day near Witney,

14 Walker, *Historical Discourses*, p.20.

where we were quartered under a hedge [for] three or four hours, it rained extremely as it had done for the most part since our advance from Farnham till then.'[15] On 4 June Waller's vanguard captured 50 Royalist stragglers at Burford, but they had missed their prize, the King, who had eaten there a few hours before. Coe recalls that they did not even have time 'to get beer, bread or water', before they set off in pursuit of the King once more. At Stow-on-the-Wold they had three days' rest, during which time Coe continues, 'a gunner of ours was hanged for violence and plundering', before marching towards Winchcombe.[16]

The King's army was suffering from fatigue. On 5 June Richard Symonds records that, 'The King and all his army marched over [the] Cotswold Downs and Broadway Hills, and came to Evesham … which was the first night's rest of our army.' The following day, Symonds continues, 'Pershore bridge was pulled down by our forces because Waller should not follow, and forty of our men lost. The bridge fell from under them into the river Avon.' Later that day the King arrived at Worcester, having travelled 'the worst way, [through] a woody and dirty country.'[17]

So far the campaign had been a great success, two major towns, Reading and Abingdon, which had been thorns in Parliament's side had fallen without a shot being fired and now the King was on the run. However, on 6 June Essex called another council of war, probably at Chipping Norton, where to his surprise Waller was told that the Earl had decided to march into the west to relieve Lyme, and that Waller was to pursue the King alone. Clarendon recalls:'The Earl of Essex, when he saw the king was got full two days' march before him, and that it was impossible so to overtake him as to bring him into their power, resolved to pursue him no farther, but to consult what else was to be done.'

At a council of war Essex resolved that Edward Massey, the governor of Gloucester, should send reinforcements to Waller who was continue pursing the King, since he 'had the lighter ordnance and less carriages'; while Essex, who had 'the greater ordnance and the heavier carriages, should prosecute the other design of relieving Lyme, and reducing the west to the obedience of the Parliament.'[18] Waller objected to this decision, claiming that the west was his sphere of influence, but Essex being his senior ordered him to obey. Even the Committee of Both Kingdoms wrote to Essex angrily demanding that he should stick to the plan of campaign, but although he acknowledged their letter he still continued his march into the West. This was a fatal blunder on Essex's part, which not only caused Parliament to lose the initiative of the campaign but also one, and nearly two, of her armies.

On 10 June Waller from Evesham wrote to the Committee of Both Kingdoms:

---

15 BL TT E 2/20, Richard Coe, *An exactdDiarie…*

16 BL TT E.2/20, Richard Coe, *An exact diarie …*

17 Richard Symonds, *The Diary of Marches of the Royal Army during the Great Civil War kept by Richard Symonds*, ed. Charles Edward Long (London: AMS Press, 1968), p.8.

18 Clarendon, ed. Lockyer, *History of the Great Rebellion*, p.209.

> I parted from the Lord General in obedience to his command… The next day was so foul that the foot and artillery could not march, whereupon leaving them with two regiments of horse and my dragoons. I marched to Sudeley Castle in some hope it might yield upon summons, but the enemy seeing no foot looked upon it as a bravado and let fly great and small shot roundly amongst us, whereupon I sent order to the army to advance to me the next day. That night the enemy burnt some houses and the stables belonging to the castle, but had not time to slight the hedges about it, so that we lodged our dragoons within little more than pistol shot of the works and laid al the passages with our horse.
>
> The next morning they craved a parley by a drum and sent out Lieutenant Colonel Sayer and Major Aldam to treat, who stood upon points of honour, that they should be allowed to march out with their full arms and conveyed to Worcester, or have parole for their safety thither; but that being refused and assurances given they should have no other condition from me but fair quarter, they parted with the resolution to hold it out to the last man, and upon their return in a bravery gave us a volley of shot. They were immediately answered with interest, and in a short time we possessed the barn which was within a stone's cast of their works. Our men were drawn up in preparation to give a general assault, and diverse of our horsemen, without orders, rode up to their works and discharged their pistols at them. Night coming on we deferred the assault until the next morning, but an hour within night their drum beat a parley and brought a letter from the governor, Sir William Moreton, and officers, signifying that they yielded upon my own conditions…the next morning I took possession of the place. We took one colonel, one lieutenant colonel, 2 majors, 5 captains, 7 lieutenants, 4 ensigns, 300 soldiers, 2 pieces of ordnance, one demi culverin the other a drake five and a half barrels of gunpowder, 1 CWT of match with a good proportion of shot.[19]

According to Richard Symonds, while Waller's army was quartered at Evesham it smashed some of the stained glass windows in the church, although Symonds could still recognise the coats of arms of various local families when he visited the building about two weeks later.[20]

Writing from Stourbridge on 16 June, Waller acknowledged that he had received a letter from the Committee of Both Kingdoms for him to march into the west, but added that it was, 'with a sad sense' of the lack of provisions in the surrounding counties. He added, 'His Majesty yesterday retired again to Worcester. I have given orders for the present reparation of Bewdley bridge, which will make me master of both sides of the river and give me a readier opportunity to follow His Majesty whensoever he dislodges. His army is mouldered away to a very small proportion, and I think it lessens every day.'[21] However, the same day Charles suddenly marched to Burford, breaking the bridges at Bewdley, Bidford and Evesham so that Waller could not pursue him. It was at Burford that Charles learnt that Essex had marched

19 *CSPD 1644*, p.206, Sir William Waller and Sir Arthur Heselrige to the Committee of Both Kingdoms, 10 June 1644.

20 Symonds, *Diary*, p.25.

21 *CSPD 1644*, p.242, Sir William Waller to the Committee of Both Kingdoms, 16 June 1644.

into the West to relieve Lyme. Encouraged by this stroke of good luck the Royalists marched to Witney, where on 18 June they rendezvoused with the rest of the Oxford Army.

Waller had expected Charles to march to Shrewsbury, but hearing that the Royalists had marched to Burford, Waller left his infantry at Stourbridge with two regiments of horse while he set off in pursuit with the rest of his horse and dragoons. He arrived at Evesham, a distance of 22 miles, on 18 June, only to discover the Royalist army had marched an additional 20 miles. 'I conceive,' he wrote to the Committee of Both Kingdoms, 'I should not ruin my horse to pursue him further and therefore I gave over the chase.' Having decided to give up the pursuit, Waller decided to 'apply myself to the service of the west.'[22]

While Waller was away, according to Richard Coe, the Tower Hamlets Regiment enjoyed their first large meal for weeks, 'we having mutton, bread, cheese and beer sent to us out of the country.' On 17 June the Regiment was ordered to march to Saltwich, but on the way:

> at Harvington we light on a Papist widow's house (but she [was] not at home) the soldiers took all in the house, as pewter, brass, bedding, great store of books etc., her name was Mistress Packington [who was] then at Worcester; we lay that night at Saltwich and lying in the salt cellars grew so dry, that we drunk the town dry.[23]

Not all of Waller's army pursued the King. Sir Arthur Heselrige with a detachment of the army had separated from Waller and would not rejoin him until the beginning of July. Heselrige had also taken the cipher used to decode the letters from the northern Parliamentarians with him, leaving Waller blind to events in the north.[24]

On 19 June the Committee of Both Kingdoms wrote to Waller:

> We have certain intelligence that the King is come back near Oxford with horse and foot. We desire you to follow him, which way so ever he takes, with as much speed as you can conveniently. If he should give you battle about Oxford, although we hope your army is able to fight with any strength the king can make in those parts where he now is, yet, because Oxford will be an advantage to him, and that the less hazard we run the better, we have appointed to be in readiness to assist you upon your command, viz. foot of Warwick, Colonel Bosseville's regiment, 240; of the castle, Major Bridges, 100; of Kenilworth Castle, Captain Needham's, 60; of Coventry, 200; of Northampton, 100; Sir Samuel Luke from Newport [Pagnell], 400; Sir Samuel Luke's from Cambridge, 400. Total 1,500 foot. Horse from Colonel Purefoy's, 250; Colonel Barker, 60; Major Bridges, 50; Northampton, 80; Sir Samuel Luke's 80; Total 520 horse.[25]

---

22 *CSPD 1644*, p.247, Sir William Waller to the Committee of Both Kingdoms, 18 June 1644.
23 BL TT E.2/20 Richard Coe, *An exact diarie ...*
24 *CSPD 1644*, p.242, Sir William Waller to the Committee of Both Kingdoms, 16 June 1644.
25 *CSPD 1644*, pp.253–254, Committee of Both Kingdoms to Sir William Waller, 19 June 1644.

How many of these detachments joined Waller is not known, because despite being promised a detachment from Gloucester after Essex's departure into the West, on 21 June Waller complained to the Committee of Both Kingdoms:'I would that you should direct your commands to them to join with me, as likewise to Colonel Massey, who promised me 1,100 men but I never yet saw one.'[26]

The same day the King marched to Woodstock where he was joined by more foot, which brought his army to a strength of 4–5,000 horse and 5,500–6,000 foot and 10 pieces of ordnance, and then marched to Bletchingdon.[27]

Waller was ready to give up the pursuit, but on 22 June the King marched to Buckingham, where he quartered for four days, before marching to Brackley. This delay gave Waller time to catch Charles up. By now the rains which had plagued the beginning of the campaign were over and on 26 June Waller requested to be:

> excused from taking long marches, without rest sometimes, [during] this extremely hot weather, especially with the foot, who are very much diminished and would quickly be ruined if I should not spare them as much as possible... I am come to Oxhill, near Kineton field [Edgehill] and the foot are at Shipston on Stour and purpose to march in the cool of the evening. I have received some supplies of horse and foot from Gloucester, Warwick and Coventry.[28]

It was hoped that Major General Browne's Army would join Waller and that Hampshire would send a party of horse to reinforce Waller.

On 28 June the King was marching towards Banbury from Thorpe Mandeville, but Waller had arrived at Hanwell, near Banbury, the night before. At last the two armies met. It was an excited Waller who wrote to the Committee of Both Kingdoms that day:

> I have only leisure to let you know that his Majesty has drawn up his army at Edgcott to hinder my march to Towcester. I am at Hanwell near Banbury. This day in all probability will prove a deciding day, the Lord prosper his own cause, for his great name's sake. I praise God I find a great cheerfulness in the army, and I doubt not we shall render you a good account of our service. We are drawing into the field, and therefore I can only give you this short assurance.[29]

However, the day passed without any action, but the same could not be said of the following day.

The next day Waller again wrote to the Committee:

> We drew up from Hanwell to the hill on this side of the town and stood there in battalia all the day, and quartered within the enclosures that night. This morning

26 *CSPD 1644*, pp.261–262, Sir William Waller to the Committee of Both Kingdoms, 21 June 1644.

27 Symonds, *Diary*, p.18.

28 *CSPD 1644*, pp.279–280, Sir William Waller to the Committee of Both Kingdoms, 26 June 1644.

29 *CSPD 1644*, p.288, Sir William Waller to the Committee of Both Kingdoms, 28 June 1644.

> we are drawn out again. The king's army is drawing up the hill, most of his horse are fallen down towards Cropredy, whether it be to secure their retreat or to make their passage that way to fight upon more equal ground is yet not certain, but we shall quickly know. If they have a mind to it they will as gladly be welcomed as ever men were.[30]

The two armies faced each other until early in the morning of 29 June. Realising that Waller would not be drawn from his strong position on Crouch Hill, and it being too steep to storm, the Royalists began to draw off. In a letter addressed to his Queen, Charles writes 'It was resolved ... to march away towards Daventry, hoping to draw him [Waller] after us into some more equal place ... which we did in the morning about seven or eight o'clock.' Symonds puts the time nearer to 5:00 a.m.[31]

Lord Forth commanded the vanguard, the King the centre. The rearguard was composed of the earls of Cleveland and Northampton's brigades of horse and 1,000 foot drawn from Colonel George Lisle's or Sir Bernard Astley's tertios.

Seeing the Royalist army draw off, Waller records, in '[all] possible haste I rose and marched to Burton, which brought me full in upon the flank of the enemy and gave me a very great advantage.'

Waller drew up his army on Bourton Hill, which according to *Mercurius Aulicus*, had the advantage of 'springs and bogs before his front, and both his flanks and back strong hedges (you know his condition of old, hills, bogs, hedges, ditches, these you must grant him, he'll not fight else.)' As he stood on Bourton Hill he could see the Royalist army marching below him on the other side of the Cherwell. There were four crossings over the river, near to where Waller had drawn up: on Waller's right was Slat Mill, to his front Cropredy Bridge, with a ford close by; and a mile and a half away up stream was Hays Bridge.[32]The bridge at Cropredy has been replaced several times since the battle. In 1886 when it was widened on the southern side some timbers were found a little downstream from the present bridge. Today's bridge dates from 1937. Another feature that has changed the battlefield is the Coventry to Oxford canal, which was extended to Cropredy in 1778 and the Banbury to Leamington Railway was built over part of the battlefield in 1852. A drainage system has not only drained the 'springs and bogs' on the battlefield, but made the River Cherwell fordable in places where it was not possible to cross in 1644. The wet weather which had plagued the campaign since it had begun was no longer an issue since according to Clarendon it was a 'very fair and very warm' day.[33]

Waller's army had suffered badly in pursuing the King during the previous month, as early as 7 June Waller and Heselrige had written, 'Our

30 *CSPD 1644*, p.290, Sir William Waller to the Committee of Both Kingdoms, 29 June 1644.

31 *CSPD 1644*, p.316, King Charles I to Queen Henrietta Maria, 4 July 1644

32 *CSPD 1644*, p.293, Sir William Waller to the Committee of Both Kingdoms, 20 June 1644; *Mercurius Aulicus*, 29 June 1644.

33 Anon., *English Heritage Battlefield Report: Cropredy Bridge* (English Heritage, 1995), the author walking the battlefield; Clarendon, ed. Lockyer, *History of the Great Rebellion*, p.216.

horse are much beaten with their march, and so are our foot.'[34] However, with reinforcements from several garrisons Waller still could probably muster an army of 8–9,000 strong compared to the king's 10–11,000 strong army. A report arrived at Royalist headquarters saying that there were 300 Parliamentarian horse about two miles away marching to join Waller. This detachment was probably from one or more of the Parliamentarian garrisons placed at Waller's disposal on 19 June. The Royalists acted quickly and sent orders to the vanguard and main body to increase their pace, hoping to cut off this detachment. Unfortunately, no orders were received by the rearguard, who continued to march at their normal pace. According to Sir Edward Walker:

> without any apprehension of the Rebels' intentions (who perceiving and interval of a considerable distance caused by this intelligence between the body and rear of the king's army) presently laid hold of the opportunity and advancing with 1,500 horse, 1,100 foot and11 pieces of cannon to Cropredy and forced that pass.

A party of Royalist dragoons was sent to secure Cropredy Bridge, while the Royalist army marched passed, however Walker continues, 'our dragoons quitting it without much resistance.'[35]

How large this gap between the main body and the rearguard was is not recorded, John Adair estimated it to be a mile and a half, although George Lord Digby estimated it to be 'about a mile.'[36] But, seeing the large gap between the main body and the rearguard, Waller was eager to engage the Royalists. In his *Recollections* he would later write that God punished him at Cropredy Bridge due to the 'presumption upon mine own strength, and former successes, justly humbled… with a dishonourable blow.'[37]

Waller's version of events is that, 'I and Lieutenant General Middleton, with some regiments of horse, advancing seized upon the bridge at Cropredy and other passes near it, and gave order to have them secured with foot and artillery. The lieutenant general fell in with some few troops and dragoons by a mill.'[38]

Lieutenant General Middleton's force numbered about 1,200 strong, consisting of Heselrige's and Vandruske's Regiments of Horse and five companies of Waller's, four or five of Jones' Regiment.

Birch's Secretary also places Major General Potley's Regiment as marching over the bridge, but according to the Parliamentariannewsbook, *Perfect Passages*, it was the Auxiliaries of the City of Westminster with their yellow ensigns:'[the] Yellow Regiment of Auxiliaries, being near, were much engaged: who being too confident of their strength, not staying till the rear of the King's forces came up, forced themselves upon the right wing of the

34 *CSPD 1644*, p.213, Sir William Waller to the Committee of Both Kingdoms, 7 June 1644.

35 Walker, *Historical Discourses* p.31.

36 Adair, *Roundhead General*, p.160; *CSPD 1644*, p.316 George Lord Digby to the Queen, 30 June 1644.

37 Waller, *Recollections*, p.131.

38 *CSPD* 1644, p.293, Sir William Waller to the Committee of Both Kingdoms, 30 June 1644.

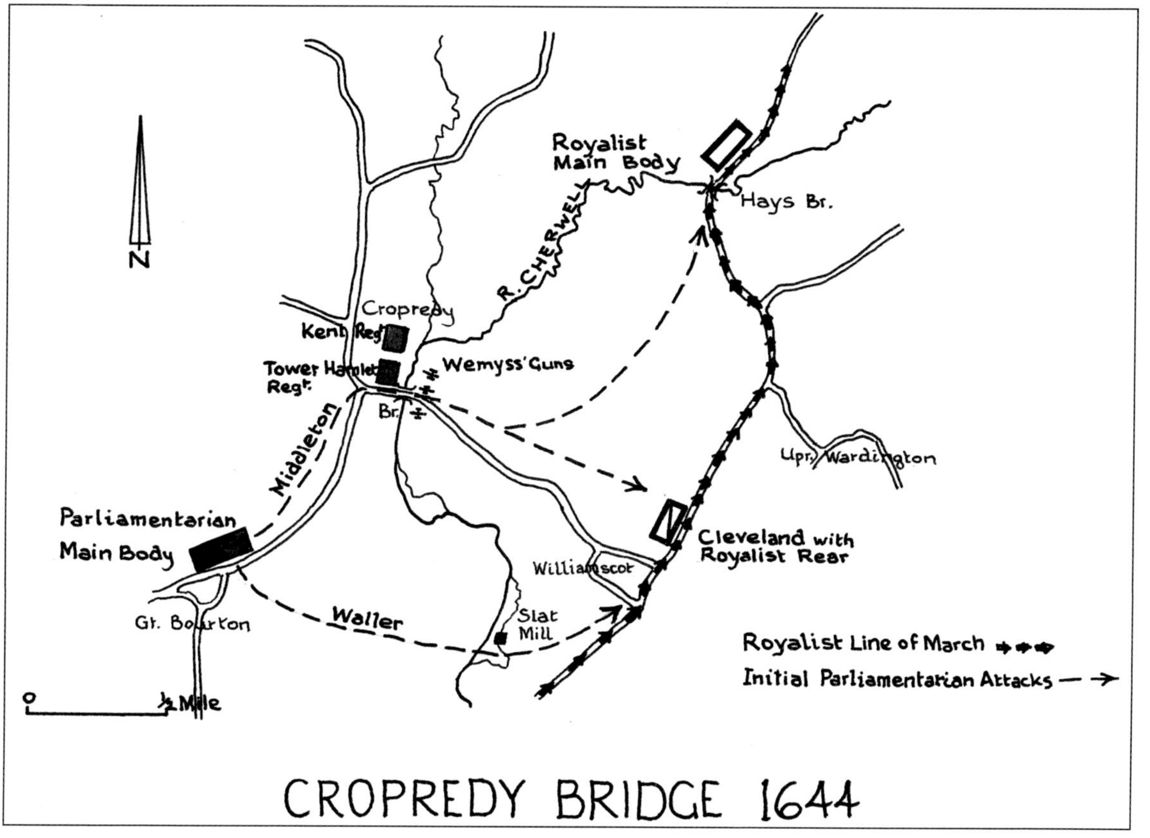

Map 6 Map showing Waller's attack at the battle of Cropredy Bridge, 29 June 1644.

King's forces.' Whether it was the Yellow Auxiliaries or Potley's is not known, but Potley's Regiment is believed to have worn yellow coats, and so possibly had yellow colours also.[39]

Meanwhile, according to Lieutenant Ellis of Heselrige's Regiment of Horse:

> Being over the river, through miss information, we too speedily pursued the enemy, (being informed that their whole body was marched away, when as a third part of them were left behind unknown to us). We pursued them above a mile, until we came to a bridge [Hays Bridge], where their foot made a stand, drew up and faced us; We being within musket shot of them, only four eldest troops (viz.) Sir Arthur's, Captain Okey's, Captain Foley's and Captain Gardiner's; They overthrew a carriage to barricade the bridge, and planted it with musketeers.

Without the support of their infantry and seeing the Royalist main body forming up on the opposite bank, the four troops of Heselrige's Regiment had little choice but to retreat. Charles ordered his own lifeguard under Lord Bernard Stuart to pursue them.

39 BL TT E.252/51, *Perfect Passages.*

The Bridge at Cropredy.
(Photo: Nicola Turton)

However, these four troops were just one prong of Middleton's attack, because as they moved north to attack the main body of the Royalist army another detachment had moved south where it clashed with the Earl of Cleveland's Brigade of Horse. According to Sir Edward Walker the Earl of Cleveland:

> drew up his brigade ... to a rising ground facing the pass [Cropredy Bridge] where under Colonel Neville that he stood too near a hedge where the rebels might place some foot he wheeled towards the right hand and took more ground, there he perceived a great body of the Rebels' horse drawn up ready to have fallen on his rear. Whereupon (not having time to expect either word or orders from the Lord Wilmot...) he gave his own word (hand and sword) and presently advancing that body of the Rebels ran, and upon that chase one cornet and someprisoners were taken...
>
> The Earl of Cleveland after his first encounter made a little stand near a great ash ... there he perceived a great body of the Rebels' horse of 16 colours (and as many colours of foot placed within hedges) all within musket shot of him, this caused him suddenly to advance, the Rebels doing the like and having stoutly stood out their musket and carbine shot, he gave the command to charge, and by his singular valour and resolution...he routed all those horse and foot and chased them beyond their cannon all which (being eleven pieces) were then taken, and 2 barricades of wood drawn with wheels in each 7 small brass and leather guns charged with caseshot; most of their cannoniers were then slain.[40]

Upon the return of the four troops of Heselrige's they not only found that the infantry that they were meant to be supporting had been routed by 'an unresistable body of the enemy's horse, of some thirty troops, and two regiments of foot', but also their way was blocked by Royalist horse and foot. Therefore:

> our four troops charged the King's own regiment, and put them to a retreat; but the other troop coming down upon us, (there being of them in all some three Regiments) with whom we were in no case able to deal, we were necessitated to retreat very disorderly, having put their body of Horse into a combustion, having slain three colonels, whereof one was Sir William Butler, a Papist of Kent, Lieutenant General of Horse, viz. Wilmot was sore wounded, and his lieutenant general taken prisoner, and committed to the custody of two soldiers, who in our disorderly retreat lost him again. We slew divers others of their officers, both in our charge and in our retreat, the way was filled with their foot and horse, many whereof were wounded sorely, slew others and took some prisoners.[41]

According to Sir Edward Walker far from being routed by these four troops the King's troop, seeing that they were about to charge Cleveland's Brigade in

40 Walker, *Historical Discourses*, p.32.

41 Ellis, Thomas, *An Exact and full relation of the last fight between the King's forces and Sir William Waller* (London, Ben Allen, 5 July 1644).

the flank 'turned their intended charge into a flight, which no question much facilitated the defeat of the Rebels.'[42]

While Middleton was crossing Cropredy Bridge Waller was fording the river at Slat Mill further downstream to attack the rear of the Royalist army, which was formed by the Earl of Northampton's Brigade of Horse. Waller records:

> I advanced with the remainder of those regiments [of horse]over a passage ... I had a steep hill to mount, not far from the top whereof the enemy was drawn up in a strong body. Some of the regiments came up slowly, whereupon I turned back leaving my regiment to march on.[43]

Waller turning away to hasten some of his regiments forward seems to have been the reason why a rumour spread in the Royalist army had he had been wounded. *Mercurius Aulicus* states that he was 'dangerously wounded' during the battle and the King records that he was 'sore wounded', but he does not appear on any casualty list, nor does he refer to it in his *Vindication* or *Recollections*. Neither does he say who commanded the force in his absence, which was reported to be about 1,000 strong. After recalling the bravery of the Earl of Cleveland's Brigade, Sir Edward Walker goes on:

> The Earl of Northampton with no less courage finding the rebels that were come over the pass below to follow him in the rear presently faced about with his own, the Lord Wilmot's, Percy's and Colonel Weston's Regiment of Horse and forced the Rebels to a speedy flight over the pass but with little loss they being not willing to abide a second charge.[44]

The other sources of the battle do not refer to this action, and Waller does not refer to it again. Except that on hearing Middleton being:

> forced ... to retreat, not without loss...Whereupon the whole army of the enemy being rallied. I thought it best to make an orderly retreat to our foot, which we did without any loss, and drew up upon the hill on the right hand of Burton, where we faced the enemy's army which was drawn up on the other side of the passage.[45]

However, it was not orderly as Waller suggests, because according to Lieutenant Ellis:

> Coming back to the bridge, the [Tower] Hamlets very honourably and stoutly made good the bridge, kept back the enemy and recovered three pieces of our ordnance, which we had lost, we having lost some half a dozen small pieces

42 Walker, *Historical Discourses*, p.32.
43 *CSPD 1644*, pp.293–294, Sir William Waller to the Committee of Both Kingdoms, 30 June 1644.
44 Walker, *Historical Discourses*, p.33.
45 *CSPD 1644*, pp.293–294, Sir William Waller to the Committee of Both Kingdoms, 30 June 1644.

> besides, which were unadvisedly drawn over before the foot were ready to march along with them, and the men running away with the horse, we could not draw them back again; being over the bridge, we rallied together and drew our body toward another place of the river, where the enemy made show of coming over, but we kept them on the other side; although we could not attain what we attempted, yet we hereby bravely caused them to draw back their whole body from their march onward toward Daventry.[46]

True, Waller's and Middleton's attacks had been pushed back over the Cherwell, but they still held the crossings of Cropredy Bridge and Slat Mill, which the Royalists decided to attack, as Sir Edward Walker records:

> By this time it was 3 in the afternoon and his Majesty having his army together resolved to attempt the passes, sending parties to both places; those sent to Cropredy Bridge were kept of all that day the Rebels relieving theirs with strong bodies of foot, but those sent to the other pass quickly gained it, and the Mill adjoining where they took some prisoners … Towards the evening we drew down most of the horse and foot below that pass nearer the Cherwell facing the Rebels who ranged their foot on the top of the opposite hill, [Bourton Hill] and drew three great bodies of their horse within reach of our cannon which being discharged amongst them made them to retire in great disorder.[47]

Night put a stop to the fighting. According to the King, Waller had lost 200 men killed, 11 pieces of ordnance, eight colours and about 1,000 deserted. *Mercurius Aulicus* records the Royalists captured 12 colours, 'four Colours of foot and eight of horse'. Richard Symonds in his diary records a blue ensign, which could have belonged to Waller's or Heselrige's Regiment of Foot and a red ensign with a white pile wavy suggesting it might have belonged to a major's company, which was taken at the 'furthest pass', suggesting Slat Mill, and a dragoon's guidon captured at the 'first pass'. Symonds also records that a French trooper captured a trumpet and white banner with 'three green snakes embowed'. This trumpet banner almost certainly belonged to Captain Parren or Parham whose troop belonged to Colonel Edward Cooke's Regiment of Horse, since his coat of arms was the same as the trumpet banner. A dragoon's guidon was captured at Cropredy bridge. On the Parliamentarian side Ellis puts Waller's losses at 100 to 120 killed and captured, and 'we took two horse colours of theirs and we lost three foot colours.'[48]

Waller had lost several senior officers including Lieutenant General Wemyss, Lieutenant Colonels Baker and Baines, three captains, two lieutenants and four cornets were captured.[49] The losses among Wemyss' firelocks, which guarded Waller's artillery, must have been particularly

46 Ellis, *An Exact and full relation of the last fight …*

47 Walker, *Historical Discourses*, p.32.

48 *CSPD 1644*, p.316, King Charles I to Queen Henrietta Maria, 4 July 1644; Symonds, *Diary*, pp.23, 24.

49 Weymss commanded Waller's artillery, Baker was the lieutenant-colonel of Waller's Regiment of Foot, and Baines was lieutenant-colonel of Colonel Samuel Jones' Greencoats.

severe when the Parliamentarian guns were overrun and their crews cut down. Eleven pieces were captured in all.

The Royalists had also suffered losing two colonels, Sir William Boleter and Sir William Clerk, both veterans of Hopton's old army; plus two majors and a captain. Lord Wilmot and Colonel Richard Neville and two captains were wounded. As to the rank and file the Royalists admit only 10 to 20, which is certainly an underestimate.

On the evening of the battle Charles sent a trumpeter to Waller so that Sir Edward Walker could publish 'a message of grace and pardon to all the officers and soldiers to that [Waller's] Army if they would lay down their arms and submit.' Waller sent the trumpeter back with his own message saying that he was unable to grant this message without the agreement of Houses of Parliament. In his letter of 30 June to the Committee of Both Kingdoms reporting the events of the previous day, Waller confirmed the King had sent a message of grace.[50]

Waller also mentions this incident in his *Recollections* but adds:

> The trumpet said he had a private message for me, and prayed me to hear him: I replied there need be no privacy, not caring to give a handle to mine enemies: but some that were near me did persuade me to hear the man, and sent out. He then presently pulled forth a letter, which to my great shame and surprise came from the Lady [blank]; in it she besought me to betray my cause; and this she did so wittily and kind, that I had much ado to be angry. Before this lady's marriage I had been her suitor, and did dearly love her and she remembered me of this, and of some soft passages. Whether or not she was put on this by some greater than herself I never knew; but I returned for [an] answer that as I had never been a traitor to my love, so would I not to my cause, which I should be, if I did as she would advise, and after this I heard no more.[51]

According to Sir Edward Walker while Waller was deliberating his answer 'either to show his anger or to colour his loss, he caused at least 20 great shot to be made at our army, many of which were levelled at the place where His Majesty stood, and some of them fell near him.' Symonds confirms this incident, but states that '10 or more great pieces' were fired, 'some of them fell near the king.'[52]

Lord Digby saw the Royalist victory '[as] if God had blessed us, as it were by [a] miracle, we had been utterly routed.'[53] Meanwhile across the field, it being a Sunday, the Parliamentarian newsbook *Perfect Passages* records:

> Sir William Waller's soldiers congregated in several places: and praised God for the great deliverances, amongst which on congregation that heard Mr Jackson who preached to one part of the army in Cropredy meadow, discerning ordnance

50 Walker, *Historical Discourses*, p.34; *CSPD 1644*, pp.293–294, Sir William Waller to the Committee of Both Kingdoms, 30 June 1644.

51 Waller, *Recollections*, p.107.

52 Walker, *Historical Discourses*, p.34; Symonds, *Diary*, p.24.

53 *CSPD 1644*, p.316, George Lord Digby to the Queen, 30 June 1644.

planted against them from the enemy were forced to remove in time of prayer to prevent the danger.

At some point the Parliamentarians held a council of war to decide their plan of action.Then, *Perfect Passages* continues:

Sir William being at his lodgings in Great Bourton to consult about business, it pleased God to show them a great deliverance, for the floor of the room in which they were; fell down and sunk into the cellar, but though God's goodness, not any one received any hurt, Major General Potley fell under Sir William Waller and Colonel Holborne fell upon him; and divers others there were in great danger: but God be praised no hurt to any one man.[54]

Waller, also records this incident: 'I escaped a great danger… being with my officers at a council of war, the floor of the room (where I was) sunk [i.e. collapsed] under me, and I lay overwhelmed with a great deal of lumber that fell upon me, and yet blessed be God, I had not hurt at all.' However, according to John Adair, Potley was badly hurt and was forced to retire from military service after this accident; yet he was present at the siege of Donnington Castle early in August, and it was not until early 1645 that Sir Hardress Waller took over his regiment.[55]

That day Waller wrote to the Committee of Both Kingdoms:

Both armies have lain facing one another within half a mile, a little brook interposing between us. The enemy has made divers offers to fall on upon me, but only offers. This night theyarose and marched away towards Banbury, but whither they intend I cannot yet discover. I am making ready to march after them.[56]

According to Richard Symonds, 'the rebels shot 30 pieces of cannon at a body of horse of ours which lay on the side [of the] hill, but did no hurt.' Despite this,'nothing of any moment done all this day.'[57]

Although Richard Coe records:

10 or 11 a clock at night a foolish fellow of our regiment [The Tower Hamlets], shot off his musket (the watch being set) which made alarms in the enemy's quarters, they shot at our Forlorn hope, which lay down by their works, and so we shot at them, but we were there over cunning for them, for our firelocks were placed under a hedge and lighted match hung alone on the palisades a musket shot off; before day they discharged a piece of ordnance, and gave us an alarm likewise, we made ourselves ready to entertain it but heard no more of them.[58]

54 BL TT E.252/51, *Perfect Passages*.
55 Waller, *Recollections*, p.107; Adair, *Roundhead* General, p.163; Spring, *Waller's army*, p.119.
56 *CSPD 1644*, p.298, Sir William Waller to the Committee of Both Kingdoms, 1 July 1644.
57 Symonds, *Diary*, p.24.
58 BL TT E.2/20, Richard Coe, *An exact diarie …*

Both sides seem to have used the lull in hostilities to bury their dead, although Cropredy Church register only records, 'five soldiers buried the last day of June', and 'Edward Webb, major of the king's horse was buried the14th day of July.' Even so, Richard Coe also records after the battle:

> we marched over the bridge, wherein our march up the lane to Moriton [Wardington], a mile off the Bridge, (which lane the enemy enjoyed before) we found many dead corpses lying naked and unburied, 40 graves in the highway... and in the church and churchyard at Moriton [Wardington] were many commanders buried, who had been slain in the fight.[59]

The parish register for Wardington does not record any soldiers being buried, which is not unusual for battle casualties. Why the five soldiers should have been recorded in the Cropredy register is not known. It has been suggested that soldiers recorded in this way were local, but if they were recognised as being from the parish then surely their names would have been known and recorded in the register.

On the evening of 30 June the Royalists received intelligence that Major General Browne's army, was at Buckingham and was marching to join Waller, Charles decided to withdraw.[60] At 4:00 a.m. on 1 July, according to Richard Symonds, the Royalist army began to depart, 'drums beating, colours flying and trumpets sounding.'[61] Later that day an exchange of prisoners took place which had been arranged by the Earl of Forth, the Royalists exchanging about 100 prisoners plus officers for 60 of their own men, plus eight or nine officers and gentlemen.

While the Royalists marched to Dedington, Waller travelled to Towcester, from where he wrote:

> During these two days march I was extremely plagued by mutinies of the City Brigade, who are grown to that height of disorder, that I have no help [*sic*: read hope] to retain them, being come to their old song of home, home. The Major General [Browne] met me here and quartered his forces within three miles of me. I found his men [in] no very good temper, some of his Essex soldiers threatening already to quit him, and the Hertfordshire men expressing their impatient suffering during a night or two's ill quartering. My Lords, I write these particularities to let you know that an army compounded of these men will never go through with their service, and until you have an army merely your own that you may command, it is in a manner impossible to do anything of importance.[62]

The following day while still at Towcester Waller wrote to the Committee of Both Kingdoms again informing them of his intention to continue the

---

59 BL TT E.2/20 Richard Coe, *An exactdiarie ...*

60 Browne's army consisted of 8 regiments of foot comprising the White, Red and Blue Regiments of the London Auxiliaries, three regiments from Essex and two from Hertfordshire, a total of about 4,000 foot. His horse mustered just 500 strong and was formed mostly of troops from the siege of Basing House.

61 Symonds, *Diary*, p.24.

62 *CSPD 1644*, pp.300–301, Sir William Waller to the Committee of Both Kingdoms, 2 July 1644.

pursuit of the King, 'with all possible speed, with my horse and musketeers, leaving some behind to line the pikes and help guard the colours.'[63]

But it soon became clear that Waller's army was in no condition to pursue the King. On 4 July Waller and Heselrige, who by now had rejoined Waller, wrote:

> Our horse being much beaten out we pray you procure us a recruit... You know the work we labour in is very difficult and not to be done without horse. We entreat your thoughts for our help, as all we are, or you can make us, will be little enough for this service. If it is possible let us have 1,000 pair of English pistols, and 1,000 saddles.

They also appealed for Colonel Norton's Regiment of Horse to march to them as well as several troops of horse which were at Farnham. Unfortunately Norton's Regiment was needed back in Hampshire, where the Royalist garrison of Winchester was plundering the surrounding countryside, including £10,000 worth of cloth.[64]

However, on 7 July Waller complained to the Committee of Both Kingdoms that:

> The meeting with Major General Browne, which I thought would have proved an addition of strength to me, has very much weakened me, for my London regiments immediately looked upon his force as sent to relieve them, and without waiting for further orders are most departed ... I am confident about 2,000 Londoners have run away from their colours. [65]

Waller probably exaggerated the number of Londoners deserting, but the fact remains what the king's army had failed to do at Cropredy Bridge, Harrington's London Brigade had succeeded in breaking Waller's army. Of course Richard Coe does not mention this, in his account he records:

> We have since our advance from Farnham marched 500 miles and upwards and lost very few of our City Brigade, no commanders except Colonel Hobland and Captain Grove of the White Auxiliaries, both good commanders, who falling sick after we came from Banbury and dying in Northampton, are both brought up to be buried in London, their whole regiment being likewise come up with the Colours; The Hamlets with Colonel Prince of the Yellow Regiment being daily expected (according to Sir James Harrington's promise.[66]

With so few foot left he had to give up the idea of pursuing the King, who was now marching into the west in pursuit of Essex's Army. On 7 July Browne's

63 *CSPD 1644*, p.303, Sir William Waller to the Committee of Both Kingdoms, 3 July 1644.

64 *CSPD 1644*, p.304, Sir William Waller and Sir Arthur Heselrige to the Committee of Both Kingdoms, 4 July 1644; Committee of Both Kingdoms to Sir William Waller, 4 July 1644.

65 *CSPD 1644*, p.323, Committee of Both Kingdoms to Sir William Waller, 6 July 1644.

66 BL TT E.2/20, Richard Coe, *An exact diarie ...*

army marched away to besiege Greenland House, which fell after a short siege.

On 13 July Waller began to reorganise his regiments of foot, he planned they should form five regiments of dragoons, each consisting of 10 companies. For this purpose a warrant was issued to the Committee of Northampton to raise 1,000 horses for Waller to mount his musketeers, 1,000 saddles with furniture and 1,000 pistols with holsters. He would later write to the Committee of Both Kingdoms asking for 50 dragoon guidons, 100 dragoon drums, 5,000 belts for their muskets and 2,000 swords.[67] However because of a shortage of horses only two regiments of foot, Waller's and Heselrige's, seem to have been permanently converted to dragoons.[68]

A mid-17th century engraving depicting an assault on a town. (The Turton Collection)

On 16 July Waller arrived at Boarstall House in Buckinghamshire and summoned it to surrender, but after this was rejected he dismounted 400 dragoons and attacked it. However the attack was repulsed and Waller withdrew leaving behind 500 horse, which next day tried to taunt the garrison into making a sally, but after this had failed they too withdrew. By this time Waller could only rely on about 2,500 horse and 1,500 foot.

On 20 July Waller again wrote to the Committee of Both Kingdoms:

> I am now come to Abingdon…I have planted myself here as in the best situation to receive additional forces as you shall think fit to send me, without which supply it will be impossible for me to attempt any considerable thing. This morning the Coventry and Warwick forces desired to be dismissed, but I persuaded them to stay for a few days, in hope of some aid from you. The Londoners will not stir one foot further, except it be towards home.[69]

67 *Commons Journal*, vol. iii, p.554; *CSPD 1644*, pp.323, Committee of Both Kingdoms to Sir William Waller, 6 July 1644; *CSPD 1644*, pp.458–459, Sir William Waller to the Committee of Both Kingdoms, 28 August 1644.

68 Waller's old regiment of dragoons passed to Lieutenant General James Holborne, who commanded it until April 1645. Waller remained colonel of his new regiment of dragoons.

69 *CSPD 1644*, pp.362–363, Sir William Waller to the Committee of Both Kingdoms, 20 July 1644.

Despite the condition of Waller's army, on 7 August it was still able to defeat a party of 1,600 horse and foot from Oxford which had tried to beat up their quarters at Abingdon.[70]

The Oxford campaign had failed in its objectives; the armies of Waller and Essex together outnumbered the King's by two to one, however Essex's marching into the west to relieve Lyme allowed the King to defeat Waller and then turn on Essex. The fall of Lyme would have been more than balanced by the destruction of the King's main army. The campaign did have one unforeseen result: on 14 June the King, while still thinking he was being pursued by both armies, had written a desperate appeal to Prince Rupert, who was soldiering in the North, to march south to his aid. Thinking his uncle was still in a desperate situation Rupert fought a needless battle on 2 July at Marston Moor, where the Royalist Armies of Rupert and Newcastle were totally defeated and the North was lost to the Royalist cause.

70 BL TT E.254/15, *A Perfect Diurnall*, 5–12 August 1644 (London: Samuel Pecke, Aug 1644)

6

The Western Relief force

After Waller's defeat at Cropredy the King's army marched into the West, where it was joined by Prince Maurice's Western Army and other Royalists regiments, bringing the total strength of the combined Royalist army to about 25,000 horse and foot. Charles' aim was to cut off and defeat Essex's army, which had successfully relieved Lyme. Upon the Parliamentarians' approach the Royalists also evacuated Taunton, which Essex quickly occupied, and the town would become a thorn in Royalist Somerset's side for the rest of the war under its governor Robert Blake. However, this was just one of a few successes Essex had, because in the face of overwhelming odds he had no choice but to retreat before the advancing Royalists and appealed for the Committee of Both Kingdoms for assistance. On 17 July the Committee wrote to Waller asking him to send a party of horse into Dorset, 'to hinder the recruiting and levies of the enemy'. On 21 July, Waller, who was still at Abingdon, replied:

> Concerning the sending of a party into Dorsetshire, I shall be ready to obey your commands, but truly unless I be immediately supplied I shall be ruined here, for those few horse and foot which I have from Warwick and Coventry are revoked and the Londoners will not stay, and if these go I shall not have enough to make good my quarter... If Major General Browne might be ordered to take up his quarter here I could leave my train [of artillery] with him, and with the train's horse mount the remainder of my foot and clear Dorsetshire.[1]

Despite these words, towards the end of July Waller was able to send Lieutenant General Middleton with a force of 3,000 horse and foot into the West, although he could not resist laying siege to Donnington Castle, near Newbury. On 2 August Middleton ordered his force to storm the castle in three places, but these attacks were repulsed. According to *Mercurius Aulicus,* Middleton lost a colonel, a major, eight captains and many lieutenants and ensigns besides inferior officers and 87 men.[2]

1 *CSPD 1644–1645*, p.9, Earl of Manchester to Committee of Both Kingdoms, 3 October 1644.
2 BL TT E.7/10 *Mercurius Aulicus,* 3 August 1644 (Oxford: Peter Heylyn, August 1644).

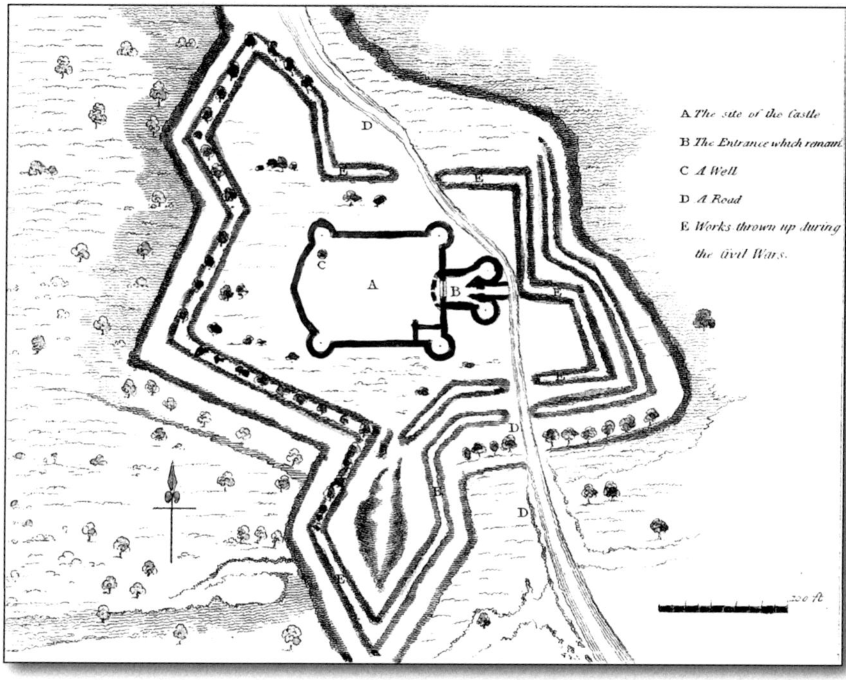

A plan of Donnington Castle defences based on a 19th-century engraving. (The Turton Collection)

After this Middleton raised the siege and continued his march into the West, but he does not seem to have received a warm welcome, as an undated Royalist account records:

> Middleton who came down hither with Waller's Brigade and hath now under his command about 3,000 horse and dragoons was marching through the north of Devon to the relief of Earl of Essex and it so conceived is so far engaged that way that there is likelihood of his return, the country being all risen and order given for the cutting down of trees and stopping all the passages and a great part of the King's forces being marched towards him.[3]

Meanwhile Essex was still retreating and on 2 August his army arrived at Lostwithiel, on the Cornish coast, where he hoped that the navy would evacuate his 8,000 strong army to safety.

After rendezvousing with a force of Dorset Parliamentarians, Middleton laid siege to Wareham, which surrendered on 10 August; its garrison, formed from Lord Inchiquin's Regiment of Foot, changed sides. Middleton then moved to Sherborne, where according to the Parliamentarian newsbook *Mercurius Civicus* on 13 August:

> After receiving information that Sir Francis Donnington and Sir William Courtneyand others, in all about 1,000 horse and dragoons were at Lampard, Middleton advanced with a party of 500 horse and dragoons to Pederton, where the enemy were now in readiness and after a violent charge the enemy were

3 BL Add ms 18981, f.241, undated account from the Earl of Bristol to the Duke of York.

> routed, whereupon they pursued them to within half a mile of Bridgwater. Took 1 major, 1 lieutenant, 2 cornets, 2 quartermasters and 40 common soldiers and killed 50 on the place. We had Major Carr and 4 commonsoldiers taken prisoner.[4]

On 20 August, while at Ilchester, Middleton wrote to the Committee of Both Kingdoms:

> I am now suppressing all levies and stopping all provisions in Somersetshire. I have driven Sir Francs Dorrington, with eight colonels, to Minehead. They intended, and would have been able in a short time, to have raised their regiments in Somersetshire, and now they have betaken themselves rather to a place to secure themselves than to raise forces. I have always parties out towards Devonshire, and am tomorrow to advance to Chard. If I should advance far into Devonshire, besides the danger, the garrison of Bristol and Bridgwater might both levy men and money.[5]

His force now consisted of only 2,000 horse and dragoons, but he was expecting a further 300 or 400 dragoons from Waller and he had ordered several garrisons in Dorset to meet him at Chard as a rendezvous, but he had to admit, 'I think their number will be inconsiderable, yet they have promised to send as many as they can conveniently spare.'[6]

By 28 August Waller had returned to Farnham, from where he wrote to the Committee of Both Kingdoms:

> [I] have despatched away directions to the Governors of Chichester and Arundel to send their several companies mounted to this rendezvous. I have not yet heard of the Kentish regiment[7]nor their horse and dragoons, but am informed that it would be quickly mounted in Kent if directions were sent down from you. How and when my ragged regiments will get to me from Abingdon I know not … the most part of them being so weak that I am persuaded they will not be able to march on foot.[8]

On 26 August the remaining elements of Waller's army had marched out of Abingdon and on 1 September 1,200 to 1,400 ragged foot arrived back at Farnham.

By now the situation at Lostwithiel had become desperate, Essex's positions on Beacon Hill had been overrun and Castle Dore was now under attack, cutting Lostwithiel off from the sea. On 31 August most of Essex's cavalry broke out of Lostwithiel and Essex escaped in a fishing boat, leaving his regiments of foot and a regiment of cavalry to their fate. On 1 September

4 BL TT E.7/3, *Mercurius Civicus, the London Intelligencer,* 15–22 August 1644 (Thomas Bates, 1644); *CSPD 1644*, pp.437–8, Committee of Both Kingdoms to the Earl of Essex, 19 August 1644.

5 CSPD 1644, pp.439–440, Lieutenant General John Middleton to the Committee of Both Kingdoms, 20 August 1644.

6 *CSPD 1644*, p.440.

7 This was Colonel John Birch's newly raised regiment of foot, which wore red coats and carried yellow colours.

8 *CSPD 1644*, pp.458–459, Sir William Waller to the Committee of Both Kingdoms, 28 August 1644.

Farnham Castle. (Photo: Nicola Turton)

the remaining Parliamentarians at Lostwithiel surrendered and the following day 6,000 foot and Colonel Leighton's Regiment of Horse marched out of Lostwithiel, as one Royalist account put it:

> The soldiers from the degree of corporal downwards should lay down their arms and march with sticks to Poole, all the other officers upward to march with their horse and arms. They are to leave all their ammunition with us some 100 barrels of powder and artillery, 32 pieces of cannon and baggage behind them.

These sticks were almost certainly white, the traditional colour for granting someone a safe passage, but they did not help Essex's infantry, since according to orders not to plunder the Parliamentarians, Symonds records that the officers had to 'perpetually beat off our foot' with their swords and hats. Another Royalist account states, 'The King's soldiers have had great booty and the Cornish dames who fell upon 300 women of the rebels that had gotten great wealth and have gotten much riches from them.' Essex's foot finally made it to the safety of Plymouth from where they were shipped to Portsmouth.[9]

9 Symonds, *Diary*, p.66; BL Add ms 18981 f.241, undated account from the Earl of Bristol to the Duke of York.

Castle Dore, an Iron Age hill fort that formed part of the Earl of Essex's positions at Lostwithiel. (Photo: Nicola Turton)

On 2 September, Waller, was still having trouble gathering his forces together, wrote:

> I do not desire to stay in these quarters nor within the Association longer than to receive those forces yourselves have assigned me… The foot, as Colonel Holborne informs me, are, with the addition of 300 out of Kent, about 1,400, so that I fall short of 300 clear. Their major informs me that the Kentish horse fall short by 100; how and when they will be supplied I know not. I have not one foot soldier mounted, Major General Browne having sent notice to the constables of the hundreds that we intended to take their horses and all they had, so you may imagine they provided for us accordingly. This day a company of dragoons under Captain Butler arrived out of Kent, and I expect 3 companies of the new Kentish regiment tonight or tomorrow. All these poor men have brought their mouths with them, and my Abingdon blades, they are the picture of famine and poverty, and I fear the money still at London will not mount to three weeks pay, for I must reserve (sufficient) for the payment of my good men in the West. I desire it may be considered that these poor creatures are to be repaired from head to foot, and I must out of this pay make provisions for a march near 300 miles, so that I cannot imagine what will be remaining to them to defray their quarters. The parts about Farnham are very poorly provided, having been exhausted when we lay here last winter, so that I thought I had done well to send for provisions further off… There are 13 wagons left behind at Abingdon for want of teams, some laden with arms, others with shirts and clothes for the soldiers, which I had in store here [Farnham] but by mistake were sent to Abingdon.[10]

10 *CSPD 1644*, pp.468–469, Sir William Waller to the Committee of Both Kingdoms, 2 September 1644.

On 6 September Waller again wrote to the Committee of Both Kingdoms informing them that:

> I have not yet one man of my [foot] mounted, and there are yet wanting 300 recruits out of Kent for Colonel Weldon's Regiment, which even then would not muster more than 500. Of the new Kentish [Birch's] Regiment there is yet wanting 200 men. Those who are here are as gallant men and as well provided as ever I saw in the field. None of the Sussex forces are come, but I have sent orders both to them and to the 400 men from the Isle of Wight to ship themselves to Poole, or the nearest landing place to Salisbury, where they are to join me with all expedition.

The following day Waller left Farnham with an army of 2,000 foot, 800 horse and 150 dragoons and the next day quartered at Wootton Bassett.[11]

On 16 September, Gerolamo Agostii, the Venetian Secretary to England, wrote to the Doge and Senate:

> Waller, who was sent that way [into the West] some days ago with a strong army, has got no further than Farnham, the soldiers being indignant at marching under the command of his wife, who being a zealous in religion, grown ambitious of the popular favour and predominant over her husband, has usurped the general's baton. To please them Parliament has recalled her, and sent fresh and urgent orders to Waller to advance without delay.[12]

Mercurius Aulicus for 6 September records that both Waller and his wife visited the besieging force at Basing House, where 'such was the soldiers longing desire to see his wonderful lady (or rather hear her) that many of the Rebels for her Ladyship's sake ran out of their trenches.'[13]

Basing House had been besieged since June after the garrison had been severely weakened, when a party of 200 foot and 80 horse sallied out on 2 June to beat up an outpost of Colonel Jones' Regiment at Wanborough Mill, near Odiham. However the raid had been betrayed by a soldier in the garrison and so the outpost had been reinforced to 200 foot and three troops of Colonel Norton's Regiment of Horse. Two days later Norton began to besiege the house, although it was not until 11 June that the garrison watched the arrival the main Parliamentarian force, which was made up of six companies of Colonel Herbert Morley's Regiment of Foot from Sussex, and from Surrey five companies of Colonel Sir Richard Onslow's Regiment of Foot and two companies of Colonel Jones, from plus three troops of horse. On 24 June Morley's Regiment took up position on the southern side of the house and Onslow's covered the western part and began digging earthworks. Basing church had already been fortified by the detachment of Colonel Jones'

11 *CSPD 1644*, pp.476–477, 482, Sir William Waller to the Committee of Both Kingdoms, 6 September 1644 and Sir William Waller to the Committee of Both Kingdoms, 8 September 1644.

12 *CSP Venice*, p.135, Gerolamo Agostii, the Venetian Secretary to England wrote to the Doge and Senate 16 September 1644.

13 *Mercurius Aulicus*, 6 September 1644.

Regiment and the horse were placed on Cowdray Down, and so the siege continued throughout the summer with additional regiments joining the besiegers.[14]

Meanwhile, on 9 September Middleton's force, by now reportedly to be 3,800 horse and dragoons, was reported to have joined with the 2,000 horse of Essex's army under Sir William Balfour. However, Middleton and Balfour hated each other, which had caused the former along with Major General James Holborne to transfer to Waller's army earlier that year, and by 12 September the two forces had separated, with Balfour reported to be at Dorchester, while Middleton was at Sherborne.[15]

After their success at Lostwithiel the King's army besieged Plymouth and due to the strength of the Royalist army in the West, Waller found that he had to distribute his meagre forces to the various Parliamentarian garrisons still holding out. To this end he sent Birch's Regiment to Plymouth, Holborne's (formerly Heselrige's) to Lyme, Weldon's to Weymouth, and Potley's to Taunton. In the case of Birch's and Weldon's Regiments they were meant to be temporary reinforcements, but were still there a year later.On 10 September Waller wrote to the Committee of Both Kingdoms that:

> I am here at Salisbury with my horse… the Isle of Wight foot and Sussex men [are] to [go] Weymouth and Lyme. Those few of my Abingdon foot I am labouring to mount, but I want 200 men of the Farnham Regiment [Jones'], which are detained at the siege of Basing [House] and will not be suffered to march to me. I hear nothing of the Malmesbury foot nor of Colonel Ludlow's horse. I have nothing in the world to keep the field with, but 700 or 800 horse, 150 dragoons and about 900 musketeers, if I can mount them. If there be not present course taken to oppose the enemy with a strong power, I know of nothing to hinder them [the Royalists] marching to London.[16]

Two weeks later the 'Isle of Wight foot and Sussex men' had still not joined Waller nor had the 200 men of Jones' Regiment.[17]

Moreover the various county committees were reluctant to raise money and horses for Waller preferring to use these resources for their own defence, and the wagons he had left at Abingdon with the supplies of clothing etc., for his men had still not arrived.[18]

Major General Richard Browne had ordered these wagons to go to Farnham, but news came that a party of Royalists under the command of Colonel Henry Gage were advancing towards Basing House. Therefore the

---

14 BL TT E.27/5 *A Description of the Siege of Basing Castle …*

15 BL TT E.256/2, *Perfect Occurances of Parliament,* 6–13 September 1644(London: Andrew Coe, September 1644); TT E.256/3, *A Perfect Diurnall* (London: Samuel Pecke, September 1644); *CSPD 1644*, pp.495–496, Sir William Waller and Sir Arthur Heselrige to the Committee of Both Kingdoms, 12 September 1644.

16 *CSPD 1644*, p.489, Sir William Waller to the Committee of Both Kingdoms, 10 September 1644.

17 *CSPD 1644*, p.523, Sir William Waller to the Committee of Both Kingdoms, 21 September 1644.

18 *CSPD 1644*, p.495, Sir William Waller to the Committee of Both Kingdoms, 12 September 1644.

wagons were forced to return to Abingdon and the horses which pulled these wagons were used as dragoon horses so that they could intercept Gage's force.

On 9 September Gage had slipped out of Oxford with 400 musketeers and 250 horse, wearing orange sashes and ribbons, the badge of Parliamentarian troops. This force marched to Aldermaston, but finding some Parliamentarians troops there, they forgot their disguises and charged the surprised Roundheads, taking six or seven prisoners. However, enough escaped to raise the alarm. The next day Gage then proceeded to Basing House, where he dispersed the besieging force. As well as the provisions Gage's force had brought with them, they seized a large quantity of provisions from Basingstoke, including 40 or 50 head of cattle, which they brought back to Basing House. Gage remained at Basing House all that day and the next, while he collected more provisions, and at about 7:00 p.m. on 12 September his force slipped out of Basing House and returned safely to Oxford.[19]

Unfortunately for Waller's men, Browne could not easily replace the horses for the wagons, complaining to the Committee of Both Kingdoms that the horses 'were so weak and tired… few of them are yet returned. This country is so emptied of horses that I much fear I shall not be able to perform your commands, unless some be sent from other parts.'[20]

Despite the cavalry from Wiltshire and Dorset not having arrived and a mutiny having broken out in Livesey's Regiment of Horse from Kent, on 24 September Waller appears to have been reinforced by some cavalry, as he writes:

> Our horse are very considerable, as good and as many as when we went first towards Oxford, with the exception of our saddles and arms. The extremely long marches our soldiers have had have drawn upon them such wants of clothes, and money to shoe their horses, that we cannot but cry out for the £5,000. Some of the horse under Captain Jervais are gone and for want of money others will follow.[21]

In a later letter Waller requested 500 back and breast plates with helmets, because, 'in the heat of the summer many of our men were unable to carry their arms, their marches being great, but now the weather is cold they exceedingly desire them.'[22]

Despite Balfour refusing to join Waller, another officer of Essex's Army, John Dalbier, was willing to join him, but '[due] to the poorness of his quarters he was necessitated to remove further off, as far as Wallop, which is halfway between Salisbury and Andover.'[23] This was the disadvantage with

19 Sir Henry Gage's account, printed in John Adair, *They Saw it Happen* (Hampshire County Council, 1981), pp.61–66.

20 *CSPD 1644*, p.509, Major General Richard Browne to the Committee of Both Kingdoms, 16 September 1644.

21 *CSPD 1644*, p.532, Sir William Waller to the Committee of Both Kingdoms, 24 September 1644.

22 *CSPD 1644–1645*, p.46.Sir William Waller and Sir Arthur Heselrige to the Committee of Both Kingdoms, 16 October 1644.

23 *CSPD 1644*, p.534, Sir William Waller to the Committee of Both Kingdoms, 25 September 1644,

cavalry, although it could cover more ground per day than the infantry, not only did the troopers have to be fed, but also their horses. Therefore an army could only campaign in an area for a short time before food and fodder ran out.

On 1 October the King marched out of Chard and began his slow march eastwards, Waller retiring before him, since despite rendezvousing with Middleton he still had only 2,000 horse and 1,500 dragoons. The same day Waller and Heselrige wrote to the Committee of Both Kingdoms appealing for Manchester and Essex to march to their aid. However, the majority of Essex's cavalry were still refusing to join Waller and his infantry were in no position to fight, since not only had they been stripped of their weapons after they surrendered at Lostwithiel, but of the 6,000 infantry which had marched out of Lostwithiel only 2,000 were reported to have reached Portsmouth, so they needed to be urgently re-equipped before they could take to the field once more.Although during the second week of October Waller, who was then at Winterbourne Stoke, was joined by 10 troops of horse and two companies of dragoons from Manchester's army.[24]

On 15 October Waller received orders for him to march east and rendezvous with Manchester's and Essex's Armies. He fell back to Andover, where he arrived that evening. The following day he reported that 'last night 500 of the King's horse came into Salisbury, but the foot were delayed by wet weather.'[25] Due to the inclement weather Waller appears to have felt safe at Andover, but on 18 October Richard Symonds recorded in his diary:

> His Majesty etc. left Sarum and marched towards Andover, Waller's force being then in Andover. Goring raised a forlorn of horse, consisting of about 200 gentlemen that were spare commanders of horse [reformadoes] beat them out of Andover, took Carr, a Scots Colonel, and another captain, a Scot, that died, who little before his death rose from under the table, saying he would not die like a dog under the table, but sat in a chair, and immediately died of his wounds. Took about 80 prisoners, followed the chase of them two miles who all ran in great confusion. Had not night come so soon, it might have made an end of Waller's army, for our intention was to engage them, but they disappointed our hopes with their heels.[26]

Waller retired to Basingstoke, from where on 20 October he reported that Manchester's army, a brigade of London Trained Bands and Essex's horse were close by. He also added that:

> 800 suits of clothes will serve us for the present. If his Excellency [Essex] has any to spare we fain would borrow them; it would be very seasonable and comfortable to the poor creatures, who are so pitiful an object that the like is not to be seen in

24 *CSPD 1644–1645*, p.41, Sir William Waller to the Committee of Both Kingdoms, 14 October 1644.

25 *CSPD 1644–1645*, p.46, Sir William Waller and Sir Arthur Heselrige to the Committee of Both Kingdoms, 16 October 1644.

26 Symonds, *Diary*, p.141.

> England… It is no little grief to us that our poor dragoons go naked this weather. Oh! That they might be thought upon for clothes."[27]

The Royalists were getting closer, and on the night of 21/22 October a party of horse commanded by Captain Fincher of Waller's horse captured 60 Royalists near Kingsclere.

According to the Royalist newsbook *Mercurius Aulicus,* the King remained at Kingsclere the following day while the Parliamentarians lay at Aldermarston Park until the evening of the 24 October; when hearing the King had marched to Newbury they forded the River Kennet near Bucklebury and drew up on Bucklebury Heath five miles from Newbury, 'having refreshed their army with what reading could afford, most of them having three days provisions prepared in their snapsacks.' From Bucklebury they sent out several parties of horse to attack the Royalists, but were repulsed. On 25 October the combined Parliamentarian armies moved to Thatcham and Shaw with the aim of giving battle to the Royalists.

Unfortunately the strength of both sides is not known, but according to Cromwell the combined armies were about 11,000 foot and 8,000 horse and dragoons. There is no way to verify this figure, but included in the strength of the Parliamentarian Army was another London Brigade which had left London on 17 October under the command of Sir James Harrington and was composed of the Red and Blue Regiments of the London Trained Bands, the Southwark Trained Bands, the Westminster Liberty Regiment and the Tower Hamlets Auxiliaries. On paper they mustered 6,000 men, but in reality mustered half that number and the brigade was further weakened when the Southwark Trained Bands were sent to reinforce the garrison of Reading. On 9 September Essex's Army was reported to be about 3,000 infantry, which had been re-equipped both in clothing and weapons and 2,000 horse. In September it is estimated that Manchester's Army was about 3,980 foot and 3,960 cavalry, although Laurence Crawford, Manchester's major general of foot, states that he had about 3,000 infantry at Newbury, and Lieutenant General Thomas Hammond states that Manchester had 7,000 foot and 7,000 horse.

As forWaller's army, he had left most of his infantry in the West to reinforce the various garrisons there and converted others to dragoons; thus he only had about 500 foot, including a detachment of Colonel Jones' Regiment which he withdrawn from the siege of Basing House and possibly Colonel Thomas Carr's Regiment of Foot, which was known as the 'Isle of Wight Foot', which had been ordered to join Waller but had joined Essex instead. On 1 October Waller was reported to have had 3,500 horse and dragoons. Therefore the combined army mustered about 9,500 to 10,480 infantry and 9,460 cavalry, although these figures are probably an overestimate since they are based on returns for September.[28]

---

27 *CSPD 1644–1645*, p.60, Sir William Waller and others to the Committee of Both Kingdoms, 20 October 1644.

28 John Bruce and David Masson, *The Quarrel between the Earl of Manchester and Oliver Cromwell* (Camden Society, 1875), p.85; Clive Holmes, *The Eastern Association in the English*

Cromwell also states that the Royalist army mustered 'not above 10,000 horse and foot', while Richard Symonds records that the King's forces mustered 5,500 foot and 4,000 horse on the eve of the battle. The foot of the King's army was commanded by Sir Jacob Astley and divided into four tertios, three from the Oxford army and one from Prince Maurice's Western army. There were also three brigades of 'Oxford' horse and at least one brigade of Western horse. Also the garrison of Donnington Castle, consisting of 200 foot of Earl Rivers' Black Regiment, could be called upon.[29]

On 25 October Symonds records:

> The rebels' whole army appeared upon the hills on the east side of Newbury, the place where the last years fight was. The King's army was drawn out upon the bottom between Newbury and Donnington. No action all this day. Toward night both sides fired upon one another from the hedges on their side of the river. We at night retired to the pass and kept it all night; by that means these was shooting all night.

The next day, 'They appeared more plain upon the hill and drew out some foot. cannon on both sides played very much. They lay quiet all night.'[30] During this time the commanders of the Parliamentarian armies held a council of war, except for Essex who was ill. According to Major General Philip Skippon:

> [Our] resolution was that all the horse and dragoons (except 1,600 or 1,800, out of all our armiesand 200 dragoons) with all my Lord General's Foot, and the four City Regiment, should march about to Speen village; and that at one the same time, as near as we could, My Lord Manchester's Forces shall [fall] upon to Enemy, to gain the passage at Shaw, and our forces that marched about to do the like at Speen; which was accordingly put in execution.[31]

It was decided that Waller would lead the largest part of the army around the King's flank and take him in the rear, while Manchester, who was the senior commander in Essex's absence, held the King's attention by a frontal assault. The signal for Manchester to begin his attack would be when he heard the sound of Waller's guns. During the night of 26/27 October, Waller began his flank march north of Newbury with the foot of his own army, Essex's, and the Red and Blue regiments of the London Trained Bands, and most of Waller's and Essex's horse, and a detachment of Manchester's cavalry, which included Cromwell's Regiment of Horse; in all about 13,000 strong. Manchester's foot regiments, with the Westminster Trained Bands, the Southwark Trained

---

Civil War (Cambridge University Press, 1974), pp.236, 238; *CSPD 1644–1645*, p.155, Second Examination of Lieutenant General Thomas Hammond.

29 Symonds, *Diary*, pp.142, 159–161.

30 Symonds, *Diary*, pp.144–145.

31 Major General Philip Skippon at Newbury to the Committee of Both Kingdoms, 30 October 1644, printed in Rushworth, *Historical Collections*, vol. 5 (London: D. Browne, 1721).

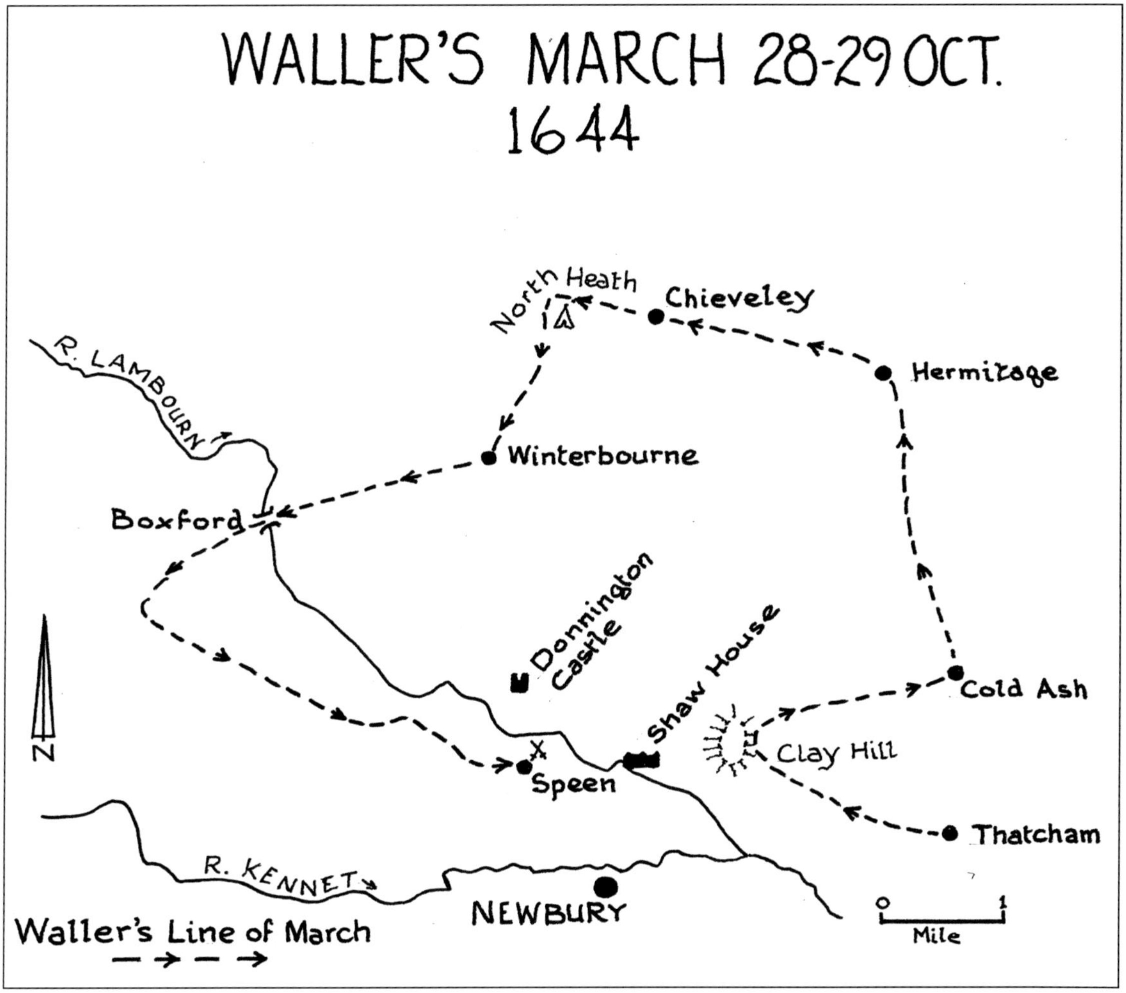

Map 7 Map showing Waller's flank march at the Second Battle of Newbury.

Bands and the Auxiliaries of the Tower Hamlets and the remaining cavalry regiments, including 600 of Waller's army, occupied Clay Hill.[32]

According to Rushworth, it was early in the morning of 27 October that Waller's men 'were on the march and in four hours' time… made their approach towards the west side of Newbury.' Waller's force had to march via Chieveley and Boxford, to avoid the ordnance of Donnington Castle, whose garrison sallied out and took some prisoners. The King had placed an outpost of 400 foot and four guns at Boxford, to protect his flank. These seem to have been quickly swept aside, but word got back to Charles of Waller's approach, so he moved Prince Maurice's Western Army and the Duke of York's Regiment of Foot to the village of Speen, where they began to dig earthworks. Lisle's 'Reading' tertio was positioned in and around Shaw House, which was owned by a Mr Doleman. The remainder of the horse and foot were placed in the centre.

32 BL Stowe ms 190, *CSPD 1644–1645*, pp.76–77. Sir A. Johnson and John Crew MP to the Committee of Both Kingdoms, 28 October 1644.

The remains of Castle Donnington Castle today (photo: Nicola Turton)

To cover Waller's departure from the Parliamentarian camp, according to Rushworth:

> Manchester the same Sunday morning commanded a party of about 400 musketeers to go over the little River Kennet, on the left hand of Shaw [House], thereby to divert the King's strength from attending Speen Hill; who advanced accordingly, and beat the King's forces out of their two works, and took some prisoners, but were at last beat back with considerable loss.[33]

This action is described by Richard Symonds, although he describes the attacking force as a whole 'tertio of foot' rather than just 400 men, who:

> [Crossed] a bridge they had made in the night intending to surprise one of our guards, but the guard retreated to the next; and joined, fell upon them, being nothing considerable in number, made two bodies retreat, killed some, took about 40 prisoners and 100 arms; then they lay quiet until 3 [in the] afternoon, only our cannon and theirs played.[34]

It was about 3:00 p.m. that Waller arrived on the western outskirts of Newbury and deployed in battle formation with the foot in the centre, commanded by Philip Skippon, Sir William Balfour commanded his horse on the right wing and Oliver Cromwell the horse on his left. His guns signalled to Manchester to attack. Waller recalls:

> After arriving on the heath about a mile and a half from Newbury at two, we fell into the lanes and hedges and marched not above one quarter of a mile before we came into sight of the enemy who had blocked up our way with a strong breastwork and in it five pieces of cannon, and for their better advantage they were under the favour of Donnington Castle, their best pieces being there. Upon our approach their cannon played hard upon us, the place being a narrow heath gave no leave to bring up our body. The hedges hindered our horse very much. Their cannon made our ground very hot. There was no way left but to fall on with horse and foot and without delay, which put in execution… his Excellency's [Essex's] foot … went on undauntedly.[35]

In a letter to the Committee of Both Kingdoms, Skippon records the bravery of Essex's infantry:

> The forlorn hope, consisting of about 800 musketeers, was led by Colonel Alridge's Lieutenant Colonel Lloyd, a worthy man who was shot in the arm, and my Lord Robert's Major, Hurry; and lodged themselves (fighting) close to the enemy's forlorne hope: His excellency's Regiment fell upon the right hand of them with great boldness; Colonel Aldrich, with his brigade consisting of his own, Colonel Davis,' Colonel Fortescue's and Colonel Ingoldsby's Regiments, fell on directly on

33 Rushworth, *Historical Collections*.

34 Symonds, *Diary*, p.145.

35 BL Harlms 166.

> their main work with undaunted resolution. His Excellency's Regiment coming upon the right hand of them, they both fell pell-mell into the same work. The Two Red and Yellow Regiments of the Citizens held the enemy [in] play on the right hand; Colonel Barclay and his brigade alone, wherein was his own, my Lord Robert's and my Regiment, most resolutely repulsed three violent charges of the enemy's horse in a plain field and after that did farther good service; The Blue City Regiment were the reserve. The sum is, (after a very sharp fight for the time) the enemy were quite driven out of all their works and the village of Speen.[36]

While Barclay's Brigade was being attacked, according to one account, the cavalry of the Eastern Association on Waller's left wing could have easily intercepted the Royalist cavalry, but it did not move:

> If Cromwell had played the part that became him, then enemy had been totally routed; all the horse under his command stood still when Colonel Barclay['s] Brigade was charged three time. Notwithstanding all that they stood still… General Lieutenant Middleton came seeing so great absurdities and oversights, and desired the said Cromwell's horse to charge, who refused him till he went with one of the squadrons and charged the enemy, who was routed and left on seconded to fly for his life, being in the middle of his enemies, so that day there was no service performed at all by Cromwell.[37]

The Earl of Manchester's chaplain, Simeon Ashe, also records that 'My Lord of Manchester's horse commanded by Lieutenant Colonel[*sic*] Cromwell (from whom very much was expected) did little service, gained no honour in this work this day.'[38]

True, these accounts were written by opponents of Cromwell's and apologists for him state that it was because his cavalry were within range of the guns at Donnington Castle, but the garrison only had four pieces of artillery and the left wing was over 1,000 yards away. If the regiments under Cromwell's command had recently been raised then there might be some truth in this argument, but they had been in many battles and included Cromwell's own Regiment of Horse. Could it be that he sulked that day? Possibly because he commanded the left wing rather than the more honourable right wing, a place given to Sir William Balfour, who was a Scottish officer.

Several of the Parliamentarian officers also only mention Skippon and Balfour as charging the Royalists in the sector of the battlefield. However, some Royalists do state that Waller's left wing did advance that day, but whether it was under Cromwell's command or Middleton's is not known.

Nevertheless despite the lack of cavalry support for Barclay's Brigade Skippon could write:

36 Major General Philip Skippon at Newbury to the Committee of Both Kingdoms, 30 October 1644, printed in Rushworth, *Historical Collections*.

37 Bruce and Masson, *The Quarrel between the Earl of Manchester and Oliver Cromwell*, pp.63–64.

38 BL TT E.22/10, Simeon Ashe, *A True Relation of the Chief Occurances at and since the late battle of Newbury* (London: Edward Brewster, 1644).

> Truly, I believe never did men perform so dangerous a service, nor come through so difficult a work with more undismayed spirits, than the poor handful of my Lord General's old foot, both officers and soldiers in the mouth of cannon and musket shot. How many the enemy lost, I cannot affirm, but I believe a far greater number than we.[39]

According to Ludlow, it was the sufferings of Essex's infantry in Cornwall that gave them courage:

> [It] being fresh in their memory, caused them to charge with such vigour, that some of them ranto their cannon, and clapped their hats upon the touch-holes of them, falling so furiously upon the enemy, that they were not able to stand before them, but were forced to quit their ground and run under the shelter of Donnington Castle, leaving behind several pieces of cannon, besides many of their men killed and taken prisoner.[40]

Various types of artillery. (Author's collection)

Skippon states that nine pieces of artillery were captured, including six sakers which Essex had lost in Cornwall. Rushworth recalls that Essex's infantry 'embraced them for joy, Saying they would give them a Cornish hug.' Why they stood out from the other three pieces, neither Skippon nor Rushworth records.[41] After an hour's desperate fight Maurice's men were driven back and Speen village was captured.

Meanwhile Waller's right wing under Sir William Balfour had come into action, as Edward Walker records:

> At this instant the right wing of the Rebels' Horse being at least 500 [*sic*?]advanced underneath the hill of Speen between that and the marsh, with 100 musketeers in

---

39 Major General Philip Skippon at Newbury to the Committee of Both Kingdoms, 30 October 1644, printed in Rushworth, *Historical Collections*, vol. 5.

40 Edmund Ludlow, ed. C.H. Firth, *The Memoirs of Edmund Ludlow, Lieutenant General of the Horse in the Army of the Commonwealth of England.* (Oxford: Clarendon Press, 1894), vol. 1, p.103.

41 Rushworth, *Historical Collections*.

> their van and came into the open field where His Majesty's Guards commanded by Lord Bernard Stuart then stood. Upon their approach Major Legge was sent with a party towards them, but being overpowered he made his retreat... and they still advanced under the favour of their musketeers. The King's Guard then wheeled about to get a more ground, and many of our horse then in our rear fled disorderly to Newbury.
>
> By that time we had gotten ground and that our faces were towards them, they were within carbine shot, were they were immediately encountered by two troops of the Queen's Regiment of Horse, commanded by Sir John Camsfield, with so much gallantry and courage as that the Rebels seeing the King's Guard coming to fall on their flank, the great body of their presently fled, we having the execution of them thence near half a mile, where we slew most of their musketeers.[42]

Mercurius Aulicus gives some additional details to this cavalry melee:

> The Rebels main body of horse advanced, with a body of five hundred horse (whereof the Earl of Essex, his lifeguard were part) and a sufficient strength of musketeers betwixt Newbury and Speen where the King's Lifeguard and Sir Humphrey Bennet's brigade were drawn up; Major Legg was sent with a party of horse towards the Rebels, who finding himself overpowered made a handsome and orderly retreat, whereupon the Rebels advanced with musketeers on their right hand towards the river, there being three small enclosure betwixt Colonel Bennet and the Rebels, which caused him to wheel off, for the better advantage to charge them... the Rebels came on, yet having attained the ground he aimed at, and his own regiment drawn up, he roundly charged the Rebels (the rest of his brigade being not then ready) and was so bravely seconded by the most valiant the Lord Bernard Stuart, [who commanded the King's Lifeguard of horse]...who fell upon their flank, that those Rebels both horse and foot were totally routed the execution followed above half a mile...and their musketeers which advanced with their horse, were almost all to a man cut off.

Richard Symonds, who was a member of the King's Lifeguard, adds:

> [At] 4 of the clock, their bodies of horse approached towards our field at the bottom of the hill near the church called (Shaw) and one body came into the field, (and) charged Sir John Campsfield's Regiment [also known as the Queen's Regiment] which stood them most gallantly. The King's Regiment being near, drove at them, which made them wheel off in confusion, and followed them in the chase, made all their bodies of horse run in confusion, killed many, besides musketeers that lined the hedges and played upon us in the chase until we cut their throats.

Walker goes on to describe the events on the cavalry wing supposedly commanded by Cromwell:

42 Walker, *Historical Discourses,* p.112.

> At the same time the Rebel's horse of the left wing were advancing towards the North side of the wheat field, but before they were got thither Colonel Goring put himself into the head of the Earl of Cleveland's Brigade, consisting of the Earl of Cleveland, Colonel Howard, Hamilton, Culpepper and Stuart's Regiment of Horse) and being accompanied by the Earl himself, he fell upon them, and forced them back in great confusion, and then got over the hedge, where he was again charged by another body, but he quickly defeated them also, and slew diverse of the rebels on the place. In this charge the courageous Earl of Cleveland engaged himself so far and by the illness of his horse which fell under him prisoner. This charge was the more gallant, because this brigade not only went over the Ditch to meet the Rebels, but passed by three bodies of the Rebels foot, who shot at them both when they pursued the Rebels and as they came back.[43]

Mercurius Aulicus continues:

> Thus the Rebels were repulsed on the west side of Speen, but those others on the east side were more confident of success, who having settled three bodies of foot in certain enclosures and ditches, advanced over a ditch, with a good body of horse, hoping thereby to break through his Majesty's guards; but this was as soon discerned and prevented by General Goring, who instantly drew up the Earl of Cleveland's brigade, put himself in their head of it...The general told them they must now charge home, and thereupon suddenly advanced up to the gap, where about fourscore of the rebels were now already come over, the rest hastening after. These he soon fell upon, and forced them back again in much confusion; As soon as he got part of the brigade over the ditch, he hastened to order them as fast as they came over, but the eager Rebels would not grant him so much leisure, and therefore a new body came to second the former, whom the general received with those horse he had already over the ditch, and then charged so home, that he made them quickly scatter and shift for themselves, many whereof were killed in the place...This charge was the more gallant, because this brigade of horse not only went over the ditch to meet the Rebels, but passed by three bodies of the Rebels' foot, who were placed in the ditches and enclosures; two of which bodies shot at his Majesty's horse as they pursued the Rebels, and as they came back.

However another Royalist, Richard Symonds, gives a very different account: 'The Earl of Cleveland before our charge was taken prisoner, and most of his officers hurt and killed, his men beaten, being overpowered with horse and foot.'

At one point Waller himself charged the Royalists:

> I fell on with my troops by the way of Speenfield, and we were mingled with the enemy, I had a great deliverance, for one of the adverse party coming behind me, and being ready to fire his pistol in my reins; in that instant one of my lifeguard killed him, or otherwise in all probability he had killed me.[44]

43 Walker, *Historical Discourses*, pp.112–113.

44 Waller, *Recollections*, p.113.

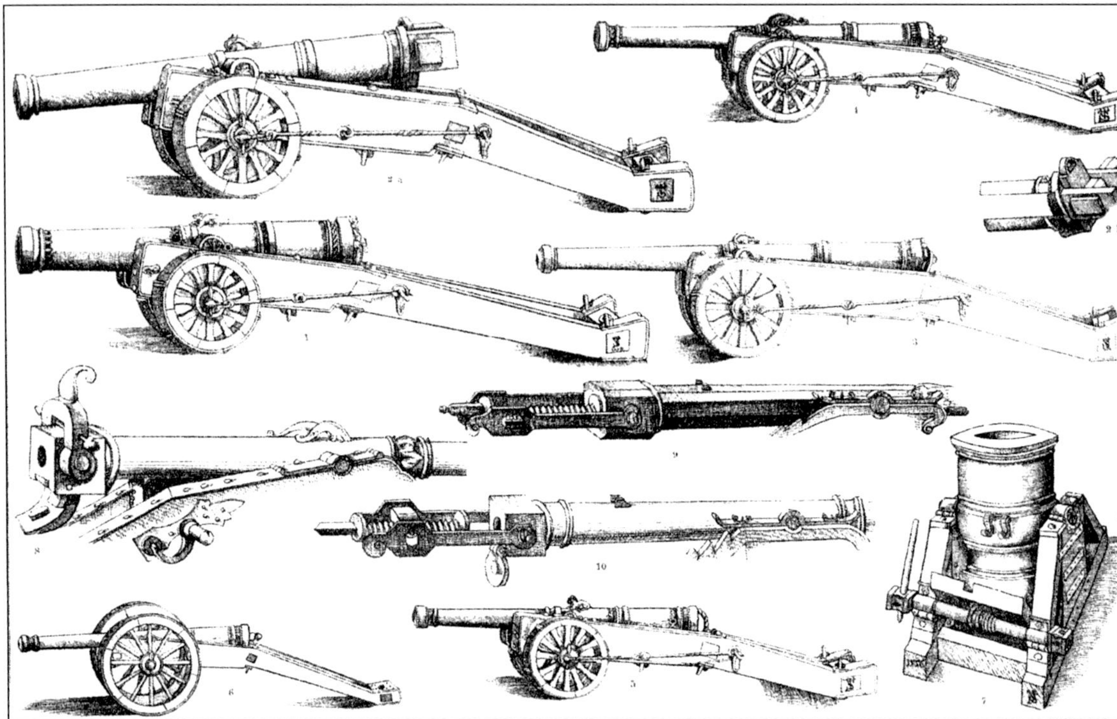

Artillery from Henry Hexham's *The Principles of the Art Militarie* …, from 1637. (Michał Paradowski's archive)

Meanwhile on Clay Hill Manchester's forces could clearly hear Waller's guns, the signal for their advance. Colonel Richard Norton, who had left the siege of Basing House to accompany the combined armies and was with Manchester during the battle, remembers that:

> About 3pm the great guns with the Parliament's forces [at Speen] open fire, at which time there were about 1,400 horse with the Earl [of Manchester], and drawn up on a hill near Shaw many of the Earl's foot. That seeing the armies engaged this examinant often expressed a wish in the Earl's hearing that these forces might engage to help those at Speen by creating a diversion and then seeing the King's forces retreating from the Parliament's, he again addressed the like speech to Captain Bettsworth [of Norton's Regiment], the Earl standing by, while the enemy were retiring towards us.[45]

Norton was not the only one to express frustration against Manchester's inactivity, insomuch that Manchester's major general of foot, Laurence Crawford, advanced without orders until he was recalled by Manchester. It was only 'towards three or four o'clock', according to Rushworth:

> hearing the cannon play from Speen Hill, Manchester drew forth two Drakes to play on Mr Doleman's House, and commanded out a party of 500 musketeers, as a forlorn hope, to attack the said House, and beat those that sallied out from thence

45 Colonel Richard Norton's evidence against Manchester, undated [1 January 1645?] printed in *CSPD 1644–45*, p.159.

The approach to Shaw House, showing part of the surviving earth bank surrounding three sides of the garden. The bank existed before the Civil War, and may have built for decoration along with the house in 1581, or was part of an existing bank and moat system around the earlier manor house. Royalist John Gwyn confirms that a dry moat was present in 1644. (Photo: Serena Jones)

> into their works; and the reason why they did not more was said to be because night came on.[46]

A letter sent to the House of Lords records that:

> The Earl of Manchester, about four of the clock endeavoured to force a passage through Shaw, a village on the other side of the field, where the King's Forces lay. Prince Maurice was on that side, and many of the King's best Foot, who maintained those passages, although they were very bravely assaulted.[47]

The Royalist news sheet *Mercurius Aulicus* takes up the narrative:

> Manchester's Army plied their work upon the north east side of Newbury near Shaw [House]… they came down the hill before Shaw [House], advancing towards those guards which Lord Astley disposed under the command of Colonel George Lisle; the colonel appointed Lieutenant Colonel Richard Page to keep Mr Doleman's house and garden, and Sir Thomas Hooper with his dragoons and other foot, to keep the hedges and lane, Colonel Thelwall with his own regiment, and others of the Reading brigade being for a reserve. The Rebels, to the number of twelve hundred horse and three thousand foot, of the Earl of Manchester's and the London Trained Bands, came

46 Rushworth, *Historical Collections*.
47 A. Johnston and J. Crewe's Letter 28 October 1644, printed in *Journal of the House of Lords*, vol. 7, p.41.

singing psalms down the hill, advancing upon Colonel Lisle's guards; At first they fell on a hedge where forty musketeers were placed, these musketeers were easily overpowered by the Rebels, who upon their quitting the hedge gave a great shout; but then that valiant gentlemen, Sir John Brown, advanced with Prince Charles, his regiment of horse, charged their foot, and did very good execution, and after received a charge of a thousand horse, whereupon he retreated by order to those foot in the garden who flanked that field, and killed many of the Rebels; this forced the Rebels horse to face about, which Sir John Brown no sooner observed, but he advanced again, and cut off very many of the rear of horse, and bravely kept the ground all day.

At the same time when Sir John Brown charged with horse, the reserve of foot came on, which was three hundred of Colonel Lisle's tertio, commanded by that experienced soldier Colonel Thelwall, whereupon were joined those musketeers in the lane, and those other forty which were driven from the hedge; and this body of foot came up so courageously, and gave such excellent fire, that the Rebels had small comfort in their new gotten hedge, shot flew extremely thick on both sides… after they had sufficiently galled the Rebels with several volleys, they fell on with the butt-ends of their muskets, and beat the Rebels not only back from the hedge, but quite out of that field: then his Majesty's forces gave a loud shout, the Rebels running off in great confusion, leaving both their colours and cannon behind them, which were not so hastily hurried away as those drakes the Rebels took at Speen. In the meanwhile another great body of the Rebels' foot fell upon those in Mr Doleman's house and garden; upon their approach a notable fine officer of the Rebels came daringly up, and commanded those in the house and garden not to shoot; Lieutenant Colonel Page bid his men to give fire upon him, who instantly shot this fine Rebel in the belly, so as he never gave more orders; which done, they poured out shot so fast upon the Rebels' whole body, that they began to run; his Majesty's forces pursued with exceeding great execution, which was greater because the Rebel race was up the hill, then his Majesty's soldiers shouted again, for the Rebels never gave shout but once, and were now so far from it, that they left here five hundred of their brethren dead within a small compass of ground, where his Majesty's soldiers had much and good pillage, divers prisoners and some colours, and then they drew off those two pieces of cannon, which they took from the Rebels.

About half an hour after, a body of the Rebels horse came down to have fetched off their cannon, but the musketeers gave fire into their body, and made them return without their errand, to their other cannon upon the hill, for these were past recovery. In this last charge, Lieutenant Colonel Page…was shot through both his thighs, besides a shot through his arm, of all which we hear he is likely to recover.

Edmund Ludlow, whose regiment of horse was with Manchester during the battle, records in his memoirs that while Manchester's infantry advanced:

Our horse had stood drawn up within a little more than pistol shot of the enemy's works all the while out foot were engaged, for their encouragement and protection against any horsethat should attack them, as also to second them in case they had made way. I had divers men and horse shot, and amongst the rest my own.[48]

48 Ludlow, *Memoirs*, vol. 1, p.104.

Shaw House.
(Photo: Serena Jones)

Colonel Richard Norton was nearby and recalls:

> Many we had wounded; amongst the number I received a fair admonition (by musket shot in my leg) for meddling where I had no charge, but I thank God my bone was too hard for the bullet and I hope I shall be upon both legs again ere it be long. I could not help it; for I thought there was need when I engaged myself to lead up Colonel Ludlow's Regiment, his horse having broken his bridle, so that he was fain to quit.

Unfortunately, Norton does not elaborate on his actions at the head of Ludlow's Regiment.[49]

Sunset is estimated to have been at 4.26p.m. and night put a stop to the fighting. Although according one letter, 'The battle lasted about three hours; they fought at least an hour by moonlight.'[50]

As in all battles of the Civil War, the figures for casualties vary considerably. On the Parliamentarian side, Lieutenant Colonel Theodore Palaologus of Colonel Francis Thompson's Regiment of Foot was killed and Major Urry of

49 BL Add ms 24860, Norton to Richard Maijor, undated.

50 A. Johnston and J. Crewe's Letter 28 October 1644, printed in *Journal of the House of Lords*, vol. 7, p.41.

Lord Robarte's Regiment of Foot was captured, both were from Essex's army. Colonel Richard Norton of Waller's army was wounded. On the Royalist side Sir Anthony St Leger, Colonel Topping, Lieutenant Colonel Leake were killed; Sir John Grenville, Sir John Campsfield, Lieutenant Colonel Page and Major Alford were wounded. The Earl of Cleveland was captured. There were possibly as many as 1,000 Parliamentarian casualties in all. The Parliamentarian account of the battle puts the Royalist figure at 200 killed and 300 prisoners, whereas Royalist accounts put it at between 60 and 100 slain.

The King's army had been lucky that day: if Manchester and Cromwell had played their parts it should have been destroyed and shortened the war by a year, and British history would bevery different since there would be no need to form the 'New Model Army'. However, Charles might not be so lucky the following day and therefore decided to withdraw. Leaving his guns at Donnington Castle the King marched to Bath, where he arrived about 4:00 p.m. the next day and was met by Prince Rupert with 3–400 horse and 600 foot. Meanwhile his army, under the command of Lord Forth, who had been slightly wounded during the battle, marched to Wallingford. The Royalists were pursued by a small party of Parliamentarian horse under the command of Colonel Birch, who captured Lady Forth. After Birch's return to Newbury he was rebuked by Manchester and Lady Forth was released.

The following day the Committee of Both Kingdoms wrote to Essex, to take measures to apprehend '[the] great number of soldiers [who] daily forsake their Colours and come from the army to London.'[51] However, a greater worry for the combined Parliamentarian armies was what the King's next movements were, and how to intercept him.On 29 October it was reported that Prince Rupert had joined the King nine miles from Bath with 4,500 foot, 3,000 horse and a train of artillery, and that the rest of his army was at Wallingford, and he then proceeded to Woodstock.

During early November there was an indecisiveness not only in Parliament itself but also the senior officers in the combined army, with some officers wanting to send 5,000 foot and 4,000 horses towards Bath, 'which they say would keep the King from raising an army, and they commend those parts for very rich quarter. Others think such a march would reduce those forces to nothing, many of the soldiers already deserting by reason of the coldness of the weather and want of provisions.'[52]

Waller and Heselrige were two of the officers who wanted to march towards Bath, and on 30 October they wrote to the Committee of Both Kingdoms:

> The King's Army is exceedingly dispersed, and of ever victory might be followed with advantage this is one. We all know the activeness of the enemy to rally, especially Prince Rupert having so good a foundation for an army atBath and the King in person with him. We conceive if you suffer your forces to disperse

51 Committee of Both Kingdoms to Essex, 28 October 1644, printed in *CSPD 1644–45*, p.78.

52 *CSPD 1644–45*, p.83. Sir A. Johnstone and John Crew MP to the Committee of Both Kingdoms, 30 October 1644.

> before they either scatter Prince Rupert's or drive them to their winter quarters, the enemy will continue masters of the west. If you command your forces to go up towards Bath, either the King will give us battle or retire to Bristol. If a battle we have cause to desire it; if to Bristol we have as fruitful parts as are in England to quarter in, and then our victory will be prosecuted to the Parliament's honour and profit. The King's contributions and levies both for men and money in the west will be absolutely frustrated, and Taunton now besieged, relieved; and so your enemies will have no army in the spring...
>
> We feel the season of the year, we see the soldiers' wants and sufferings, yet our sensibleness of the desolation and utter ruin which falls upon all sorts of people where armies come makes us more earnestly desire to end the war than to enjoy our own ease.[53]

Taunton had been besieged since the 23 September, but after considering what to do, the Committee of Both Kingdoms decided that it was best to keep their forces together, although to proceed to Abingdon until the King's movements were known, and then act accordingly.Only two regiments of London Trained Bands were to be left to secure Newbury and Waller was ordered to send 1,000 horse to relieve Taunton which might also 'hinder the levies and contributions made for the King'. Despite being eager to march into the west, Waller now made his excuses, even though he was 'sensible to the sad condition of that poor town of Taunton, and the good people in it', but he continues:

> The continual duty and service we have been upon has extremely weakened my troops, insomuch as if you deduct 1,000 horse from them, the remainder will be so small as I cannot with any countenance stay with them. Besides, we are in such want that there is necessity for an instant supply; those former little payments for a fortnight in three or four months being utterly insufficient to recruit them with necessaries, and their discontents are increased by seeing other forces paid in greater proportion than they are...
>
> My horse have been in constant service ever since the first Battle of Newbury, both winter and summer. After the business of Alton and Arundel in the winter and the battle of Cheriton in the spring, the House of Commons was pleased to provide £10,000 towards the recruiting of my horse, but I never received one penny. I have at least 500 men on foot, and as many unserviceable horse.[54]

However, on 5 November the Committee of Both Kingdoms decided it was best for the combined armies to remain at Newbury, and the forces that had marched away should return. For over a week the King's intentions were unknown to Parliament, but on 8 November Manchester wrote to the Committee that he had intelligence that 'the King is come to Wallingford with his whole army, and that intends to march to Donnington Castle. Their

53 *CSPD 1644–45*, p.83, Sir William Waller and Sir Arthur Heselrige at Newbury to the Committee of Both Kingdoms, 30 October 1644.

54 Committee of Both Kingdoms to Waller, 6 November 1644; Waller at Newbury to the Committee of Both Kingdoms, 11 November 1644, printed in *CSPD 1644–45*, pp.102, 113.

The Earl of Manchester, commander of the Eastern Association Army. (The Turton Collection)

opinion is that it is not safe to divide our forces until we know for certain what the intentions of the enemy are. I hope [in] a day or two [we] will discover.'[55]

The combined armies would discover that evening that the King was within five or six miles of Newbury and the following day between 10:00 and 11:00 a.m. arrived at Donnington Castle, and 'from thence both horse and foot drew off into a plain field between Newbury and the Castle.' A plan by Bernard de Gomme puts the Royalist army at 4,200 horse and 5,000 foot drawn up in two lines, on the left wing was seven bodies of cavalry with a body of 100 musketeers behind five of these bodies. There were four bodies of infantry in the front line and three covering the gaps in the second line. Sir William Blakiston's Brigade of Horse was drawn up between these two lines of infantry. Behind the foot battalions were two more regiments of horse and Colonel Gage's Regiment of Foot in two bodies as a reserve, along with three regiments of cavalry. The right wing was the same as the left wing with seven squadrons of cavalry supported by musketeers.[56]

De Gomme's plan shows the combined armies deployed within the town of Newbury itself, with a few battalions in the field nearby. This does not appear to be artistic licence on De Gomme's part, since Manchester, Waller and Balfour wrote to the Committee of Both Kingdoms later that day that, 'it was not considered safe for us to draw out in regard of the castle's ordnance, therefore we resolved to make good the town.'[57]

However, Ludlow records that:

> The enemy contrary to all expectation, appeared again in a body near Newbury, where our army lay, who drew out to oppose them. Some small skirmishes happened between them, but a general engagement was opposed in a council of war by some of the greatest amongst us… things were managed with such heat as created great differences between the principal officers of the army, by which this favourable conjuncture was lost.[58]

At the council of war Waller, Heselrige and Cromwell argued with Manchester to give the order to attack. Manchester's exact words are not known for certain, but according to Waller:

55 *CSPD, 1644–45*, p.106, Edward, Earl of Manchester at Newbury to the Committee of Both Kingdoms, 8 November1644.

56 BL Add ms 16370, plans of fortifications and plans.

57 *CSPD, 1644–45*, p.108, Manchester, Waller and Balfour at Newbury, to the Committee of Both Kingdoms, 9 November 1644.

58 Ludlow, *Memoirs*, vol. 1, pp.105, 106.

> A proposition was made to fight, saying that the King had hopes of a foreign aid, and particularly out of France. The Earl of Manchester then declared his opinion against engaging, saying to his knowledge there were no forces coming out of France and that if we beat the King never so often yet he will be king still, but if we are once beaten we shall be hanged, and our posterity will be slaves.[59]

Sir Arthur Heselrige also presented evidence against Manchester, claiming that after hearing that French or any other foreign forces being sent to England, Manchester replied:

> 'Upon my credit you need not fear the coming in of the French, I know there is no such thing.' The Earl afterwards said, 'That if we beat the King 99 times yet he is King still, and so will his posterity be after him, but if the King beat us once we shall be all hanged, and our posterity be made slaves.'[60]

Colonel Samuel Jones recalls that, 'he seemed to have a dislike for this discourse, saying that he had more reason to return with his army to his own Association and there take up winter quarters for his army could not subsist without covert.'[61]

With the army commanders arguing among themselves Ludlow continues: 'The King, in the face of our army, twice as numerous as his, had time to send his artillery from Donnington Castle towards Oxford. Without any opposition ... by this time it was clearly manifest that the nobility had no further quarrel with the King."[62]

However, Richard Symonds records in his diary for 9 November does record that at least some fighting did take place that day:

> At about 4 the enemy drew [out] of Newbury two bodies of horse and lined hedges with musketeers, played upon our horse with their cannon as they marched up to them. And because the Queen's Regiment of Horse was drawn within some danger of some musketeers which they drew down below Mr Doleman's house... and a body of the enemy's horse drew boldly out, the Prince Rupert commanded the Queen's Regiment of Horse and Prince Maurice his Regiment of Horse to charge them, no sooner drew up to them but the Rebels wheeled off behind their own cannon and musketeers, which galled that body of ours. Captain Fitzmaurice of the Prince's regiment, and divers more killed and hurt. Their cannon played on both sides and their muskets; little hurt on our side. A musket bullet in volley shot the king's horse in the foot as he stood before his own regiment in his arms.[63]

Despite this skirmishing there would be no third battle of Newbury, due to the infighting of the senior Parliamentarian officers and with the King having achieved his aim of recovering his artillery. Symonds continues:

59 *CSPD 1644–45*, p.148, Sir William Waller's evidence against Manchester, undated.

60 *CSPD 1644–45*, p.151, Sir Arthur Heselrige's Evidence against Manchester, 6 December 1644.

61 *CSPD 1644–45*, p.160, Colonel Samuel Jones' evidence against Manchester, 2 January 1645.

62 Ludlow, *Memoirs*, vol. 1, p.105.

63 Symonds, *Diary*, p.148.

> It growing night, the whole army marched off in full bodies, drums beating and colours flying, trumpets prattling their marches, all in the face of the enemy, who followed not but with some piquering rouges. Our army drew up to the castle hill, and lay in the field all night; the king lay in the castle. [The next day] the King took [blank] pieces of his cannon which he left the last time in the castle…Relieved the castle, and marched off with his whole army to Lambourne… Some of the enemy followed the rear, but Prince Rupert set some horse in a barn and they fell behind them, the others charged before them, killed 15, and took more.[64]

In their correspondence to the Committee of Both Kingdoms neither Waller, Manchester or Balfour mentioned the events at the council of war, but the quarrel which started at Newbury would continue in Parliament between the factions of Cromwell and Manchester.

Even if the combined armies had given battle there was no guarantee that they would have been victorious, since many of the soldiers had been sleeping in the open in freezing weather, which made desertion rife. According to Skippon, 'Sir William Balfour says, all your Excellency's Horse are not about 800 and Colonel Barclay (who calculated their numbers in the field this day) said, that the Foot (I mean your Excellency's) were not above 1,200.' In another letter dated the same day, Manchester, Waller and Balfour informed the Committee of Both Kingdoms that a battle 'might break our army, the officers of the foot complaining of the lessening of their foot, and many hundreds of our horses be already dead, and the living very weak, and many of the troopers run from their Colours.' This letter also states that 'the weather [was] turning bad'.[65]

In another letter written five days later, the senior Parliamentarian officers reported:

> We hold it our duty to represent the state of the army… The horse are so tired out with hard duty in such extremity of weather as hath seldom been seen, that of much more service be required of them you will quickly see your cavalry ruined without fighting. The foot are not in [a] better case, besides the lessening of their numbers through cold and hard duty; sickness also is much on the increase, which we dare not conceal from you, daily regarding their extreme sufferings with not a little sorrow. The places we are in do not afford firing, food or coverings for them, [the soldiers] nor is the condition of the people less to be pitied, who both within our horse and foot quarters are so exhausted that we may justly fear a famine will fall upon them.[66]

Of course it could be argued that they exaggerated the poor conditions of their army to cover up their failings at Newbury, but in other letters they

64 Symonds, *Diary*, p.148.

65 Rushworth, *Historical Collections*, vol. 5, Major General Philip Skippon at Newbury to the Earl of Essex, 10 November 1644; *CSPD 1644–45*, p.110, Letter from Manchester, Waller and Balfour to the Committee of Both Kingdoms.

66 Manchester, Waller and Balfour at Newbury, to the Committee of Both Kingdoms, 15 November 1644, printed in *CSPD 1644–45*, p.125.

confirm the hardships their armies had been through. Winter was setting in and Donnington Castle still defiantly holding out, despite several appeals for it to surrender. Therefore between 15 and 18 November the armies finally broke camp and Waller set out for Farnham with the remnants of his brigade, which could no longer be referred to as an army.[67]

67 *CSPD 1644–1645*, pp.113–114.

7

Waller's Last Campaign

As the remnants of Waller's army marched through the streets of Farnham, they were in a very different mood from that previous May when they had high hopes of defeating the King's Oxford Army. On 15 November it had been stated that one of the objective of the combined armies at Newbury was to send one of the City regiments and three belonging to Manchester to reinforce the besieging force of Basing House. However on 19 November the siege diary, which was kept by the governor of Basing House, the Marquess of Winchester, recalls:

> The enemy wearied with lying 24 weeks, diseases, with winter seizing them, his army wasted from 2,000 to 700, fearing the forces of his Majesty now moving about Hungerford, raised his leaguer, and at this morning drew off his wagons and two guns, three days before brought in. The foot at noon marched towards Odiham, the huts being fired, and some troops of horse left to secure their rear, on whom a party of our horse with Cornet Bryan waiting their opportunities disorder their retreat.[1]

The Royalist garrison had not escape the effects of war, by 1 November the garrison's supply of bread, corn and beer were exhausted and the soldiers were described as:

> Spent and naked, and the numbers few, having besides our hurt and maimed, and such as runs from us, lost near 100 men by sickness and the siege, whereof a lieutenant colonel, two ensigns, three sergeants and seven corporals.[2]

The day after the siege was raised Colonel Gage arrived at the house once more, with a 1,000 strong relieving force and much-needed provisions. Once the garrison had recovered it could launch raiding parties into Surrey and the parts of Hampshire controlled by the Parliamentarians.

On 22 November Colonel Jones reported to the House of Commons, 'that a body of the Enemy's Horse and dragoons to the number of seven

1 BL TT E.27/5, *A Description of the Siege of Basing Castle.*
2 BL TT E.27/5, *A Description of the Siege of Basing Castle.*

thousand were advanced to Odiham.' This force may have been Colonel Gage's force which had been sent to relieve Basing House. This news sent the Committee of Both Kingdoms into a panic since they believed that the King's Army had gone into winter quarters. Orders were sent to the various County Committees within the Southern Association to 'send all the foot and horse they can with all possible speed to Farnham'. [3] These regiments included Colonel Richard Whitehead's and Herbert Morley's which had until recently been besieging Basing House and so were very weak, insomuch that the Committee of Sussex was ordered to bring Morley's Regiment up to 800 by using members of the Sussex Trained Bands, until recruits could be found to replace them. Fortunately, the Royalist force soon retired and the emergency was over for the moment.

However, Waller had not forgotten Taunton. On 11 November he had suggested 'Colonel Ludlow's and Colonel Fitzjames' Regiments with 200 commanded horse of mine own under Commissary General Vandruske' should be sent to join the Dorset horse. Waller also suggested that he would send Major General Holborne as their commander, who was also to withdraw detachments of foot from the various garrisons in the West.[4] However, it was not until the end of November that Waller finally ordered Holborne into the West. Holborne entered Somerset at the beginning of December and after joining Sir Anthony Astley-Cooper's Dorset brigade and Vandruske's force he relieved Taunton on 14 December. Holborne made the town his headquarters, so that he could launch attacks against the Royalists in the West, in what would become a war of attrition. Ludlow recalls:

> At my return into Wiltshire I received orders fro the Committee of Both Kingdoms to send what men I could spare out of my regiment to reinforce a party commanded by Major General Holborne … I drew out 200 horse for that service and was necessitated to march with them myself, my major who had got possession of good quarters at Dean, a house belonging to Sir John Evelyn, being not willing to remove … In our march we were joined by the forces of Dorsetshire. When we were advanced near the enemy, my troop was ordered to a quarter of which they were in possession, but quitted it upon our approach … We made use of the opportunity and furnished the town with provisions and all things necessary which being done, the forces of Wiltshire and Dorsetshire marched back to the said counties.[5]

Ludlow's major was Francis Dowett, who had change sides several times during the war and had sided with the Parliamentarians just before the Second Battle of Newbury, possibly thinking Charles' cause was lost. Ludlow had written sarcastically of Dowett's part in the battle that he had kept his troop in the rear so that the whole regiment would not be lost.

3 *Commons Journal*, vol. iii, p.703, *CSPD 1644–1645*, pp. 134, 140, 142.
4 *CSPD 1644–45*, pp.113–114, Sir William Waller at Newbuy to the Committee of Both Kingdoms, 11 November 1644.
5 Ludlow, *Memoirs*, vol. 1, pp.107–108.

On 23 December the Committee of Both Kingdoms informed Holborne that they had given orders that 1,200 horse and dragoons, plus 600 foot be sent to him so that he could garrison Ilminster 'or other places as you shall think fit'. These forces appear to have been the remainder of Waller's force. In the meantime the regiments of Colonels Fitzjames and Ludlow, and the Plymouth horse were to remain with Holborne for their own security.[6]

Waller's movements during December are obscure. He is known to have been at Petersfield on the 7th and 20th, before returning to Farnham, where he stayed throughout January 1645. The soldiers lacked pay and with morale low the soldiers took their frustration out on the civilians, which prompted Waller on 7 December to issue the following order:

> That no soldier upon any pretence whatsoever shall henceforth plunder, seize or take away any of the Goods, sheep, cattle, horse or horses whether by enchanting or otherwise from any Countryman or other Traveller upon the road, nor molest in their person or Goods any man or woman coming to or from the Market without express order from the General or other superior officer having power thereunto, upon pain of death without mercy.[7]

Despite this order being read at the head of every regiment, plundering continued. 'Scant one day [passes],' wrote John Wight in December, 'but we hear of some robbing. There are many foot soldiers yet about Bramley and Wonersh and these parts who are much suspected. I pray do not ride late.'[8]

On 21 December, with the Parliamentarian forces in turmoil, King Charles appointed George Goring Lieutenant General of Surrey, Sussex, Hampshire and Kent, a position Waller still held for Parliament. If the Royalists could control at least part of these counties then they could recruit from this area. Therefore Goring lost no time preparing to march on this territory. On 8 January 1645, having intelligence that the Royalists had marched to the borders of Sussex and Hampshire, the Committee of Both Kingdoms wrote to the various county committees of the Southern Association:

> The enemy being drawn near to your parts, we have designed a considerable strength both of horse and foot to march towards you for your defence, and to oppose the enemy. We desire you to draw together all the forces of your county to be in readiness to join with the forces to be sent to you. We need add nothing further to move you to all care and expedition herein, the nearness of the enemy being as we conceive a sufficient motive.[9]

The Kent, Sussex and Surrey trained bands were called out to meet this new threat and the garrison on the Isle of Wight was ordered to send 200 men to reinforce the garrison at Portsmouth, along with Colonel Whitehead's

6 *CSPD 1644–45*, p.196, Committee of Both Kingdoms to Holborne, 23 December 1644.
7 Court Martial Papers of Sir William Waller's army, printed in Adair, *Cheriton*, pp.212–213.
8 LM Cor 5/57, John Wight to Sir Poynings More, December 1644.
9 *CSPD 1644–1645*, pp.239–240, Committee of Both Kingdoms to the Committees of Surrey and Sussex, 8 January 1645.

Regiment. However, on 9 January it had advanced only as far as Fareham, when his men mutinied. On that day Goring wrote to the King:

> I esteem myself very unhappy to be diverted from the pursuit of a distracted enemy, by that which is a greater misfortune, a want of arms, disorder in the train and a universal deadness in the officers of foot to undertake any action without refreshment. I was necessitated to call a council of war, rather to please some of them than to hear them and I find so many difficulties and objections raised in all things I propose of action.[10]

Goring was forced to retreat on this occasion, but on 27 January Gerolamo Agostini, the Venetian Secretary in England, wrote to the Doge and the Senate, 'The king's forces are making themselves felt in the West, in Sussex and elsewhere, but particularly towards Portsmouth.'[11]

Waller had set up a cavalry screen in Hampshire, but this did not prevent Goring from sweeping through the county at the end of January with a force of cavalry and dragoons, and he was able to attack Aldershot and Crondall on 27 January. On 29 January 1645 Goring wrote to Sir Edward Walker:

> Having had certain notice how the enemy was quartered both horse and foot. They being spread very much about the country presuming upon the distance of our troops, their foot being in Farnham and villages thereabouts and their horse being spread almost from Alton to Southampton so that they hindered provisions and contributions to come into Winchester, I drew out all the horse from about Salisbury, but only a few to guard the foot, which were left behind and after a great march I divided the troops so that I preposed to fall upon most of all their quarters upon Monday night last, but their horse quarters had notice of our march and removed towards Sussex at four o'clock in the afternoon but we found their foot about Farnham unprovided for us, there were three companies at Crondall which were about 200 and there were about 100 more about Aldershot both which quarters were beaten up at the same time, those at Crondall were most killed or taken, their three colours taken and at Aldershot very few escaped, but some that were quartered with a major in a house which was defensible against our horse, and the few dragoons that were there, It fell out that the foremost parties which were to fall on both quarters were Irish and they gave no quarter to any man, which I can hardly blame them for considering the inhumane usage of the other party to their countrymen upon cold blood, which I am very confident we shall make them weary of.

Goring added that he had not received any orders from Oxford lately so he had, 'drawn most of the horse about Salisbury which is the only place about which we can refresh with ease and security … for all Hampshire is so eaten up that very few of our troops can subsist in it.'[12]

10 BL Add ms 18982 f.11, George Goring at Fareham to King Charles, 9 January 1645. Several secondary accounts have mistaken this town for Farnham.

11 *CSP Ven. 1643–1647*, p.172, Gerolamo Agostini, the Venetian Secretary in England wrote to the Doge and the Senate, 27 January 1645.

12 BL Add ms 18982, f.30, General George Goring to His Majesty's Principle Secretary of State, 29 January 1645.

On the same day that the counties of the Southern Association were warned about the imminent advance of the Royalists into its borders, Holborne's force routed a party of Royalists near Bridgwater and pursued them back there, but failed to capture the town. He again sallied out of Taunton on 16 January to beat up the quarters of Colonels Windham and Hawley's regiments, who had mutinied near the town. These actions may have prevented Goring marching east until the end of the month.[13]

Goring's raid into Hampshire prompted the Committee of Both Kingdoms to order Waller to undertake counter measures by creating a force of 6,000 men and pursue Goring into the West. However, this was easily said than done since due to the lack of provisions around Surrey and Hampshire which forced Waller to disperse his regiments over a wide area. On 2 February Waller wrote:

> I have had conference with Colonel John Greaves and the foot officers, from whom I have this information, that the Lord General's Horse are about 600, his and Manchester's foot 2,000 and Manchester's horse near 700. I cannot yet give a particular account of my own forces, both in regard they are quartered more remote from me, and I know not to what proportion they are recruited. Tomorrow morning I propose to take a view of the foot, and in the afternoon of the Lord general's and Manchester's horse. On Tuesday I intend to be at Petersfield and to muster my own horse and dragoons, and on Wednesday or Thursday, if money be sent down to advance to Alresford and Bishop's Waltham, from whence I can move as you may direct me …
>
> [However], it is in vain to talk to the soldiers of marching till they money comes. The officers this day represented some particulars wherein their regiments were defective, viz., 600 pikes, 1,000 sword, 1,000 bandoliers, 2,000 knapsacks and 2,000 pairs of stockings.

Waller was also expecting detachments from Newport Pagnell and Aylesbury to bring his force up to strength, but at least 100 of the 300 from Newport had deserted, and Waller believed the rest would follow.[14]

After reviewing his forces, on 7 February Waller wrote that Manchester's horse:

> fall [far short] of your reckoning, and you will perceive by the Commissioners that the Lord General's troops hold out no better. It was your resolution that these troops in all should make up 1,500 horse, besides 7 troops which were appointed of the remainder of Lieutenant General Cromwell's Regiment to join with me by way of addition to my forces. If they should only amount to a little over the half, I desire to known how far you will think fit I should engage, and beg to have some instructions to direct me. The Commissioners have not yet gone through with their musters. The Sussex Regiment will be ready to march the beginning of next week. I hear nothing of the Aylesbury Regiment, which I requested might

13 BL TT E.27/7, *Mercurius Aulicus*, 5–12 January 1645.
14 *CSPD, 1644–45*, p.282, Sir William Waller at Farnham to the Committee of Both Kingdoms, 2 February 1645.

be stationed at Reading, and in lieu of it Colonel Alexander Berkeley sent to me which would greatly advantage the service and not weaken at all the garrison of Reading. Expecting your commands I rest.[15]

On 13 February Waller wrote to the Committee of Both Kingdoms:

> Mine own forces are quartered in Hampshire as far as Aylesford, I have already sent orders to all the regiments of horse to advance, assigning them their particular quarters, This enclosed from Colonel Fortescue will inform you in what condition my Lord General's foot are, which I humbly conceive I cannot but this it was your intention that those horse and foot of His Excellency that were immediately to be put upon action should be have at the least as much, if not more than they that were to be still in their quarters, but contrarily those at Reading (whither all the money is sent) have received ... three weeks pay and we are here offered one weeks pay. This is the right way to put them all into mutiny. I must needs be say Colonel Fortescue and the chief officers have done, and do their parts to acquaint the soldiers and express the noble readiness to advance the service, but truly Sir this discontent hath wrought a pre-indication in the soldiers and inferior officers against me imputing this unhappiness of their condition unto the infection of being put under my command, I fear the consequence will be very ill. I have but two things to offer unto you upon this. The first is there may be an immediate despatch of so much monies as may make our pay equal with that received at Reading. The next is that which I humbly presented unto you yesterday, that I may have the honour to have a full commission (according to the latitude expressed in that letter) whereby I may be vested with a fit power to command as the importance of this service will require. Or if that will not so well conform with your present councils, I shall but offer it and that with all humbleness and submission that there may be some person of honour and merit ... appointed to this command against me.[16]

Unfortunately, Fortescue's letter does not appear to have survived so we do not know what condition Essex's foot were in, but later that day Waller marched out of Farnham intending to be at Aylesford that evening. He left behind the mutinous troops of Essex's army. Originally it had been intended that he should relieve Taunton, but now Weymouth was seen as being in far greater danger, with some reports suggesting that the outer works had already been captured. Also on the same day to quell the mutinies within his army the Committee of Both Kingdoms ordered the officers to obey his commands since he was on 'very important service, which admits not delay'.[17]

However, not all were willing to do so. On 15 February it was reported to the House of Commons that three cavalry regiments which belonged to Essex's army and quartered at Leatherhead in Surrey, refused to march,

15 *CSPD, 1644–45*, pp.291–292, Sir William Waller at Farnham to the Committee of Both Kingdoms, 7 February 1645.

16 BL Harl ms 166, f.185, Waller to the Committee of Both Kingdoms, 13 February 1645.

17 *CSPD, 1644–45*, p.304, Committee of Both Kingdoms to the Officers of Waller's army, 13 February 1645.

saying that 'they would rather go under any [commander] who the Lord General should appoint without money, than [serve] with Sir William Waller with all the money in England.'[18] Essex's infantry allocated to Waller felt the same, insomuch that Skippon and Balfour had to be sent into Surrey to try and persuade these regiments to serve with Waller, but their efforts appear to have been in vain.[19] These detachments of Essex's army were not the only problem: on 21 February Sir Samuel Luke wrote to Gunner Thomas Wright, that 'Sir William Waller could not get an able gunner to go with him although he offered great advance and certain pay so he is fain to make matrossess to serve for gunners.'[20]

On 19 February, while at Petersfield, Waller wrote to Speaker Lenthall:

> I am so far from being retarded in your service by this distempers that have unhappily fallen out amongst us, that I am resolved to advance though none but mine own troops should follow me, and what difficulties soever it shall be my fortune to meet with in my way, by God's Grace … I shall give them a cheerful welcome. This night upon the coming of my Lord of Manchester's and Lieutenant General Cromwell's horse I advance my quarters to Bishop's Waltham, the dragoon horses from Sussex are appointed to be brought in tomorrow morning, when likewise the arms and pistols for Sir Arthur Heselrige's Regiment and Colonel Thompson's will be with me also. I came the last night hither from Chichester, whether I was fain to go myself unto the Committee [of Sussex] (unto whom I had written diverse times before) to press them to a present despatch of their recruits.[21]

In another letter he informed the Committee of Both Kingdoms that he had:

> given order for the transportation of Colonel Morley's Companies (which make up near 350 good men and commanded by a gallant man the lieutenant colonel [John Drake] from Portsmouth thither with a months provision with them and myself with the greatest part of my horse and dragoons will immediately advance.[22]

Drake's detachment was intended to sail to reinforce the garrison of Weymouth, which 'I received intelligence from thence last night that the town holds out bravely, I shall neglect no opportunity to relieve it.'[23] The Committee of Both Kingdoms received this letter the following day and sent orders for him to halt his advance until further notice because Goring was once again threatening Hampshire. They also sent orders that Morley's

18 *CSPD, 1644–45*, p.307, Proceedings of the Committee of Both Kingdoms, 15 February 1645; Luke, *The Letter Books of Sir Samuel Luke, 1644–1645* (London: HMSO, 1963) ed. H.G. Tibbutt, nos. 304, 1077, 1097.

19 *CSPD, 1644–45*, p.307, Proceedings of the Committee of Both Kingdoms, 15 February 1645.

20 Luke, *Letter Books*, nos. 304, 1077, 1097.

21 BL Harl ms 166 f185, Waller to Lenthall, 19 February 1645.

22 BL Harl ms 166 f185, Waller to the Committee of Both Kingdoms, 19 February 1645.

23 BL Harl ms 166 f185, Waller to Lenthall, 19 February 1645.

Regiment was to sail from Portsmouth for Melcombe Regis, which was in need of infantry, rather than Weymouth.

The garrison of Weymouth seems to have enjoyed a period of peace with its neighbouring Royalist garrison at Portland, according to Peter Ince, the chaplain of the Weymouth garrison: 'we were in as sweet a quiet and security as any garrison in the Kingdom.'[24] Then at midnight on the 9 February, Sir Walter Hastings, the governor of Portland, with a detachment of his men slipped over the walls of Chapel Fort with little resistance, since most of its garrison were sleeping. Finally when the alarm was raised the Parliamentarians counter-attacked, but were repulsed with loss, including Major Sydenham who was mortally wounded. Sydenham, the brother of the governor of Weymouth Colonel William Sydenham, would die a few days later. The Royalists also captured Nothe Fort, which protected Weymouth harbour. Having been repulsed, the Parliamentarians evacuated Weymouth and retired to neighbouring Melcombe Regis, which the Royalists believed was indefensible.[25]

Originally the plan was that Sir Lewis Dyve, the governor of Sherborne, with a force of 1,500 horse and foot, would also attack Weymouth, but he arrived at midday on 10 February; knowing the importance of the town Charles ordered Goring, who was then at Salisbury with 3,000 horse and 1,500 foot, to support Dyve and Hastings, although he appears to have left most of his force at Dorchester and proceeded to Weymouth with a small detachment. That evening they fired 'a multitude of great bullets and iron bars, hot and cold', which according to Peter Ince did little damage to Melcombe Regis, while Parliamentarian cavalry sallied out to harass the enemy. On 13 February Peter Ince records:

> Our enemies began to fire [at] us; and by small iron slugs heated in a forge, which they shot from their muskets, set fire on a thatched house, over against the Chapel Fort; from when they shot about the house continually to hinder us from quenching the flames, but without the least hurt to any man. This fire was soon put out, it only consumed two houses, blessed be God: Upon this we fell (though unwillingly) to the like course, and fired a house in Chapel Fort; but being little delighted with such sad spectacles, we sent to the enemy, that there might be no more such work, on either side, they sent us word, they scorned to parley with us, and would so what they pleased.[26]

The artillery dual continued the following day with houses on both sides being burnt down. After which this dual ceased.

On 15 February, Lieutenant Colonel Haynes managed to break through the Royalists' lines and join enter Melcombe Regis with a valuable addition of 100 cavalry. The following day he sallied out and routed a party of Royalist horse at Radipole and captured about 45 prisoners, including a captain and a cornet. After this the Royalists appear to have partly withdrawn from their

24 BL TT E.274/7, Peter Ince, *A Brief Relation of the surprise of the forts of Weymouth, the Siege of Melcombe Regis, and recovering of the forts* (London: Luke Fawne, 1645).

25 Ince, *A Brief Relation…*

26 BL TT E 274/7 Ince, *A Brief Relation…*

original stations. At the beginning of the second week of the siege another sally managed to bring back 900 sheep for the garrison of Melcombe Regis. Peter Ince also records at this time that:

> In both towns there was every day a new expense of shot and blood on both sides; but considering the many advantages they had continually upon us, it did daily cause in us an admiration, that our loss should be so little. Every night we were molested with the loud blasphemies and revellings of our enemies; but the worse we found them, the greater was our hope of deliverance from them.[27]

About the 23 February Goring arrived at Weymouth that evening began to cast up a fortification on the north side of Melcombe Regis, which was quickly captured the following day.

On 26 February some Royalist cavalry escorting some provisions to Weymouth were set upon by Parliamentarian cavalry and chased them back to Weymouth. To all in tense and purposes it seemed like any other skirmish, but seeing what was happening the commander of Chapel fort sent out about 100 musketeers to cover the retreating cavalry. However, seeing that the Royalists were distracted with this skirmish, 150 musketeers from Melcombe Regis under the command of Major Wilson and Captain Langford were sent to recapture Chapel Fort, 'the enemy,' according to Peter Ince, 'not discovering our men, till they were upon the outworks, ran into the Chapel and after a shot or two cried [for] quarter. Thus had we now again regained the command of the town of Weymouth.'[28]

On 26 February, Sir Lewis Dyve wrote to Sir John Berkeley and tried to make the best of 'the disaster that happened to us this day' by stating that 'the two principal forts, where our provisions and ammunition lies we still maintain and doubt not be God's assistance to keep them still. Hoping that this misfortune will turn [to] our advantage.' This and a similar letter to John Digby never reached their intended recipients as they were captured and sent to London.[29] The Royalist commanders could not let this humiliation pass and Goring also wrote to Berkeley ordering him to bring his forces to Weymouth, while those men Goring had left at Dorchester were also to come to town since they intended to make a night assault on it.

The plan was to assault Melcombe Regis and the part of Weymouth held by the Parliamentarians simultaneously. In the evening of 27 February preparations for the attack were made in secret to assault the towns early the following morning. Unfortunately for the Royalists their efforts were in vain, as the Parliamentarians were forewarned by an escaped prisoner of war, so when the attack came they were ready for them. 'We quit the west-guard of Weymouth,' recalls Peter Ince:

> and made a barricado below in the street beneath Chapel Fort, planted a gun there and ordered all the other guards, so as might serve best for the repulse of them that

27 BL TT E 274/7 Ince, *A Brief Relation...*
28 BL TT E 274/7, Ince, *A Brief Relation ...*
29 *Lord's Journal*, vol. 7, p.260.

> were coming against us. About one or two of the clock the night, (it being light) on they come, the most considerable part of them of the west-side, where entering the work (which we quit) so easily, they thought all their own and gave a loud 'hoop'... They had not come in a body far down the street, but their presumption was confuted and they wished themselves further off. A long time shot was going on both sides; but at last seeing they got nothing but wounds, by staying, they began to run away, and be quiet, leaving five dead men in the streets ... On the other side from Northpoint, the Irish rebels, and others of their fraternity fell in, and the Barricado made that way, lying below the houses under the hill, the enemy broke in within the Barricado though the houses, and put our men to a somewhat disorderly retreat thence; but they fell back to a second Barricado, where a gun was planted, which they had been in a way to desert too, but that the governor came seasonably in, and commanded them to make it good; so they fired the gun upon the enemy, whereupon they fled back and were followed by a party, taken off from the main guard, to the further barricado formerly quitted ... Those on the north end of town did only lie behind a bank, firing at a distance and came not up, yet left some of their blood behind them. So after about two hours fight, they very silently stole away, that we might not fall upon their rear.[30]

Attempts to retake the town being unsuccessful later that day Goring and Dyve decided to abandon the parts of Weymouth they still held and marched away. According to the Earl of Clarendon, Weymouth was:

> [A] place of so vast importance was, by most supine negligence at best retaken by that contemptible number of the enemy, who had been beaten into the lower town [Melcombe Regis] and who were looked upon as prisoners at [the] mercy [of the Royalists]. The mysteries of which fatal loss were never inquired into.[31]

While Colonel William Sydenham set about finding the Royalist sympathisers in Weymouth, several of which were hanged, the Committee of Both Kingdoms does not seem to have had information of the Royalists surrendering the towns, as on 4 March they ordered Waller to relieve Melcombe Regis and he resumed his march into the west once more.[32]

On 5 March Waller mustered his forces near Winchester, which amounted to 3,000 horse and dragoons and Cromwell's force, which 'was to make all possible expedition to join with Waller's forces', mustered a further 2,000 horse and dragoons. On 12 March Goring planned to oppose Waller's westward march, hoping to join with Sir John Berkeley's force, which would bring their combined strength to around 2,500 foot and 3,500 horse, although the rendezvous did not take place. Sir Richard Grenville, who had originally been Waller's lieutenant general of horse was also soldiering in the West with a small army.[33]

---

30 BL TT E.274/7 Ince, *A Brief Relation ...*

31 Clarendon, *History of the Rebellion*, vol. 5, p.139.

32 *CSPD 1644–45*, p.334, Committee of Both Kingdoms to Waller, 3 March 1645; *CSPD, 1644–45*, p.318, Committee of Both Kingdoms to Waller, 21 February 1645.

33 *Calendar of the Clarendon State Papers*, vol. 1 p.259, Lord Goring to the Prince of Wales, 12 March 1645.

Winchester's West Gate. (Photo: Nicola Turton)

On 8 March it was Waller's turn to beat up the Royalists' quarters at Andover. Among the prisoners of Lord Percy's Regiment Cromwell noticed:

> A youth of so fair countenance, that he doubted of his condition; and to confirm himself willed him to sing; which he died with such daintiness that Cromwell scrupled not to say to Lord Percy, that being a warrior, he did wisely to be accompanied by *Amazons*: on which that Lord in some confusion, did acknowledge that she was a damsel; this afterwards gave cause for scoff at the King's party, as that they were loose and wanton, and minded their pleasure, more than either their country's service or their master's good.[34]

This young woman was Lord Percy's mistress rather than a trooper.

This success was followed four days later by Waller and Cromwell destroying a Royalist regiment of horse, under the command of Sir James Long, in a series of skirmishes between Westbury and Steeple Ashton.[35] Two days later Holborne's force fell upon Goring near Crookham and killed, according to Parliamentarian sources, 300 Royalists and captured 300 more, although the Royalist news sheet *Mercurius Aulicus* denies that this skirmish ever took place.[36]

Much of the Parliamentarian forces being in the West, the garrisons of Winchester and Basing House had more freedom to patrol in Hampshire and west Surrey; which prompted the Committee of Both Kingdoms to order, on 14 March 1645, Colonel Edmund Ludlow's Regiment of Horse to garrison Odiham and Blackwater, 'to preserve the country thereabouts'. The troops of Captains Ramsay, Stevens and Bruce along with Essex's Lifeguard were ordered to support Ludlow in his mission and he could call upon Colonel Jones' Regiment of Foot at Farnham if needs be. However the regiment's position was too exposed to hold for long, and it was forced to retired to Godalming. Ludlow records in his memoirs:

> After we had been there a few days, my major, who had more wit than courage or honesty, prevailed with the council of officers to vote our lying there unsafe and inadvisable. I being unwilling to stay contrary to their advice, without an especial order, acquainted the Committee of Both Kingdoms with the result of the council of officers, who approving their reasons, sent me orders to draw off: in obedience to which I marched into Surrey, and the first night arrived at a place called, as I think, Godalming, near Guildford. Sir John Evelyn endeavoured to persuade me to join Lieutenant General Cromwell, who was ordered into the West; but being engaged to attend our committee about the recruiting of my regiment, I was not willing to stir till that business was effected, that I might not leave so many honest men who had lost their horses in the service, before I had procured some provisions to be made for them.[37]

34 Waller, *Recollections*, pp.125–126.

35 BL TT E.274/14, *A Copie of Sir William Waller's letter of the great victory obtained by Sir William Waller and Lieutenant General Cromwell against Colonel James Long (High Sheriff of Wiltshire) who was driven from Devizes and his whole regiment taken* (London: Robert Austin, 1645).

36 BL TT E.279/8, *Mercurius Aulicus*, 6–13 April 1645.

37 Ludlow, *Memoirs*, vol. 1, pp.113–114.

Even Ludlow's presence on the border of Surrey did not prevent the garrison of Basing House imposing taxes on the county. On 30 April John Wight reported to his friend Sir Poynings More, that a new tax had been imposed on Surrey:

> On Sunday last, there was brought to our High Constable a warrant subscribed 'Marmaduke Rawdon' for the levying of £280 upon our Hundred for the advance of the King's army, to be paid in to Basing the 8th of this instant. I doubt their mercies will be cruel enough. I shall be afraid to live in my house after the date of the warrant. The like warrants are come to the Hundreds of Woking and Godley.[38]

It is not known whether the Royalist tax collectors returned, though it is doubtful.

By the 21 March Waller had resumed his march westwards and it was when he came near Devizes that a party of horse sallied out of the town to fall on his rear, but after a short fight the Royalists were routed and pursued into Devizes, one lieutenant-colonel and several other officers and many soldiers were taken. On the same day Colonel Percy's Regiment of Horse with Goring's troop of horse was routed by a party of 300 Parliamentarian horse at Pitmaster.[39]

After his success at Devizes Waller then marched to Bristol, but he was desperately short of infantry, so on 23 March after facing the city he drew off to Marshfield, from where he wrote to the Committee of Both Kingdoms:

> I cannot but lament my want of foot, and dare speak of with confidence that if I had but those 3,000 that were assigned unto me you might be masters of the west and of the places of the greatest importance in it the people being universally disposed to receive us, but unwilling to engage till they see me with such a body as y give them assurance I mean to stay with them and not be gone tomorrow. I hope that Lieutenant General Cromwell and Major General Holborne are joined before then, I am like to have the hardest task to get to them. The enemy interposing between me and them at Shaftesbury. If your lordships think fit to send down foot or to command them that were at Farnham with some other regiments in addition to march to me I shall be in the way to receive and secure them about Wimborne.[40]

He also adds:

> There is a party in Herefordshire and Gloucestershire that have besieged Hereford near 16,000 strong and that they have 6,000 muskets among them. They will not yet declare of either side but only for the defence of their own county. The people

38 SHCLM Cor 5/66, John Wight to Sir Poynings More, 30 April 1645.

39 BL TT E.276/6 Bernard Alsop, *The Weekly Account*, 26 March 1645; TT E.278/8 Richard Collings, *The Kingdome's Weekly Intelligencer* (London, 8–15 April 1645); TT E.279/8 Peter Heylyn, *Mercurius Aulicus* (Oxford, April 1645).

40 BL Sloane ms 1519 f.66, Waller to Committee of Both Kingdoms, 23 March 1645.

> in all these counties are likewise prepared to rise and if I had a body of foot in the field I am confident they would speedily be with me.[41]

This party became known as the Clubmen; they had first appeared in December 1644 from war-weary inhabitants who opposed both sides. Two notable parties were in Shropshire and Worcester, led by the parsons of Bishop's Castle and Shelsley Beauchamp. Both sides tried to negotiate with these Clubmen, but when this failed often they were disarmed by force.

On the 26 March Waller set out for Downton, six miles from Salisbury, but Goring was uncertain whether he should pursue him since, according to Goring, he was much stronger than he had anticipated and advised that he should continue besieging Taunton.[42] In 1645 Charles Prince of Wales had been sent into the West to give the 14-year-old more military experience, with a council of war to advise him. Based at Bristol this council met to discuss the situation, and on 28 March John Lord Culpeper informed Goring of their decision:

> Sir Richard Grenville may be oppressed before your Lordship's approach to his succour, or that he retiring towards Exeter, the garrisons of Langport, Borough and Ilchester may be in danger by the enemy on their backs. The means to prevent both as conceived to be your Lordship's very speedy march to the West with all your forces, whereby probably you on the one side and Sir Richard Grenville on the other or both joined may take the advantage to finish the work which Cromwell and Vandruske, before Waller … can be joined with him and advanced to them.
>
> The business of Taunton we conceive is not to be farther thought upon until the decisive[ness] of a battle shall give it … [or] there may be an opportunity offered to surprise and burn the town … [Alternatively] if the forces of Taunton, Cromwell and the Weymouth men shall march towards Wimborne to join with Waller they will thereby give Sir Richard Grenville liberty to burn Taunton without resistance and afterwards will all the Western forces may march after them towards Yeovil and Wincanton, where the worst that can happen will be a fair field with them in such ground as you will choose the advantage of provisions and they having none but bare naked quarters left them.[43]

Here we see the burning of Taunton being openly discussed, no longer was it seen as a 'war without an enemy' but a savage war. As a Frenchman fighting in the French Wars of Religion during the sixteenth century put it, 'We fought the first year like angels, the second like men and the third like devils.'[44]

The same day Culpeper wrote his letter to Goring, Sir Richard Grenville with 800 horse and 2,000 foot defeated a force which had sallied out of

41 BL Sloane ms 1519 f.66, Waller to Committee of Both Kingdoms, 23 March 1645.

42 *Calendar of Clarendon State Papers*, vol. 1, p.261. Lord Goring at Shafton to Lord Culpeper, 26 March 1645.

43 BL Tanner 60A/27–28, Sir John Culpeper to George Lord Goring, Bristol 28 March 1645.

44 Ronald Hutton, 'For King and Country', in *The Making of Britain, the Age of Expansion*, (Basingstoke: MacMillian Education Ltd, 1986), ed. Lesley M. Smith, p.66.

Taunton in three engagements, and they had now retired to Exminster where they expected to join with the forces of Lyme and those of Cromwell. This left Taunton with a garrison of just 400 foot and three troops of horse.[45]

Goring does not seem to have received Culpeper's letter at this stage, and he sent his infantry to reinforce the besiegers at Taunton, while his cavalry with 200 mounted foot straddled the Dorset–Wiltshire border in an attempt to stop Waller's movements. On 27 March Grenville, having engaged a combined Parliamentarian force from the garrisons of Taunton, Weymouth and Poole at Exminster, had arrived at Chard, just 15 miles from Taunton; however when ordered to march further east he wrote that, 'his men would now not stir a foot and that he had promised the Commissioners of Devon and Cornwall that he would not advance beyond Taunton till Taunton were reduced.'[46] Moreover, fearing that Cromwell might also join with this force and invade Cornwall, Grenville decided to fall back to Honiton. A decision supported by the Prince's council, who advised Goring and Berkeley to march to Grenville's assistance.

However, about this time Goring reported that he was ill. What this sickness was he does not say, but on 29 March he wrote to Culpeper, that 'an indisposition [is] upon me that I am not able for the present to dispatch any business in the least kind', and that he was, 'very much perplexed at my want of health at this time of action.' On the other hand Goring was able to recall his infantry and was well enough to muster his army at Yeovil on 29 March, 'where if God gives me health I shall not fail to be, though for the present I want it very much.'[47]

Meanwhile Waller had written from Downton the day after his arrival:

> Our duty and marches have been extreme, so that we are here a tired company and necessitated to make some stay for our refreshing. Lieutenant General Cromwell I presume, is this day joined with Major General Holborne for he was last night at Bridport. I hope General Goring's drawing down after me towards Mere and leaving [Sir Richard] Grenville with his and Berkeley's forces at and about Chard, may afford our forces some good opportunity. I have sent an express with all speed after Lieutenant General Cromwell to know where and how I may join him, and I shall apprehend the first opportunity to do it. I cannot but advise you that since my coming thither I have observed a great smoke of discontent rising among the officers. I pray God no flame break out. The ground of all is the extremity of want that is among them, indeed in an insupportable measure.[48]

45 *Calendar of Clarendon State Papers*, vol. 1, p.261, Sir Richard Grenville at Chard to Lord Goring, 28 March 1645; Clarendon, *History of the Rebellion*, vol. 5, p.144.

46 *Calendar of Clarendon State Papers*, vol. 1, p.261; Clarendon, *History of the Rebellion*, vol. 5, p.145.

47 Florene Memegalos, *George Goring 1608–1657, Caroline Courtier and Royalist General* (Aldershot: Ashgate, 2007), p.232.

48 BL Tanner ms 60/15, Sir William Waller to the Speaker of the House of commons, William Lenthal, 27 March 1645.

On 28 March Waller proceeded to Calne, while the forces of Cromwell and Holborne had joined at Bridport, together their forces were about 4,500 strong. On 29 March *Mercurius Aulicus* records:

> Cromwell lying at Dorchester with all his own horse and the united forces from Taunton, Poole and Weymouth, 4,000 in all. Goring had notice of it and advanced towards them with 1,500 horse the rest of the Royal cannon and army being ordered to follow for securing the retreat. 800 of the Parliament horse disputed a pass up on a little river; but some of Goring's horse facing them there whilst others got in behind them, they presently quitted the pass and fled. Whereupon Goring chased them four miles; took many, with two colours of horse and great store of carbines and pistols and slew more. Their forces were so beaten and scattered that, of 4,000 at first they durst not next morning draw out of the town against 1,500 of Goring's horse; although his horse, foot and cannon were full 6 miles behind.

It seems that Cromwell and Holborne had slipped away from Dorchester because later that day they were reported to have joined Waller at Cerne Abbas, bringing their combined strength to about 8,000 horse and foot.[49] Now that these forces had united, the Royalists feared an attacked on either Bath or Bristol, so Grenville was ordered to join Goring and the siege of Taunton should 'for the present be laid aside'.

On 1 April Goring reported that Sir John Digby with about 1,000 cavalry had beaten up Waller's quarters at Cucklington, near Wincanton and several officers had been taken.[50] The following day Goring was ordered to chase Waller 'out of those parts' and Culpeper hoped for another Roundway Down; but Goring dismissed the idea since although he was 'strong enough to keep Waller in check', he was not strong enough to 'force his quarters' until Grenville had joined him. Despite Goring's claim one Royalist officer wrote: 'General Goring … sent out parties almost every night to beat up the enemy's quarters in Wiltshire, which was done with such good success that in a short time we took many prisoners and colours.' According Sir John Digby's biographer, Edward Walsingham, Digby gave Waller 'leave neither night or day, but still plied upon him and wearied him out with almost continual alarms.' True, Walsingham was apt to exaggerate, but even Clarendon states that Waller lost 1,000 men in just two encounters.[51]

One of these raids occurred on 12 April when an outpost of Waller's army near Sturminster Newton was beaten up. The Royalists captured a colonel's colour and about 30 prisoners, but two troops of Cromwell's regiment arrived and drove the Royalists off, claiming to have taken two of the enemy's cornets. Waller admits that this was unlikely because colours were not usually taken on raids. On the same day Colonel Popham's[52] Regiment of between 180 to

49 BL TT E.278/8, *The Kingdomes Weekly Intelligencer,* 8–15 April 1645.

50 *Calendar of Clarendon State Papers*, vol. 1, p.262, Culpeper to Goring, 1 April 1645, and Lord Goring at Bruton to Lord Culpeper, 1 April 1645.

51 *Calendar of Clarendon State Papers*, vol. 1 p.262, Culpeper to Goring, 1 April 1645, quoted in Adair, *Roundhead General*, p.183; Walsingham, *Hector Britannicus or Sir John Digby*, p.109.

52 It is unclear whether this was Alexander Popham's or Francis Popham's Regiment, both of whom commanded regiments of horse.

400 horse, which was quartering on the Wiltshire border, had their quarters beaten up by a Royalist force under Lieutenant General Porter. After the Royalists had killed 40 men the whole regiment surrendered.

The losses sustained by Waller's forces at this time are also confirmed in a letter from Sir Samuel Luke to his father:

> If I should tell of Waller and Cromwell losing 800 or 900 horse and foot you will hardly believe it, and though I heard of it about seven nights ago yet I perceive it is not yet come to London, though bonfires were made at Oxford on Friday last and bells rung for it also ... I fear the cavaliers have had good success which makes your Diurnals so silent in London.[53]

With these losses Waller slipped away and through night marches to conceal his movements from Goring, retired to Salisbury.

A short time later Waller and Cromwell parted, Waller heading for Reading, while Cromwell marched into Oxfordshire. On 24 April Symonds recalls in his diary that:

> Cromwell's horse and dragoons ruined some of our horse quartered about Islip of the Lord of Northampton's command. 21 buried in Islip, 18 buried in [blank] over against Kidlington; and this day they demanded up Bletchingdon, a house belonging to Sir Thomas Coghill, where in Colonel Windebank had 200 foot, sans works, and provisions only for two or three days ... About two or three of the clock, Friday [25 April] the colonel valiantly gave up the house and all his armed, besides 50 horse that came thither for shelter; and this without a shot.[54]

On 3 May Symonds continues: 'Cromwell's forces removed to Faringdon, else if they had stayed Prince Rupert and General Goring had fallen upon them. They were twice repulsed by Farringdon men with great loss to them.'

Years later Waller would look back on this campaign and write:

> When I was commanded to march without delay to the relief of Taunton, with a body of horse and a few dragoons, and a vote for 3,000 foot (of which I never received the benefit of one man): and this against a complete[ly] formed army, far exceeding my strength, in a deep enclosed country; where it was known, that every field was as good as a fortification, and every lane as disputable as a pass. So that in effect, I was in no better condition than those gladiators of old among the Romans, preserved awhile, to perish in the end and kept only to be lost. This was the friendship I parted with.[55]

Of course by the time Waller wrote these words the political scene had shifted greatly and he was accused of being an opponent of the army and

53 Luke, *Letter Books*, no. 540, Sir Samuel Luke to Sir Oliver Luke, 21 April 1645.

54 Symonds, *Diary*, pp.163, 164.

55 Waller, *Vindication of the Character and conduct of Sir William Waller Knight ... Explanatory of His conduct in taking up arms against King Charles the First* (London: J. Derrett, 1793), pp.18–19.

even imprisoned. Writing about Cromwell, he said that 'as an officer he was obedient, and never did dispute my orders, nor argue upon them.' However, when Waller was interrogated by Cromwell as Lord Protector in March 1657, he records that he 'did examine me as a stranger, not as one whom he had aforetime known and obeyed.'[56]

---

56 Waller, *Recollections*, pp.116, 125.

Conclusion

Since the Second Battle of Newbury the Earl of Manchester and Lieutenant General Oliver Cromwell, supported by their various factions in Parliament, had been quarrelling about their performance during and after the battle. The quarrel spread to other senior officers within the army and in December 1644 motions were put forward for an ordinance that MPs serving in the army should resign their commands. At first this 'Self-Denying Ordinance' was thrown out by the House of Lords on 13 January, but it was finally passed on 3 April 1645.

However, it had become clear that the three main Parliamentarian armies of Essex, Manchester and Waller needed reforming if Parliament was to win the war. As early as 2 July Waller had written about the London Brigade under his command:

> My Lords, I write these particularities to let you know that an army compounded of these men will never go through with their service, and until you have an army merely your own that you may command, it is in a manner impossible to do anything of importance.[1]

He was not the only commander to be dismissive of these London regiments. A petition of senior officers in Essex's army dated 8 January 1645, records:

> These additional forces sent forth for our supply out of the Trained Bands and Auxiliaries of London are found to be more destructive then supporting to us for their great pay in hiring soldiers they entreat ours away and do but give us old soldiers put under new commanders.[2]

Unfortunately for Essex and Waller, they could not take the field without the support of these London brigades.

Moreover, the soldiers within these armies saw themselves as an individual army and there are various reference in letters referring to the 'our troops' as compared to 'Waller's troops', so making co-ordination between

1 *CSPD 1644*, pp.300–301, Sir William Waller to the Committee of Both Kingdoms, 2 July 1644.

2 Harl ms 166 f.174, Petition of the colonels and other chief officers of his Excellency's Infantry, 8 January 1645.

the armies difficult if not impossible. Therefore it was decided to establish a new army of 22,000 men. These would be divided into 11 regiments of horse, each 600 strong, 12 regiments of foot of 1,200 men and a regiment of dragoons 1,000 strong. However, of the 14,400 foot, just 7,174 would come from the three Parliamentarian armies. Essex's Army could only supply 3,048 foot, and Manchester's 3,578, leaving just 548 infantry from Waller's army. Therefore Parliament would have to recruit a further 7,226 to bring the army up to strength.

After Waller had retreated to Salisbury, he received the following command:

> For the more convenience and security of reducing the forces under your command, we have thought fit they should be brought from Salisbury towards Reading to such a place as Sir Thomas Fairfax shall appoint, whither you are to march accordingly … The officers who are to be reduced, but who are not to be of the new army, shall have the same pay upon their reduction as the other officers were are (not) reduced. They are to be recommended to the Committee of the West to employ such of them as they may occasion to use. We desire you to send such foot as you can spare for the security of the garrisons, especially of Poole and Wareham. So that they be not of those two regiments which are to be of the new army.[3]

At the end of April most of Waller's army were disbanded at Wokingham, some regiments soldiering on in Major General Massey's Western Association, others becoming independent of any army, being dispersed in various garrisons. The regiments of Heselrige and Livesey became Butler's and Ireton's regiments within the New Model Army. Originally it had been intended that Heselrige's Regiment would be commanded by John Middleton, and Livesey was to continue commanding his regiment, but their nominations were rejected for political reasons. On 14 April Waller wrote to the Speaker, William Lenthall, of his disappointment that:

> his own regiment had not been so much as taken into the New Model, which was not only a discouragement to them but a dishonour to him and he desired therefore he might be called home to serve them in the House since he had been so unfortunate in their service abroad and the letter was referred to the Committee of Both Kingdoms.[4]

At a muster at Wokingham, Holborne's (ex-Heselrige's) and Potley's Regiments formed Sir Hardress Waller's Regiment, Sir Hardress was Sir William's cousin and had spent much of the war soldiering in Ireland before returning to England at the beginning of 1645 to take command of Potley's Regiment. Among the counties chosen to recruit his regiment was Surrey, who clothed their recruits in red coats faced orange. The other regiment of foot to enter the New Model Army was Colonel Ralph Weldon's Regiment,

---

3 *CSPD 1644*–1645, p.415, Committee of Both Kingdoms to Waller, 17 April 1645.
4 Harley ms 166, Sir Simond D'Ewes' Commons Journal, 16 April 1645.

which appears to entered it unchanged. The rest of the foot, like Birch's and Jones' regiment remained in their garrisons and would not be disbanded until the end of the Civil War.

After much debate it was decided to appoint Sir Thomas Fairfax to command the New Model Army. He had distinguished himself serving in his father's Northern Association and was also the only acceptable candidate to both factions. Oliver Cromwell was appointed lieutenant general of horse: there were no other suitable candidates since both Sir William Balfour and John Middleton were Scottish Presbyterians, while Philip Skippon was appointed major general of foot.

It was with this new national army that Parliament would win the war. However, this new army needed time to organise itself, therefore Waller's and Essex's Regiments of Horse were ordered into the West, along with Cooke's, Fitzjames', Popham's, the Plymouth Horse; the remains of Behre's and Dalbier's Regiments were placed under Major General Edward Massey's command. Massey would be joined by a brigade under Colonel Ralph Weldon, which would pin down the remaining Royalists for the rest of the war and prevent them from levying recruits and money after the battle of Naseby.

Even so, it would be two long years before the last Royalist garrison surrendered. In the years that followed some of Waller's men would become prominent in British history: Sir Michael Livesey, John Okey, Edmund Ludlow, and Richard Horton would sign the King's death warrant; Holborne, Middleton and Vandruske would join the Scottish army, while Sir Arthur Heselrige would play a leading role in the Commonwealth, and would die in the Tower of London in 1661. The majority of Waller's army faded into obscurity again. As for Waller, he would be imprisoned by Cromwell and flee to Europe, but would take part in the procession at the Restoration; however during the reign of Charles II he retired from public life and died on 19 September 1668, and was buried in the New Chapel of Westminster Abbey aged 69.

Colour Plate Commentaries

Plate A – The infantry of Waller's Armies 1

1. A pikeman of the Westminster Liberty Regiment. He wears his civilian clothes, a quality buff coat, Tower Pattern pikeman's helmet and decorated back and breast and tassels. He is also depicted in coarse heavy-duty linen overhose, worn over finer woollen hose.

1a. Alternative, common style of pikeman's 'Pot'.

1b. Continental style 'Cabasset'.

2. A musketeer from Samuel Jones' Regiment, green coat, pale 'Venetian' style breeches, woollen hose, wool felted 'Monmouth 'cap. Raised in early 1643, the regiment was the garrison for Farnham Castle in Surry. The regiment saw action in most of Waller's later campaigns. It fought at Cheriton and Cropredy Bridge and besieged and blockaded Basing House throughout most of the war.

2a. Greencoat wearing 'Montero' cap, with linen or wool lining, in contrasting colour.

2b. Redcoat in knitted cap.

3. Ragged Pikeman during Alton Campaign. Observers noted that the Royalist prisoners were well equipped and clothed in comparison to the poor condition of many of the Parliamentarian troops.

3a.b.c. Various types of hilt on soldier's swords.

Plate B – The infantry of Waller's Armies 2

1. Musketeer of Haselrig's Regiment, wearing blue coat over a linen doublet, he is equipped with hanger belt, natural woollen breeches and dark hose. He carries a bandolier of charges and a matchlock Musket. Formed in the middle

of 1643, Haselrig's infantry regiment helped lay siege to Basing House in the autumn of the year, before taking part in the storming of Alton Church. The regiment also saw action at Cheriton and Cropredy Bridge in 1644. In early 1645, the regiment was reduced into Sir Hardress Waller's Regiment of Foot in the recently formed New Model Army.

1a. Red, linen lined, coat.

2. Pikeman Springate's Regiment, in red coat, lined in linen, wearing a back and breastplate. He has been issued a sword on baldrick. Springate's Regiment was raised in 1642 in Kent. In 1643, it took part in the relief of Gloucester and fought at the First Battle of Newbury. In December, the regiment fought at the storming and capture of Arundel. It was reduced into Weldon's Regiment in early 1644.

2a. Soldier's leather snapsack.

3. London Trained Band Musketeer, probably from the White or Yellow Regiment, wearing a civilian doublet, green 'venetian' breeches, felt or beaver hat, matchlock Musket.

3a. Matchlock Musket

3b. Alternative trigger mechanism.

3c. Flintlock mechanism.

Plate C – Officers, Ensigns and Musicians

1. Senior Regimental Officer, in Waller's Army. Quality buffcoat, with cloth or thin leather sleeves, decorated with metallic braid, red breeches, with boot hose held up with 'points'. The front of the coat held together with hooks and eyes, contrived to look like lacing. He wears a tawney coloured scarf, the colours of the Earl of Essex. He is carrying a Leading Staff indicating his rank.

1a. Alternative scarf and baldrick, buff coat tied with ribbons, larger falling band.

2. Ensign with colour, sleeved buff coat, long legged 'Dutch' breeches, red hose with turned down boots and laced boot hose.

2a. Alternative hat style with 'tied up' falling band.

2b. Officer in Montero, with falling band.

3. Company Drummer, in red soldier's coat and felt hat.

Plate D – Cavalry and Dragoons of Waller's Armies

1. Trooper, Waller's Horse, buff coat, back and breast, possibly with helmet as per the Cuirassier below, slung from a hook. Commonly known as Arquebusier, after the common armament, the arquebus, he would also, ideally carry a pair of pistols. Raised in 1642, the regiment was active in all of Waller's campaign and marches. It was disbanded in April 1645 and its personnel used to man New Model Cavalry Regiments.

2. Cuirassier of Haselrig's Regiment, or Balfour's Lifeguard troop, he wears three quarter armour, a tied falling band and pistol. Haselrig's Regiment may have been equipped as cuirassiers after Ripple Field. Current thinking argues that they were reequipped as a standard cavalry formation in time for Cheriton in March 1644, following their rout at Roundaway Down in July 1643. The Regiment was reduced into Butler's New Model Cavalry Regiment in April 1645.

2a. Wheelock pistol.

2b. English Doglock mechanism.

2c. Pistol holster variants.

3. Trooper, Waller's Dragoons, coat, slung weapon, bandoliers, heavy weight over hose, pointed to breeches, worn with shoes. Like Waller's Cavalry Regiment, his dragoons took part in all of his campaigns. It was reduced into Okey's New Model Regiment of Dragoons in April 1645.

3a. Alternative to bandolier, cartouche, or cartridge box.

Plate E – Cavalry Standards

Captain Fines, second son to Lord Viscount Seye and Sele
Captain Morley of Sussex
Colonel Sir William Waller
Captain Pennyfather, under Sir Arthur Hesselrige

Plate F– Cavalry Standards

Sir Arthur Hesselrige
Captain Norton of Hampshire
Captain Butler, Sir William Waller's Regiment
Captain Hawley, Sir Robert Hawley's Regiment

Plate G – Infantry Colours

Colonel, James Carr's Regiment
Colonel, Herbert Morley's Regiment
Colonel, Samuel Jone's Regiment
Colonel, Richard Onslow's Regiment

Plate H – Infantry Colours

The White Regiment, The London Trained Bands
The Yellow Regiment, The London Trained Bands
The Westminster Liberty Regiment, The London Trained Bands
The Green Auxiliary Regiment, The London Trained Bands

See Appendix One for further details of these regiments

Appendix I

Regiments Which Served with Sir William Waller

Unfortunately there is no complete list of which regiments served with Waller in the Western or Southern Associations, so the following list is by no means comprehensive, while other regiments that were ordered to join him did not necessarily do so.

Regiments of Horse	Notes
Sir Edward Apsley's troop	Raised March 1644 and disbanded July 1644 after opposition from the gentry of Sussex.
Sir William Balfour	Part of Essex's army, served at Cheriton.
Colonel John Barker's troop	Part of the garrison of Coventry, on 19 June 1644 it was placed at Waller's disposal.
Colonel Hans Behre	Part of Essex's army, served with Waller at the siege of Arundel from 22 December 1643, returned to Essex's army before the Cheriton campaign.
Colonel John Bingham's troop	Garrison of Poole, probably attached to Holborne's force in December 1644.
Major John Barker's troop	Garrisoned Warwick Castle. On 19 June 1644 placed at Waller's disposal.
Colonel Robert Burghill	Raised in 1642 and served in all of Waller's campaigns. After Burghill was wounded at Lansdown the regiment passed to his major, Jonas Vandruske.
Colonel Robert Butler	Garrisoned Wareham and probably served with Holborne late in 1644.
Colonel Thomas Ceeley	Garrisoned Lyme, probably served with Holborne in December 1644 when he relieved Taunton.
Colonel Richard Cole	Raised early 1643 and formed part of the garrison of Bristol before being sent to Waller.
Colonel Edward Cooke	Raised December 1643 and served in all of Waller's campaigns. With Middleton's force in August 1644, then in March 1645, Waller sent it to join Cromwell's force.
Lt Gen Oliver Cromwell	Part of Manchester's Eastern Association, served with Waller early in 1645.
Colonel John Dalbier	Part of Balfour's Brigade at Cheriton.

Regiments of Horse	Notes
Colonel Francis Dowett	Raised 29 August 1643, disbanded 17 October 1643
Colonel Thomas Essex's troop	Raised 1642 and after Edgehill was sent to Bristol, joining Waller just before or after Lansdown.
Colonel John Fiennes	In February 1645 was part of Cromwell's force in the West.
Colonel Nathaniel Fiennes	Raised February 1643 from the troop he had commanded the year before. It garrisoned Bristol and supplied a detachment to Waller's Western Association.
Colonel John Fitzjames	Raised 20 May 1644, joining Waller in September 1644 and later attached to Holborne's force.
Sir William Gould	Raised Devon in 1642 and joined Waller in time to take part in the battle of Roundway Down.
Sir Richard Grenville	See Cooke's Regiment.
Sir Arthur Hesselrigge	Originally raised as cuirassiers, but re-equipped as harquebusiers after Roundway Down. It served in all of Waller's campaigns.
Colonel Thomas Hume	Raised 20 November 1643, but disbanded on 18 March 1644.
Colonel Samuel Jones' troop	Garrisoned Farnham Castle and served at the siege of Basing House in 1644.
'The Kentish Horse'	It joined Waller in April 1644 and appears to have been absorbed into Sir Michael Livesey's Regiment
Sir Michael Livesey	Raised Kent and carried red cornets. It served in all of Waller's campaigns.
Colonel Edmund Ludlow	Raised June 1644, transferred to Massey's force in September though joined Waller in time to serve at the Second Battle of Newbury.
Sir Samuel Luke	Garrisoned Newport Pagnell, on 19 June 1644 Waller was given permission to draw out 80 men.
Colonel John Meldrum	Part of Balfour's Brigade at Cheriton.
Colonel John Middleton	Formed part of Balfour's Brigade at Cheriton.
Lt. General John Middleton	Raised Summer of 1644, serving at the Second Battle of Newbury and later in the West.
Colonel Herbert Morley	Joined Waller in November 1643, serving at Arundel, becoming the castle's garrison. At least 1 troop served at the siege of Basing House in 1644.
Colonel Richard Norton	Served at Cheriton, Second Siege of Basing House, Second Battle of Newbury and in the West in 1645.
Colonel Alexander Popham	Raised June 1644. A Colonel Popham had joined Waller by 11 October 1644, so was probably present at the Second Battle of Newbury. It also served in the West during 1645.
Colonel Francis Popham	See Colonel Alexander Popham's Regiment.
Colonel William Purefoy	On 19 June 1644 the regiment was put at Waller's disposal.
Colonel William Strode	An independent troop which served with Waller in the West during 1643.

Regiments of Horse	Notes
Colonel William Strode	Raised June 1644, joining Waller in time for the Second Battle of Newbury, served briefly at Basing House before becoming part of Holborne's force.
Colonel William Sydenham	Probably join Waller in April 1644 and served until early June, becoming part of the garrison of Weymouth. A detachment served with Middleton in August 1644. In December it became part of Holborne's force.
Colonel George Thompson	Joined Waller in March 1644 in time for Cheriton and served on all of Waller's subsequent campaigns.
Colonel Jonas Vandruske	Served in all of Waller's campaigns.
Sir William Waller's Lifeguard	Served in all of Waller's campaigns.
Sir William Waller	Served in all of Waller's campaigns.
Colonel Nathaniel Whetham	Garrisoned Northampton. On 19 June 1644 Waller was given permission to draw out 80 horse, who had joined him by 17 July.

Regiments of Dragoons	Notes
Colonel Adam Cunningham	Part of Essex's army as a regiment of foot, was temporarily mounted and served at Cheriton.
Colonel Richard Browne	Raised 1642 and served with Waller at the storming of Farnham Castle, Winchester and his early campaigns in the West.
Colonel Anthony Fane	Raised in Surrey in 1642 and was with Waller at the storming of Farnham Castle, where Fane was killed. The regiment was disbanded shortly afterwards.
Major General James Holborne	Formerly Waller's own regiment of dragoons
'The Kentish Dragoons'	At least one company served on the Western Relief expedition.
Colonel Richard Norton	An obscure regiment.
Sir William Waller	Served on all of Waller's campaigns. Later taken over by Holborne
Sir William Waller	Formerly his regiment of foot, though converted to dragoons during the summer of 1644.

Regiments of Foot	Notes
Sir Edward Aspley	Raised March 1644 and disbanded July 1644 after opposition from gentry of Sussex.
Colonel Thomas Ayloffe	Part of Manchester's Eastern Association and garrisoned Newport Pagnell. On 19 June 1644 it was placed at Waller's disposal.
Colonel John Barker	Garrisoned Coventry, on 19 June 1644, 200 men of the regiment were put at Waller's disposal.
Colonel John Bingham	See his troop of horse
Colonel John Birch	Waller 'New Kentish Regiment' joined Waller in September 1644 and garrisoned Plymouth, later Hereford. Disbanded October 1648, the last of Waller's old regiments.
Colonel Godfrey Bosseville	Garrisoned Warwick. On 19 June 1644 Waller given permission to draw out 240 men of the regiment.

Regiments of Foot	Notes
Major John Bridges' company	Garrisoned Warwick Castle. On 19 June 1644 Waller was given permission to withdraw 100 foot from Castle.
Colonel Robert Butler	Possibly grey coats. See also his regiment of horse.
Colonel Horatio Carey	Raised from Royalists captured at Higham, which was apt since Carey later changed sides, nevertheless the regiment continued to serve with Waller's Western Association until the summer of 1643.
Colonel Thomas Carne (or Carr)	Garrisoned the Isle of Wight, probably present at Second Battle of Newbury.
Colonel James Carr	Raised 29 August 1643, disbanded March 1644.
Colonel Thomas Ceeley	Garrisoned Lyme, probably served with Holborne's force late 1644.
Colonel Edward Cooke	Raised 29 August 1643, and was disbanded early in 1644.
Colonel Robert Cooke	Raised Spring 1643, possibly at Lansdown and Roundway Down. After it was disbanded during the summer of 1643 at least one officer appears in his son Edward's regiment.
Colonel Nicholas Devereux	Garrisoned Malmesbury, 100 men possibly at Cropredy Bridge, and a detachment joined Waller on 21 March 1645.
Colonel Thomas Essex	Raised in 1642 as Oliver St John's Regiment it formed part of the garrison of Bristol and served with Waller on his Welsh campaign, Lansdown and Roundway Down.
Colonel John Fiennes	Raised in 1643 and garrisoned Bristol and so may have supplied a detachment to Waller's Western Association.
Colonel Nathaniel Fiennes	Raised 1643 as part of the garrison of Bristol and supplied a detachment to Waller in time for Roundway Down.
Green Auxiliaries of London	Formed part of Harrington's London Brigade in late 1643, which served at Basing, Farnham and Alton.
Colonel Edward Harley	Raised on 29 August 1643, but served with Waller only briefly, being sent to garrison Plymouth.
Sir Arthur Hesselrigge	After joining Waller in December 1643 the regiment served in all his campaigns. In about July 1644 Holborne took over the regiment.
Major General James Holborne	See Heselrige's Regiment of Foot.
Colonel William Jephson	Garrisoned Portsmouth and supplied a detachment to the siege of Basing House in 1644.
Colonel Samuel Jones	It garrisoned Farnham Castle, but supplied a detachment to all Waller's campaigns from November 1643 until late 1644.
Kent Trained Bands	Composed of about 20 regiments of trained bands of horse and foot, auxiliaries and volunteers. A brigade under Sir Henry Heyman served at the siege of Arundel Castle.
Sir Samuel Luke	Garrisoned Newport Pagnell. On 19 June 1644 Waller was given permission to draw out 300 men of the regiment.

Regiments of Foot	Notes
Colonel Edward Massey	Garrisoned Gloucester. 270 men from Gloucester were present at Cropredy Bridge.
Colonel Edward Massey	Garrisoned Gloucester and was known as the Governor's regiment. See Massey's other regiment.
Sir John Meyrick	Raised in 1642. Two companies appear to have served with Waller in his Welsh campaign and at Lansdown and Roundway Down.
Colonel Herbert Morley	Raised March 1644 to garrison Arundel Castle. Six companies served at the siege of Basing House in 1644, and 100 men for the Western Relief expedition. Later joining Waller for the campaign in the West in 1645, reinforcing the garrisons of Melcombe Regis and Weymouth.
Colonel Richard Norton	Garrisoned Southampton, a detachment beat up the Royalist quarters at Romsey in December 1643 and a least one company present at the siege of Basing House from July 1644.
Sir Richard Onslow	Raised 1642 and was also known as Surrey Auxiliaries, served at siege of Basing House in 1644.
Colonel Alexander Popham	Served in Waller's Western Association and garrisoned Bristol. After Roundway Down and Bristol's surrender it garrisoned Lyme.
Major General Christopher Potley	Raised August 1643, joining Waller for siege of Arundel and served in all of Waller's campaigns. Part of Middleton's force in August 1644. Early in 1645 it was taken over by Sir Hardress Waller.
Southwark White Auxiliaries	Formed part of Harrington's London Brigade on the Oxford Campaign.
Sir William Springate	Present at First Battle of Newbury, before joining Waller in time for the storming of Alton. Present at the siege of Arundel, although it was disbanded shortly afterwards due to the death of its colonel.
Colonel Anthony Stapley	Garrisoned Chichester. A detachment served at the Siege of Arundel. In September 1644 5 companies, mounted as dragoons joined Waller. A detachment also served with Waller in the West early in 1645.
Colonel Robert Stephen	A weak regiment raised in April 1643 and served with Waller's Western Association.
Sussex Trained Bands	Served at the siege of Arundel Castle.
Colonel William Sydenham	Raised summer of 1644 and garrisoned Weymouth, serving with Holborne's force from late 1644.
Tower Hamlets Regiment	Formed part of Harrington's brigade on the Oxford Campaign.
Sir William Waller	Raised 29 August 1643 and served in all of his campaigns. It was converted to dragoons in the summer of 1644.
Colonel Ralph Weldon	Raised early in 1644 and served in all of Waller's campaigns until January 1645 when it was sent to garrison Weymouth. Absorbed into the New Model Army.

Regiments of Foot	Notes
Lt. General James Weymss	Raised on 29 August 1643 to guard Waller's artillery, and so were armed with firelocks. It was badly cut up at Cropredy Bridge. Waller left it in the west after the Battle of Cropredy Bridge
Westminster Auxiliaries	The regiment formed part of Harrington's London Brigade on the Oxford Campaign.
Westminster Liberty Regiment	Formed part of Harrington's London Brigade in 1643.
Colonel Nathaniel Whetham	Garrison of Northampton. On 19 June 1644 Waller was given permission to draw out 100 men.
Colonel Richard Whitehead	Raised Hampshire in 1644 and served at the siege of Basing House in 1644.
White Regiment of the London Trained Bands	Formed part of Browne's London Brigade which was present at Cheriton.
Yellow Auxiliaries of the Tower Hamlets	Formed part of Harrington's brigade in 1643.
Yellow Regiment of the London Trained Bands	Formed part of Browne's London Brigade which was present at Cheriton.

Appendix II

Logistics

Waller's army was like other armies of the day, were divided into infantry, cavalry, artillery and a baggage train. The infantry, or foot, was divided into pikemen and musketeers, in theory the ratio was two musketeers to one pikeman, certainly Colonel Edward Harley's Regiment had this ratio, but others had a far greater number of musketeers to pikemen. When Major Thomas Smith's company in Major General Potley's Regiment mustered on 1 August 1644 it was found to have 75 musketeers and 28 pikemen, and some garrison regiments, such as Colonel Samuel Jones' Regiment, seem to have been armed entirely with muskets. Whereas Colonel John Birch's company on 26 August 1646 mustered '84 private soldiers, whereof 12 of them were pikemen and the rest musketeers.' His lieutenant-colonel's company mustered 58 private soldiers, whereof 11 were pikemen. True, this might be a higher ratio of musketeers to pikemen from when it was first raised.[1]

A musketeer was armed with a matchlock musket, a sword and a rest to steady his aim. Although by 1645 the rest appears to have been discarded. The musketeer was also issued with a powder flask and a bandolier with bottles to hold the powder which was poured down the barrel of the musket. Attached to this bandolier was a bullet bag where the musket balls were kept. It has been suggested that these were called 'apostles' since there were usually 12 of these bottles, but there is no contemporary evidence to suggest they were known by such a name and these bandoliers could have between 10 and 15 bottles. The musket was fired by a length of match, hence the name 'matchlock musket', and it was estimated that each musketeer needed about 12 feet of match per day, since it had to be lit not only in battle, but also on guard duty and when marching along. True, the musketeers could extinguish their match, but if they were attacked then there would be a desperate scramble for them to light their match again. Since James Wemyss' Regiment was raised to protect the artillery and baggage train, where large amounts of gunpowder were stored, it was armed entirely with 'firelocks' or flintlocks. The flint striking the metal frizzen would cause sparks which would ignite the powder in the pan, which in turn would ignite the powder in the musket

1 TNA SP 28/177; BL Add ms 70061.

barrel and so propel the musket ball down the barrel. There is also some archaeological evidence that musketeers inscribed their initials on their muskets, but how widespread this was is unknown.

In theory pikemen wore armour, which was a helmet, backplate and breastplate, and tassets to protect the thighs, although by the time of the formation of the New Model Army the armour appears to have been discarded. The pike itself could be 16 to 18 feet long. Pikemen would also carry a sword, and in the early part of the seventeenth century a dagger, but this seems to have been discarded by the time of the Civil War.

One unusual warrant, dated 20 April 1644, was to deliver to the Committee of Militia of London '5,000 long bow arrows, 5,000 musket arrows and 500 leather quivers to be employed in the service of the State.' Another dated 26 April 1644 was for 'the remainder of those musket and longbow arrows with bow cases and shooting gloves … and other things as belong unto archery as are now in your custody to be employed in the state service.' Which regiments they were to be delivered to is not specified, but both Waller and Essex employed London auxiliary regiments for the Oxford campaign of 1644 and there were also three London auxiliary regiments sent to Major General Richard Browne which garrisoned Abingdon.[2]

Each county had its own trained band regiments, which could be called upon in the event of danger. At the beginning of the war there were four London Trained Band Regiments, the North, South, East and West, but on the outbreak of war these were reorganised into six regiments, the first to the sixth, although they are better known by the colour of their ensigns, the first being the Red Regiment, the second the White Regiment etc.[3] There were also six auxiliary regiments raised which were also known by the colour of their ensigns, plus the Westminster Auxiliary Regiment (or the Red Regiment), the Tower Hamlets Regiment, Southwark Trained Bands, the Westminster Auxiliaries, and Southwark Auxiliaries.

Why these regiments should be known by the colour of their ensigns is not known; over the years it has been suggested they had the same colour coats as their ensigns, i.e. white coats etc., but other regiments are known to have had red coats with red ensigns but have not been referred to as the Red Regiment. In recent decades it has been suggested that they wore red coats, but this does not stand up to argument either because Colonel Mainwaring's Regiment of Foot was known as the 'London Red Coats', and they would not be referred to this if there was more than one red-coated London regiment. The only references to any uniformity comes from the Royalist newsbook *Mercurius Aulicus*, which for first battle of Newbury, records that 'much of the slaughter fell upon the London Trained Bands and their Auxiliaries, many of whose buff coats our soldiers have now.' While for the second battle of Newbury *Aulicus* records that Sir Bernard Astley's brigade captured from the Parliamentarian soldiers with the Earl of Manchester, a 'great store… [of] Trained Band buff (for many of these were Londoners).' A Royalist spy reported that at Abingdon Major General Browne's garrison was formed of

2 TNA WO 47/1/14, Warrants to deliver arms, 20 April 1644 and 26 April 1644.
3 TT E 669 f.6 [8], *A list of the names of the several colonels and their colours* (London, 1642).

three regiments, including Colonel George Paine's regiment of blue coats. Paine's Regiment had been formed in December 1644 or January 1645 by amalgamating the White, Red and Blue Regiments of the London Auxiliaries.[4]

Clothing

To raise a company, regiment or even an army was easy, the difficulty lay in keeping it supplied with clothing, food and ammunition. To administer supplies to the army the Committee of the West was established. Exactly when the Committee was formed is unknown, but it certainly existed by 3 August 1643. On the formation of the Southern Association the 'Committee of the Four Associated Counties of Sussex, Surrey, etc.,' was established, which on 14 May 1644 was ordered by the House of Commons to liaise with the Committee of the West, 'to consider of some things of absolute necessity for Sir William Waller's march.'[5]

Beneath these two committees were various county committees which administered their own county's war effort. In addition to these committees was the 'Committee of Militia of the City of London and parts adjacent, within the Lines of Communication and Parishes with the Weekly Bills of Mortality', or the 'Committee of the Militia' for short, which was responsible for the London Trained Bands.

Unfortunately, very few records of these committees survive which would have recorded the issuing of arms and clothing to Waller's army. One such warrant is dated 10 August 1643 which ordered that:

> Whereas there is a present necessity of making provisions of coats, shirts, shoes and snapsacks not only for the soldiers of the several regiments in the army of his excellency the Earl of Essex but likewise for such as shall recruit that army as also for such regiments of foot as are forthwith to be raised under the command of Sir William Waller. It is therefore ordained by the Lords and Commons in parliament assembled That Stephen Estwick, Francis Pecke and Captain Player senior be desired forthwith to furnish the said coats, shirts, shoes and snapsacks to the number of ten thousand of each sort at the rate of sixteen shillings for each soldier. And it is further ordered by the said Lords and Commons that the two months weekly assessment upon the county of Essex shall be set apart toward the payment of the said provisions of coats, shirts, shoes and snapacks and it is to be further ordered that Sir Gilbert Gerard treasurer at Wars shall from time to time pay unto the said Stephen Estwick all such money as shall come in upon the said assessment and the said Sir Gilbert Gerard shall not suffer any part thereof to be employed for any other use.[6]

---

4 BL TT E.68/18, Peter Heylеyn, *Mercurius Aulicus* (Oxford: 23 September 1643), and TT E.22/3, Peter Heylеyn, *Mercurius Aulicus* (Oxford: 2 November 1644); BL Add ms 18982 f.409. The other two regiments were Rainsborough's redcoats and Browne's greycoats.

5 *Journal of the House of Commons* (London: HMSO, 1802), vol. 3, 1643–1644, p.492.

6 SP 28/9/316, Order by John Brown, Clerk to Parliament, 10 August 1643.

A warrant for Essex's Army shows that it was issued 3,440 coats, 6,000 pairs of shoes, 3,000 knapsacks and 1,700 shirts. This order appears to have included 740 red coats, lined red or white and 1,600 grey coats, lined red, yellow or white, making a total of 2,340 coats. The colour of the remaining 1,100 is not recorded.[7] However, the merchants supplying these clothes were having difficulty supplying all the clothes needed:

> Worthy Sirs. My services to you we have sent for the army of His Excellency, in part these coats, shirts and shoes and snapsacks underwritten for the remainder we work night and day to send the full, we shall send more shirts and coats with all speed. [However], there is scarce any cloth, woollen [*sic*] or linen to be had for money, yet we shall endeavour … to supply all things.[8]

If the entire order of 10,000 coats etc., were completed this leaves 6,560 coats, 4,000 pairs of shoes, 7,000 snapsacks and 8,300 shirts to be distributed among the regiments of Waller's army. Unfortunately, it is not known which regiments benefited from the issue of this clothing, but must have included Sir William Waller's own regiment of foot and that of Sir Arthur Heselrige, since both were raised on 29 August. The latter regiment is known to have worn blue coats at the siege of Arundel in December of that year. In June 1644 at Lyme they are recorded as the 'valiant blue coats of Sir Arthur Heselrige's Regiment'.[9] Colonel James Wemyss' Regiment of Firelocks, which was also commissioned to be raised on 29 August 1643 also wore blue coats, but there is no evidence to suggest Waller's also wore them. There was also an unidentified yellow-coated regiment with the army in April 1644, which could have been either Waller's or Major General Christopher Potley's Regiment of Foot, which was also entitled to the 10 August issue of clothing.

On the other hand the regiments raised in Kent appear to have been clothed in red coats and Surrey supplied Colonel Samuel Jones' Regiment with 700 'soldiers coats of green cloth', which cost 11s 6d each or a total of £402 10s, plus 15 shillings for packing and carriage. No other types of clothing are mentioned.[10]

Why some regiments were issued with clothing centrally, while others were supplied locally is unknown. It could be that since Waller had commissioned these regiments to be raised and so he was responsible for their welfare, whereas those raised by the county committees were responsible for their own regiments.[11] The clothing supplied by a county were more likely to keep the same colour coats than those supplied centrally which might change from issue to issue. For example, the coats for the Kent regiments seem to

7 Stuart Peachey and Alan Turton, *Old Robin's Foot, the army of the Earl of Essex, 1642–1645* (Nottingham: Partizan Press, 2017), pp.15–16.

8 BL Tanner ms 62B f.650.

9 BL TT E.252/41, *A Perfect Diurnall of some passages in Parliament,* 3 June 1644.

10 TNA SP 28/244, part 4 unfolio. 300 coats were made in October 1643 and 400 the following month.

11 In late 1644 Waller had an argument with the Wiltshire Committee over Colonel Ludlow's troop, saying it was raised by his commission, whereas the rest of Ludlow's Regiment was raised by the Wiltshire Committee so they could command it as they wished.

have been supplied by Captain John Taylor of London who on 4 March 1645 was paid for supplying 3,052 redcoats at 10s 4d each, as well as 2,400 shirts at 3d each. At this time breeches were not usually supplied, but Taylor also supplied 600 pairs of breeches at 9s and 3,350 pairs of stockings at 15d each and 900 pairs of shoes for 2s 8d per pair. Ferdinando Appleby, shoemaker, was also paid £50 on 2 November 1644 for 400 pairs 'of neats leather shoes' at 2s 6d a pair. Jonathan Tilecoate was also paid £187 18s 4d on 12 February 1645 for 600 shirts at 2s 10d each and 100 shirts for 2s 9d each, plus 200 pairs of stockings at 8d a pair and 50 pairs of shoes at 2s 8d.[12]

Unfortunately, all too often when it comes to clothing issued to the soldiers no colour is mentioned. For example on 28 September 1642 a payment was made of three shillings to the person 'that brought the soldiers' coats that were delivered at Portsmouth'. While on 15 August 1644 £2 3s 4d was paid to Captain Peck, 'for making 100 shirts and for bringing down of coats and snapsacks' for Colonel Stapeley's Regiment of Foot, which garrisoned Chichester.[13] The clerk compiling the accounts was only interested in the quantity of clothing that he was paying for rather than whether they were of a regimental colour, although in 1642 Stapley's Regiment were issued with red coats faced yellow.[14] In theory clothing was meant to be issued once a year, preferably just before winter, but on 16 February 1646 Colonel John Birch desired that 'my regiment may be clothed who are in extreme necessity having had no clothes near these twenty months.'[15]

It is usually suggested that the officers and sergeants supplied their own clothing, but Richard Clapp's account book for the garrison of Plymouth records suits being made for these ranks; for example:[16]

> 19 October 1644 '10 yards of cloth to Lieutenant Colonel Fitch to make his 3 sergeants and 2 drummers each of them a suit.'
> 23 October 1644 '34 yards cloth to Major Haines for 17 suits for the officers of Colonel Rowse's Regiment.'
> 6 November '2 yards cloth to Sergeant Selwood to make him a suit.'

Two yards seems to have been the amount of cloth used to make a sergeant's suit of a coat and breeches, although on 11 November 1644 four yards of cloth was issued for a sergeant in Captain Cambrill's company. On the other hand a soldier's suit was usually made from two yards of kersey, although one or two were made from two and a half yards.

Despite the order for clothing in August 1643, on 23 November William Cawley wrote from Farnham, 'The soldiers both horse and foot, want clothes,

12 SP 28/130/62, 67, The accompt of Captain Charles Bowles, commissary for the county of Kent, 1644.
13 TNA SP 28/129, Part 8 folio 7, Sir William Lewis' his disbursements from 1 August 1642; SP 28/130/95 Account book for the Sussex Regiments, 1644.
14 TNA SP/28 part 17, The accompt of Richard Clapp Deputy Treasurer, muster master and commissary of provision in the garrison of Plymouth, 24 May 1643 to 8 Jul 1649.
15 Tanner 60B/449 Desires of Colonel Birch, 16 February 1646.
16 TNA SP/28 part 17, The accompt of Richard Clapp Deputy Treasurer, muster master and commissary of provision in the garrison of Plymouth, 24 May 1643 to 8 Jul 1649.

boots, shoes and almost all necessaries for their subsistence.' In desperation Waller sent some parties 'to Godalming and Midhurst to take up some coarse cloths, linen, shoes and stockings for the soldiers.'[17] Although raised in August 1643, Colonel Edward Harley's Regiment of Foot had not received its allocation of 'caps, coats, shoes, stockings and knapsacks', or 'drums, colours and other necessaries', by 11 December when the regiment was preparing to embark at Deal for service in the West.[18] If, or when, the regiment finally received their clothing, is not recorded.

It appears to be rare for caps or hats to be issued to Parliamentarian soldiers, and it is usually presumed that the soldiers supplied their own headgear. When it comes to caps being issued they were probably Monmouth caps, which were supplied to English regiments before the Civil War and those being sent to Ireland. Unfortunately, such was their popularity during the early seventeenth century that no one thought to describe them in detail, although Richard Symonds, when referring to the town of Bewdley, states that their local economy was:

> making of caps called Monmouth caps. [These were] knitted by poor people for 2d a piece, ordinary ones sold for 2s, 3s 4s. First they are knit. Then they mill them, then block them, then they work them with tasels [?teasels], then they shear them.

Their design has been debated extensively. However, a tax introduced in July 1644 refers to 'Monmouth caps of all sorts', suggesting that there was more than one type and in 1663 the House of Commons referred to 'Bewdley and Monmouth caps, and other woollen caps'.[19]

According to the Colonel Harley's account, to arm the regiment he would need '800 muskets, of which 150 are desired to be firelocks, 400 pikes, 1,200 swords and belts', even though his regiment appears to have only mustered 300 men. Therefore the regiment would have a ratio of two musketeers to each pikeman.[20] These arms came from a variety of sources, including Bristol and Europe, but the Parliamentarians had the advantage of controlling London with its various arms factories. In April 1642 the following merchants estimated that they could supply the following:[21]

17 HMC 13th Report, Appendix Part I, *The manuscripts of his Grave the Duke of Portland presented at Welbeck*, vol. 1 (London: HMSO, 1894), p.159, William Cawley to William Lenthall, 23 November 1643; p.160 Sir William Waller to William Lenthall, 23 November 1643.

18 HMC 14th Report, Appendix Part II, *The manuscripts of his Grace the Duke of Portland presented at Welbeck*, vol. 3 (London: HMSO, 1894), pp.119–120.

19 Symonds, *Diary*, p.14; *Lords Journal* vol. 6 (London HMSO, 1802), p.624; *Commons Journal*, vol. 8 (London: HMSO, 1802), pp.492–493.

20 HMC 14th Report, Appendix Part II, *The manuscripts of his Grave the Duke of Portland presented at Welbeck*, vol. 3 (London: HMSO, 1894), pp.118–119.

21 BL MS Tanner ms 63/15, Estimate of arms which can be supplied per month, April 1642.

Names	No. per month
John Edwards and Robert Thacker	500 pikes and 1,000 musket rests
John Gace and William Beacham	2,000–2,500 bandoliers
Benjamin Stone	200 pikes, 2,000 swords, 200 halberds and 100 partizans
John Dickenson and Leonard Hickford	5,000 sword belts and 2,000 carbine belts

All these items were to be of the 'same goodness, proof and rate they formerly contracted to service his Majesty'.

There was also to be a standard price set for these arms:[22]

Weapon	Price each
Long pike (land service)	4s 6d
Long pike (sea service)	3s 2d
Short pike	2s 4d
Muskets furnished with worms and scourers	16s 6d
Bandoliers (land service)	3s
Bandoliers (sea service)	2s 6d
Ordinary swords (infantry)	7s 6d
Ordinary swords (cavalry)	10s
Belts for swords	1s 8d
Belts for carbines	2s
Girdles and hangers (infantry)	2s
Girdles and hangers (cavalry)	2s 5d
Girdles and hangers (dragoons)	2s 0d
Firelock carbines	£1 10s
Snaphaunce carbines	£1 2s
Pair of firelock pistols	£2 16s
Harquebusier arms consisting back and breast plates with headpiece (light)	£1 15s
Harquebusier arms consisting back and breast plates with headpiece (heavy)	£2
Halberds (white and plain)	8s
Halberds (guilt)	13s 4d
Partizans (white and plain)	14s
Partizans (with tassels)	17s 6d

However, as the war dragged on the price of weapons appears to have varied.

During summer of 1644 the Committee of the West was ordered to supply 500 swords and 300 bandoliers for the Isle of Wight Foot and on 9 February 1645 the House of Commons received a letter from Sir William Waller asking for 200 back, breast and pots [helmets] and 400 pairs of pistols. The Commons ordered, 'that it referred to the Committee of the West to take care to provide these backs, breasts, pots and pistols'. These weapons appear to be for Heselrige's and Thompson's horse regiments, which Waller acknowledged as receiving on 19 February.[23]

Individuals were sometimes expected to supply their own weapons. On 25 February 1644 the High Constables of the administrative district of the Hundred of Elmbridge in Surrey were ordered to:

22 BL ms Tanner ms 63/16, Prices for weapons, 14 April 1642.

23 Rev. G.N. Godwin, *The Civil War in Hampshire and the Story of Basing House* (Alresford: Laurence Oxley, 1904), p.233; *Commons Journal*, p.44.

> warn all men within your Hundred from 16 to 60 years of age that are able to bear arms to assemble themselves with all their best arms at the Crane in Kingston by eight of the clock on Tuesday next in the morning and those that have none to appear and receive arms at the rendezvous appointed.[24]

Some were willing to sponsor the arming of soldiers. On 29 November 1643 Lady Littcott of East Molesey in Surrey provided 'two men complete with muskets', whereas the Widows Brean and Teme, Thomas Finch and William Starr of Walton on Thames could only afford to arm 'one man complete'. It was estimated that the musket would cost 30 shillings and each soldier would have 18 shillings and 6d pay per month.[25]

Like the infantry, the cavalrymen could also be sponsored by an individual, including Sir William Waller who in 1642 supplied four cavalrymen on, 'bay horses with stars on their forehead … armed with carbines, pistols, and buffcoats and swords', to the value of £104. Whereas Essex supplied 20 cavalrymen armed with 'pistols, head piece, back and breast [plates] and swords', to the value of £560. Although most just supplied one horse and rider, or even just a horse.[26]

Arguably one of the most famous regiments to serve with Waller was Sir Arthur Heselrige's Regiment of Horse, which were armed as cuirassiers, i.e. they wore armour from head to knee, with a pair of riding boots. Originally Heselrige's troop had been harquebusiers, but when he raised his regiment they were converted to cuirassiers.[27] In the Earl of Clarendon's history of the war he recalls that before the battle of Lansdown:

> Waller received from London a fresh regiment of five hundred horse, under the command of Sir Arthur Heselrige, which were so prodigiously armed that they were called by the other side *the regiment of lobsters*, because of their bright iron shells with which they were covered, being perfect cuirassiers. They were the first seen so armed on either side, and the first that made any impression upon the king's horse, who, being unarmed, were not able to hear a shock with them; besides they were secure from hurts of the sword, which were almost the only weapons the other were furnished with.[28]

The phrase, 'first seen so armed on either side' suggests that there were other regiments to be armed as cuirassiers, but none has been identified. However, this is not to say that there were not troops of cuirassiers, the colonel's troop of Sir William Balfour's Regiment of Horse were described as cuirassiers from it first being raised in 1642 until 18 May 1644, after this it referred to as a 'troop of horse', suggesting it had abandoned its cuirassier armour. The colonel's troop of Sir Philip Stapleton's Regiment was also described as cuirassiers

---

24 TNA SP 28/244/2, Order to the High Constables of Elmbridge, 25 February 1643.

25 TNA SP 28/244/2, Return of the Hundred of Elmbridge

26 TNA SP 28/131, Return of horses and riders supplied from London, 1642.

27 TNA SP28/3B/313, Receipt for payment of Sir Arthur Heselrige's troop of horse, 11 November 1643.

28 Clarendon, ed. Lockyer, *History of the Great Rebellion*, pp.134–135. Clarendon's italics.

until 16 July 1644, when it was afterwards referred to as Essex's 'lifeguard' or by the Earl of Essex as 'my troop of guards'.[29] There was at least one troop of 100 cuirassiers with the King's Oxford Army commanded by Colonel Blague, and a commission to raise a troop of 80 horse for Newcastle's army stated that 40 were to be cuirassiers and the other 40 were to be harquebusiers.[30]

Clarendon also refers to the Heselrige's Regiment at the battle of Cheriton, that 'Sir Arthur Heselrige's Regiment of cuirassiers, called the *Lobsters*, were so formidable that the king's naked and unarmed troops (amongst which few were better armed than with sword) could not bear their impression.'[31] However, Clarendon is wrong on this point because according to the pay warrants for the officers of the regiment, from 29 August 1643 the captains of Heselrige's Regiment were commanding troops of harquebusiers and not cuirassiers.[32]

There were also sound logistical reasons for abandoning their cuirassier armour, because not only were the horses needed to mount a cuirassier in short supply in England, but also the London armourers estimated they could either make 300 harquebusier arms per month or 500 sets of infantry armour, but just 60 sets of cuirassier armour.[33]

But what did harquebusiers look like? According to the contemporary manuals of the time they wore a backplate and breastplate, a helmet and a buff coat for protection. However, the evidence suggest that it was either a back and breast plate, or a buff coat, as a receipt dated 15 November 1642 records:

> received of Richard Maijory of Huesley in the said county [Hampshire] Esq., four horses completely armed with great saddles, pistols and carbines and buff coats valved with furniture at £20 a piece which with £20 in money then reckoned of him amounteth in the whole to £100 which were employed in the troop of Captain Francis St Barbe for the service of the Parliament.[34]

This troop served in Colonel Richard Norton's Regiment of Horse which was raised in Hampshire. Others may be issued with backplates and breastplates and a headpiece or helmet. Rarely do you find a trooper being issued with a buffcoat and a headpiece. Some accounts do not even mention buffcoats or armour. Richard Clapp's account book for the garrison of Plymouth records the issue of the kersey for following issues to the cavalry:[35]

29 TNA SP 28/15/226, SP 28/17/85, Warrants for payment of Sir William Balfour's troop; SP 28/15/219, SP28/17/79, SP 28/19/67 and P 28/28/122, warrants for payments of Sir Philip Stapleton's Troop of Horse.

30 TNA WO 55/423 305, Warrant signed by Sir Edward Walker on 2 May 1644.

31 Clarendon, ed. Lockyer, *History of the Great Rebellion*, p.195. Clarendon's italics.

32 TNA SP 28/35/375, Captain Edward Foley's arrears of pay; SP 28/266/86, Captain John Butler's arrears of pay; SP 28/267/209, Colonel John Okey's request for arrears of pay.

33 BL ms Tanner ms 63/14, Estimate of armour produced by the London armourers, 13 April 1642.

34 BL Add MS 24,860, Receipt signed by John Eiste, Robert Wallop and Edward Hooper, 15 November 1642.

35 TNA SP/28 part 17/13, The accompt of Richard Clapp Deputy Treasurer, muster master and commissary of provision in the garrison of Plymouth, 24 May 1643 to 8 Jul 1649.

15 April 1644
Cornet Thomas Wansey for the troopers of the late Captain John Wansey for the clothing of the soldiers in kersey, 70 yards

Lieutenant William Bodley for the clothing of the soldiers of Major Leighton's troop, 70 yards

Captain Chaffin for the clothing of the soldiers [of the] late Colonel Goules', 70 yards

16 April 1644
Captain Halfe for the clothing of the soldiers of his troop, 84 yards

Five yards of kersey was issued on 15 July 1644 to 'William Upton, a trooper to make a suit of clothes'. Unlike the infantry clothing for troopers was made from 3¾, 4 and 4¼ yards of kersey per suit, suggesting that there were at least four sizes of clothing issued to the cavalry. Trumpeter Lebb Kennedy of Captain Carr's troop had a suit of clothes made for him from four yards of kersey, although what colour this cloth was is not recorded. Suits were usually a coat and breeches. The soldiers of the garrison were also issued with shirts, stockings and shoes. In January 1645 '13 capes for soldiers to stand sentinel' were received, 'in which were afterwards tarred'. [36]

Snapsacks or knapsacks were issued to the soldiers for 'the carriage of small provisions of victuals for their better accommodation in their journey'.[37] Despite the hundreds of thousands of knapsacks known to have been issued to soldiers during the early seventeenth century, both in Britain and Europe only one is known to still exist, which was recovered from a shipwreck in the Netherlands. This is a tubular leather bag fastened at each end by a leather strap which was long enough for the soldier to carry the bag over his shoulder. This knapsack is similar to those depicted in contemporary paintings. Although most of the sources suggest that these knapsacks were made of leather, there are a few references to them being made of canvas.

Regimental Colours

Each company of foot and troop of horse and dragoons carried a regimental colour. For infantry these were ensigns, which measured six foot by six foot, plus a sleeve to attach the colour to a staff. According to Thomas Venn:

> The Colonels Colours in the first place us of a pure and clean colour, without any mixture. The Lieutenant Colonels only with Saint George's Arms, in the upper corner next the staff; The Major's the same, but in the lower and out most corner

36 TNA SP/28 part 17/1, The accompt of Richard Clapp Deputy Treasurer, muster master and commissary of provision in the garrison of Plymouth, 24 May 1643 to 8 Jul 1649. Between December 1644 and January 1645 100 soldiers and troopers were issued with waistcoats which were made from one yard of cloth, but this item of clothing does not appear to have been standard issue to soldiers of the Civil War period.

37 *Calendar of the Cecil Papers in Hatfield House*, vol. 22 (London: HMSO, 1971), p.299, King Charles to the Earl of Salisbury, 18 February 1639.

> with a little steam blazant. And every captain with Saint George's Arms alone, but with so many spots or several Devices as pertain to the dignity of their respective places.[38]

These devices could be roundels, stars, diamonds or 'piles wavy' etc., and if the ensign was a 'medal colour' i.e. yellow or white, then the devices were to be red, blue, green etc., whereas a coloured ensign was to have a 'metal' device so the White Regiment of the London Trained Bands had red diamonds, whereas the Blue Regiment had white devices. The London Trained bands also did not conform to Venn's system since the major had one device, the first captain, two devices etc. Judging by the surviving examples of infantry colours there was no regulation size for the St George's Cross.

Unfortunately, none of the ensigns carried by Waller's Western infantry are known, but for his new army the following can be identified.

Colonel John Birch's (New Kentish Regiment)	Yellow
Sir Arthur Heselrige's Regiment	Blue
Colonel Samuel Jones' Regiment	White
Colonel Richard Onslow's Regiment	Red
Colonel Herbert Morley's Regiment	Blue
Colonel William Springate's Regiment	White
Colonel Ralph Weldon (Old Kentish Regiment)	Red
Unidentified Regiment	Yellow

The regiment with yellow colours may have been either Waller's or Christopher Potley's Regiment. None of the devices of these regiments which distinguished each company are known.

Among the accounts for Kent is the following payment for ensigns:

> For Mistress Hollingworth of London, the 20 December 1644 for the price of 18 crimson ensigns, of her had, £3 15s each £67; more one yellow ensign £3 more, nine white ensigns and four crimson ensigns at £3 3s 6d each £41 5s 6d more for mending of ensigns, etc., 10s total £111, 0s 3d.[39]

38 Thomas Venn, *Military and Maritine* [*sic*] *Discipline in three Books* (London: F. Tyler and R. Holt, 1672), p.181.

39 TNA SP28/130/61

These accounts also mention the following:

> To Master Allen of London the 6th June 1644 for [the] price of nine colours for Sir Michael Livesey's Regiment [of Horse] £11 00 00.

The colours or cornets of Livesey's Regiment of Horse are known to have been red with various mottos in a white scroll to distinguish each troop, for example Captain Owen's cornet had the motto, 'Vita, Veritati, Omniaq' and Captain Sir Thomas Piers troop carried the cornet with the motto, 'Finis, Coronat, Opus'. On the other hand Captain Thomas Skinner's troop had an arm emerging from a cloud holding a flag with the motto, 'Aut: Autsuper, hunc.'[40]

An arm emerging from a cloud was a common device, usually holding a sword, but sometimes a flag or a pair of scales. Cornets often had religious or political themes and could either have a motto either in English or more commonly in Latin.

Although Waller seems to have preferred yellow cornets for his regiment of horse, Captain Butler's troop carried a blue cornet and Captain William Gwilliam a black one. Waller's own standard had a shield hanging from a tree, with the motto, 'Fructus Virtutis'. Whereas Heselrige's Regiment carried green cornets, with his own having an anchor hanging from a cloud with the motto, 'Only in Heaven'. The regiment originally raised for Lieutenant General Sir Richard Grenville had red cornets, as did Colonel Richard Norton's Regiment. The only known cornet for an officer in Vandruske's Regiment was black. This was for Captain St George's troop which depicted St George slaying the dragon with the motto, 'Soyes, mon Dieu, ma garde et Mon Apuy Salies'.[41]

Although he did not serve with Waller, Hugh Croxton's bill to Lionel Copley is an excellent example of the cost of a cavalry cornet:[42]

22 March 1643	
For ¾ Damask	£0 07s 06d
For 1½ ells of taffeta	£0 19s 06d
For 4 ord of fringe	£0 10s 00d
For a pair of cornet strings	£0 03s 06d
For 2 pair of cordwell strings	£2 12s 00d
For 8 pairs of ribbon	£0 02s 00d
For painting the banners and cornet with a horseman & horse & a motto	£2 00s 00d
For making the cornet and banners	£0 10s 00d
	£12 04s 06d

40 BL Add ms 5247, Regimental Banners, Temp Charles I.

41 BL Add ms 5247, Regimental Banners.

42 TNA SP 28/42.

Croxton also supplied Copley with a second cornet on 18 December 1644:

For ¾ of orange damask	£0 11s 00d
For 1½ ord of silk and silver fringe	£0 08s 06d
For a pair of silk and silver cornet strings	£0 16s 00d
For painting the cornet	£0 15s 00d
For the cornet staff and case with belt, boot and swivel	£1 08s 00d
For making the cornet	£0 03s 00d
	£4 02s 00d
The embroidering of your cornet cost	£1 09s 00d

The standards of the cavalry were about two feet by two feet, with a sleeve where the standard's pole was inserted.

Dragoons were mounted infantry who rode on inferior horses to the cavalry to fight and then dismounted. Such were their usefulness that in July 1644 Waller had planned to convert his entire infantry to dragoons, but due to lack of horses this task proved impossible. Even so he converted his own regiment of foot to dragoons and his old regiment of dragoons passed to Major General James Holborne. Originally dragoons were formed from both pikemen and musketeers, but the pike was too unwieldy to carry on a horse so was quickly dropped. Even so, on 1 December 1642 Captain Thomas Moore's company of Sussex dragoons were issued with 40 hatchets and axes and 103 Swedish feathers. These were also known as 'swine feathers' and were similar to pikes albeit five feet in length, with one end being stuck into the ground and the other with a pike head pointing towards the enemy to protect the firer against cavalry.[43]

Dragoons carried guidons, which were a similar size to the cavalry cornet, but with a swallow tail. On 26 September 1643, Waller's Regiment of Dragoons was seen in the Artillery Yard in London, where its guidons were observed to be plain yellow with one to five black roundels as a device.[44]

No army would be complete without an artillery train and there was a variety of guns to choose from, from siege artillery, like the cannon royal, to field pieces such as the demi-culverin. According to Colonel Robert Ward, who wrote the *Anim'adversions of War*, there were the following pieces of artillery:

43 TNA WO 55/387/47, warrant to supply Captain Thomas Moore's company of dragoons with Swedish feathers, hatchets and axes, 1 Dec 1642.

44 BL Harl ms 986 pp.111–112, Richard Symonds, *The King's Army*.

Type	Weight of shot in pounds	Diameter of shot	Range in paces	Weight of powder (pounds)	No. of horses need to pull the piece
Cannon Royal	64	7¾	300–1,500	40	16
Cannon Serpentine	52	6¾	340–1,600	25¼	14
French cannon	46¾	7	360–1,740	25	12
Demi-cannon eldest	36¼	6½	370–1,800	20¾	11
Demi-cannon ordinary	32	6¼	350–1,700	20	10
					9
Demi-cannon	24½	5¾	340–1,600	18	8
Whole culverin	19	5¼	420–2,100	16	8
Culverin	16¼	5	400–2,000	15	7
Demi-culverin	11¾	4½	380–1,800	9	6
Demi-culverin lesse	9	4	320–1,600	8	5
Saker	5½	3¼	300–1,500	5½	4
Minion	5	3	280–1,400	5	3
Falcon	2½	2½	260–1,200	2½	2
Falconette	1½	2	220–1,000	1½	2
Rabinet	¾	1¼	150–700	¾	2
Base	½	1	100–560	¼	2

However, one type of artillery piece that Ward does not mention, but is known to have been used by Waller's Southern Association Army, was the leather gun. It was once believed they were invented by James Wemyss, Waller's lieutenant general of the ordnance, but they are known to have existed in the early 1620s; the inventor and country of origin is uncertain, although they are usually associated with Gustavus Adolphus' Swedish Army. Even their name is misleading, since the barrel was made with either a wrought iron or copper tube about 2 mm thick, hammered into shape and then soldered together. The tube was then tightly bound with iron wire and finally covered with leather. Some surviving examples have more than one barrel.[45]

The True Informer for 9 December 1643 records that on 5 December Wemyss:

> with wagons laden with leather pieces of ordnance and much other ammunition and is by this time at Farnham with Sir William Waller. These leather pieces are of very great use, and very easy and light of carriage. One horse may draw a piece which will carry a bullet of a pound and a half weight and do execution very far.[46]

For every artillery piece not only were a certain number of horses needed to drag it, but also a number of supporting wagons which carried the ammunition and gunpowder for it. The number depended on the size of the artillery piece. Wagons were also need for ammunition and gunpowder for the infantry and cavalry, but also carried the provisions for the army.

45 Stephen Bull, *The Furie of the Ordnance, artillery in the English Civil War* (Woodbridge: Boydell Press, 2008), pp.10–11.

46 Godwin, *The Civil War in Hampshire*, p.96.

Provisions

In theory a soldier received two pounds of bread and a pound of meat per day. Despite being a Protestant country Britons were still forbidden to eat meat on Wednesdays, Fridays and Saturdays, so soldiers were issued with cheese instead. This was washed down with two bottles of beer, or a bottle of wine. Bread could be substituted with biscuit, which was probably like a hard tack biscuit popular with the army and navy in later centuries.

Among the entries in the account book of Waller's commissary general, Nicholas Cowling, for 2 January 1644 records, 'paid for 4 fat sheep for sick soldiers, £1 6s 8d'. Another entry for 17 May 1644 records, 'paid to the butchers in Farnham for 3 sheep and a half for the officers and sick soldiers £1 17s'. Sometimes a particular regiment is mentioned such as, 'Paid William Edward for 82 lbs of pork for the London Red Regiment, £1 0s 0d'. Since it is not described as fresh meat it could have been salted to preserve it, although this would mean that it would have to be soaked in water to wash the salt away to make it edible. Payments for bread and beer are also common, for example 'Paid for beer for the Green and Yellow Regiments of the London Brigade £6 0s 0d', and on 29 January 1644 5 shillings was paid for beer for the 'Blew Regiment', which was presumably Heselrige's Regiment of Foot. As to cheese there are payments for Holland, Cheshire and Suffolk Cheese, which was supplied by Thomas Stanley of Bread Street, London, between February and May 1644. On 2 July 1644 Cowling paid £4 'at Daventry for 20 lambs to the yellow coats', and £9 for '28 sheep for the use of the train and blue coats'. These were Lieutenant General Wemyss' Regiment of Firelocks.

Between 24 December 1643 and 31 March 1644 Cowling's account book also contains payment for for the following loaves of bread:[47]

24–30 Dec 1643	Jan 1644	February 1644	March 1644
4,188 loaves	12,304 loaves	28,560 loaves	23,064 loaves

Each loaf cost a penny, although on 14 March 1644 Cowling paid £3 4s to Widow Cole for 'bread for the officers'. Unfortunately the amount of bread Widow Cole supplied is not recorded but it must have been a better quality than the loaves for the soldiers. Other entries for officers included:

47 TNA SP 28/135, Nicholas Cowling's Account Book, unfolio.

Date	
9 Jan 1644	'Paid Mr Powell of London for wine for the general officers, £12 10s 0d'
18 Jan 1644	'Paid for fowls and eggs for the chief officers, £0 5s 6d'
22 Jan 1644	'Paid for 2 sides of veal, 2 sides of pork, 4 sides of mutton, a calves head and feet for the officers, £3 10s 9d'
2 Feb 1644	'Paid to Mr Gilbert Keite for 168 pound of loaf sugar at 12d per pound £8 6s 0d'
	'Paid Mr Smith in the Old Bailey for strong waters for the officers of the Army, £1 19s 7d'
17 Apr 1644	'Paid for 4 roasting pigs for the chief officers £0 12s 0d'
25 April 1644	'Paid in Farnham for veal, mutton, and lamb for the colonels and other officers, £3 0s 0d'
	'Paid for roasting pigs and pigeons and chickens for the chief officers in the army £0 16s 0d'
4 May 1644	'Paid for 3 roasting pigs and pigeons and chickens for the chief officers in the army £0 13s 6d'
	'Paid for beef, veal and lamb for the officers £8 2s 0d'
8 May 1644	'Paid for wine beer and dressing the dinner for the Council of War, £1 13s 6d'

The account book also shows that provisions were transported great distances, such as on 1 February 1644, 'Paid for the carriage of 3 loads of cheese and other things from Guildford to Arundel, £5 0s 0d' and for the 2 February 'paid to Mr Thomas Stanley of Bedstreet, in London for 30 Holland cheeses and 10 Cheshire Cheeses £8 9s 11d, for 40 cwt of cheese at 21s per cwt, £42 0s 0d'.

What is clear that despite all these entries that there were not enough provisions for the whole army, so the soldiers must have relied on regimental commissaries to supply them with food. However, commissaries of cavalry regiments also had to worry about feeding the horses, and the artillery, including the baggage train had three commissaries who were responsible for either ammunition, draught horses and provisions for the men.

A typical warrant was one that was delivered to the High Constables of the Hundreds of Kingston and Elmbridge in Surrey on 2 December 1643 which read:

> By virtue of a commission unto me directed from the honourable Sir William Waller knight, Sergeant Major general these are to will and require you forthwith upon sight hereof that you levy upon your several parishes and tithings within your Hundred 30 loads of hay and 30 quarters of oats and that you bring or cause the same to be brought to me or my deputy to the sign of the Lamb in Farnham or were the army shall be advanced the 6th of December with a with a return of this warrant and the names of those that refuses to pay or those that seek to hinder you in this service and thereof fail not as you will answer the contrary at your utmost peril. [signed] William Jones, Commissary.[48]

Warrants like this would be sent to other areas controlled by Waller and on more than one occasion. However, campaigns were fought not just for strategic gain, but also where the provisions and fodder were in abundance.

48 TNA SP 28/244/2 unfolio.

Appendix III

Captain Edward Harley's Troop in Waller's Regiment of Horse, July to 3 August 1643

After the battle of Roundway Down Captain Edward Harley wrote to his father, 'I lost ten horses and two men in the fight last week and last time I have lost five or six more so that my troop is now very weak.' The following is compiled from three muster rolls for his troop.[1]

Captain Edward Harley
Lieutenant William Baas; shot through the foot at Lansdown.
Cornet Robert Harley
Quartermaster Francis Cook
Corporal John Osborne
Corporal Edward Noble
Trumpeter John Willing
Farrier William Wood
Trooper Thomas Rea; lost a pistol at Lansdown.
Trooper Richard Massey
Trooper Andrew Barker; lost his pistols at Roundway Down.
Trooper John Taunton; lost his headpiece and carbine at Roundway Down.
Trooper Edward Kettlewell; horse killed at Lansdown and he lost his back and breast plate. He also lost his sword at Roundway Down.
Trooper Robert Jones; He lost a pistol at Roundway Down.
Trooper Hugh Acton; horse killed at Lansdown and he lost his pistols and saddle.
Trooper Richard Skews; lost his headpiece at Roundway Down.
Trooper Robert Lewis; horse killed at Lansdown and lost a pistol.
Trooper David Price; horse killed at Lansdown as well as losing a pistol.

1 HMC Portland Manuscripts, p. 113, Edward Harley to Sir Robert Harley at Westminster, 15/25 July 1643; BL Add ms 70004 ff.123, 124 A list of Captain Edward Harley's Troop, July and 3 August 1643.

Trooper Basil Warren; lost his pistols at Roundway Down.
Trooper Robert Rudshall
Trooper Thomas Price; lost his pistol and saddle at Lansdown.
Trooper Peregrine Foley; lost his back and breast plates at Roundway Down.
Trooper John Wantleigh or Whiteling; lost his pistols at Roundway Down.
Trooper Jeffrey Lovett; shot in the thigh at Lansdown and lost his pistols. At Roundway Down he lost his pistols again.
Trooper Thomas Rudge
Trooper Thomas Knight
Trooper William Burch
Trooper Gerard Evans; lost his pistols at Roundway Down.
Trooper William House; cut over the hand at Lansdown and his sword was broken. At Roundway Down he was 'cut over the face'.
Trooper Edward Horne
Trooper Roger Evans; cut over the face at Lansdown and lost a pistol.
Trooper Philip Luke
Trooper Benjamin Goodspeed
Trooper Baldwin Green; broke a pistol at Roundway Down.
Trooper Edward Peeks
Trooper John White
Trooper George Leydman
Trooper Richard Meredith
Trooper George Thorneton; Wounded by a sword thrust in the neck at Roundway Down and lost his horse and [blank – weapons]
Trooper Thomas Legg
Trooper Thomas Woodward; lost his head piece and saddle at Lansdown and was 'shot in the back and in diverse places of his body at Roundway Down', where he also lost his horse. Lost his pistols at Roundway Down.
Trooper John Blackbrick
Trooper Thomas Pole
Trooper Richard Farmer; 'cut over the head, sorely' at Roundway Down where he also lost a horse and all his weapons.
Trooper John Banks; lost a pistol at Lansdown, reported missing at Roundway Down.
Trooper Edward Black; shot in the thigh at Lansdown and lost his pistols.
Trooper William Damm; reported missing after Roundway Down.
Trooper William Lincoln; horse killed at Lansdown and lost his pistols. He lost all his weapons at Roundway Down.

Troopers recorded to be in the troop but not mentioned in the 3 August muster roll

Trooper James Harris; horse killed at Lansdown and lost his horse and all his weapons at Roundway Down.

Trooper Samuel Hicks; horse killed at Lansdown and lost all his arms. Was taken prisoner but since escaped. Reported missing after Roundway Down.

Trooper Thomas May; horse killed at Lansdown and he was shot through the shoulder and lost all his arms.

Trooper Thomas Riddick; hurt in the thigh with a sword at Lansdown and lost his head piece and a pistol.

Trooper George Anderson; lost his carbine, pistols and saddles at Lansdown.

Trooper Thomas Powell; lost a pistol at Lansdown, reported missing after Roundway Down.

Trooper Thomas Curtis; Lost his pistols at Lansdown.

Trooper William Thorpe; 'cut over the head and hand' at Roundway Down, where he also lost his horse and all his weapons.

Trooper Morgan Vaughan; reported missing after Roundway Down.

Trooper Matthew Jones; lost his arms at Lansdown and was reported missing after Roundway Down.

Trooper Thomas Williams; reported missing after Roundway Down.

Trooper James Williams; reported missing after Roundway Down.

Trooper John Holding; reported missing after Roundway Down.

Appendix IV

The Armies' Movements During the Oxford Campaign

A. A List of the Several Quarters of Sir William Waller's Army[1]

18 to 20 May Waller's army at Bagshot
22 to 23 May Waller's army spends two days at Basingstoke
24 May, Waller's army at Aldermaston. (f)
25 to 26 May, Waller's army spends two days at Compton (f)
27 to 28 May Waller's army spends two days at Marcham (t)
29 May Waller's army at Nuneham (f)
30 May Waller's army at Standford on Thames (t)
31 May to 1 June Waller's army quarteres at Abingdon (t)
2 June Waller's army at Appleton Woods (f)
3 to 4 June Waller's army quarters at Newbridge for 2 days (f)
5 June Waller's army quarters at Witney (f)
6 June Waller's army quarters at Fifield (f)
7 June Waller army quarters at Stow on the Wold (t)
8 to 9 June Waller's army quarters at Winchcombe for 2 days (t)
10 to 11 June Waller's army quarters at Evesham (t)
12 June Waller's army quarters at Norton field (f)
13 June Waller's army quarters at Bromsgrove (t)
14 to 15 June Waller's army quarters at Stourbridge (t)
16 June Waller's army quarters at Droitwich (t)
17 June Waller's army quarters at Pershore (t)
18 to 19 June Waller's army quarters at Tewkesbury (t)
20 to 21 June Waller's army quarters at Gloucester (t)
22 to 23 June Waller's army quarters at Dowdeswell (f)
24 June Waller's army quarters at Stwo on the Wold (t)
25 to 26 June Waller's army quarters at Shipton (t)
27 to 28 June Waller's army quarters at Hanwell (f)
29 to 30 June Waller's army quarters at Great Bourton (f)

1 BL Harl ms 378

1 July Waller's army quarters at Great Preston (f)
2 to 3 July Waller's army quarters at Towcester (t)
4 to 6 July Waller's army quarters at Northampton (t)
7 to 9 July Waller's army quarters at Great Preston (t)
10 to 12 July Waller's army quarters at Daventry (t)
13 July Waller's army quarters at Towcester (t)
14 July Waller's army quarters at Buckingham (t)
15 to 16 July Waller's army quarters at Bicester (f)
17 to 18 July Waller's army quarters at Woodstock (f)
19 July Waller's army quarters at Newbridge (f)
20 July onwards Waller's army quarters at Abingdon (t)
(t) = quarters in the towns (f) = quarters in the fields

B. The King's Movements[2]

16 May, the king leaves Oxford for Reading
17 May, the king leaves Reading
31 May, king at Islip
2 June, the king at Woodstock
3 June, the king marches to Oxford via Islip
3 to 4 June, the king marches to Burford, via Wolvercote
5 June, the king marches to Worcester, via Evesham (garrison withdrawn)
6 June, the king arrives at Worcester
12 June, the king leaves Worcester and marches to Bewdley via Shrawley
15 June, the king leaves Bewdley and marches back to Worcester
16 June, the king marches to Brodway, via Eversham
17 June, the king marches to Burford, via Stow on the Wold
18 June, king rendezvous with his foot regiments at Witney
21 June, the king marches to Bletchingdon, via Woodstock
22 June, the king marches to Buckingham, via Bicester
26 June, the king marches from Buckingham to Brackley
27 June, the king marches to [blank], neat Thorpe Mandeville
28 June, the king marches towards Banbury
29 June, the king at Cropredy
31 June, the king marches to Deddington, via Fathingo, Aynhoe on the Hill and Abberbury
1 July, the king marches to Morton on the Marsh
2 July, the king marches to Worcester, via Brodway and Eversham
5 July, the king marches from Worcester to Coberly, via Brodley and Sudeley Castle
12 July, the king marches from Coberly to Sapperton
13 July, the king marches to Badmington
14 July, the king marches to Bath, via Marshfield and Lansdown
16 July, the king marches from Bath to Wells

2 Symonds, *Diary*, pp.3–82.

18 July, the king marches from Wells to Nunnery
20 July, the king marches from Nunnery to Ivelchester/Kingsmore
24 July, the king marches from Kingsore to Chard
25 July, the king marches to Honyton
26 July, the king marches to Exeter
28 July, the king marches from Exeter to Crediton
29 July, the king marches to Bow/Spreyton
30 July, the king marches to Oakhampton
31 July, the king marches to Lifton
1 August, the king marches to Trecarell in the parish of Lezant
2 August, the king marches to Liskard, Lostwithiel
5 September, the king marches to Liskard to Taverstock, near Plymouth
17 September, the king marches to Oakhampton.

C. The Movements of Essex's Army[3]

This is a copy of the late Earl of Essex his march from St Albans into Oxford etc 1644, as it was found in one of the pockets of their soldiers at Lostwithiel.

Hertfordshire
From St Albans to Beaconsfield
from B. to Henley
from H. to Reading
from R. to Wickham, in Oxfordshire
from W. to Bradfield in Berkshire
from B. to Bluberry
from B. to Abingdon to my Lady Powell's house; from thence we faced Oxford,
and so to Islip, where Sir Ralph Hopton's army lay within two miles of us, and next morning being Holy Thursday, we had a skirmish with them until next Monday.

Oxfordshire
From Islip to Woodstock
from W. to Chippin Norton
from C. to Barfoot (Burford?)

Berkshire
From B. to Farindon, June 8
from F. to Lamburne, June 10
from L. to Bedding (Bedwin?) June 11
from B. to Amfield (Amport?) June 13
from A to Compton (Compton Chamberlain?) June 14
from C to Blanford

3 Symonds, *Diary*, pp.97–98.

Dorsetshire
From B. to Dorcester
from D to Bridport
from B. to Crewkerne, June 23

Somersetshire
From C. to Chard, June 24
from C. to Axminster, June 30
from A. to Honiton, July 1

Devonshire
From H. to Colhampton, July 2
from C. to Tiverton, July 3
from T to Kirton, July 20
from K. to Bowe, July 21
from B. to Okehampton, July 22
from O to Tavistock, July 23
from T. to Horsebridge, July 26

Cornwall
from H. to Lincolnhelne, July 27
from L to Bodmin, July 28
from B. to Lostwithiel, August 2
'from thence like rouges to the Devil', added Symmonds.

Select Bibliography

British Library

Add ms 5247, Regimental Banners, Temp Charles I
Add ms 16370 A Collection of coloured plans of fortifications etc., 1644-1670.
Add ms 18980, letters from senior Royalist officers, vol. 1 1642-1648.
Add ms 18981, letters from senior Royalist officers, vol. 2 1642-1648.
Add ms 18982, letters from senior Royalist officers, vol. 3 1643-1648.
Add ms 24860, Letters to Richard Major alias Maijor. 1639-1959.
Add ms 70004, Portland papers, 1642-1647.
Add ms 70061, papers relating to Colonel John Birch's Regiment, x.1646-1647.
Harley 166 Journal of the House of Commons, 15 February 1644-3 November 1645
Harley ms 382 Letter book containing correspondence written by the sisters of Sir Symonds D Ewes.
Harley ms 384, Letter book containing correspondence written by relations of Sir Symonds D Ewes.
Harley ms 986 Symond, Richard *The King's Army, 1643*
Harley ms 3783 Collections of letters to Dr William Sandcroft, 1628-1668
Harley ms 6804, Papers relating to the affairs of Charles I
Stowe ms 190, Letter book of Sir Samuel Luke, Oct 1644-March 1645
Film of Tanner ms 61-63 originals at Bodleian Library
Thomason Tracts, see footnotes in each chapter for details.
A True relation of the several passages and proceedings of Colonel Goring at Portsmouth (London: E G for John Benson, 1642)

East Sussex Record Office

475/37, John Coulton, clerk under Captain William Morley to Henry Jeake, 8 January 1644.

Hampshire Record Office

48M80/F1 Letter from the Marquess of Winchester at Basing to King Charles I about the danger to basing in the Civil War, 2 December 1642
40M83/1 The humble Declaration of Sir Marmaduke Rawdon, Colonel, undated

Surrey History Centre

G52/6/2 (1) A True Relation of the Marchings of the Red Trained Bands of Westminster, the Green Auxiliaries of London and the Yellow Auxiliaries of the Tower Hamlets, under the command of Sir William Waller from Munday the 16 October to Wednesday 20 December 1643 (London, 1643)
LM/Cor 5/- Correspondence from John Wight to Sir Poynings More

The National Archives

SP 16/- State Papers of Charles I
SP 21/- Correspondence of the Committee of Both Kingdoms (Derby House Committee)
SP 28/- Commonwealth Exchequer Papers, 1640-1674
WO 47/-, Minutes of the Office of the Ordnance
WO 55/-, Miscellaneous Entry Books and papers of the Office of the Ordnance

Printed Primary Sources

Anon Historical Manuscripts Commission 13th Report, Appendix 1, *The Manuscripts of His Grace The Duke of Portland, preserved at Welbeck Abbey,* (London: HMSO, 1891),
Anon HMC 15 Report Appendix viii
Anon HMC *Calendar of the Cecil Papers in Hatfield House* vol. 22 (London: HMSO, 1971)
Anon *Journal of the House of Lords vol. 6* (London: HMSO, 1802)
Anon *Journal of the House of Commons* vol. 8 (London: HMSO, 1802)
Adair, John (ed.), *They Saw it Happen: Contemporary Accounts of the Siege of Basing House* (Hampshire County Council, 1981)
Atkyns, Richard, 'The Vindication of Richard Atkins', in *Military Memoirs, the Civil War, Richard Atkyns and John Gwyn* (London: Longmans, Green and Co. Ltd, 1967)
Bruce, John and Masson, David *The Quarrel between the Earl of Manchester and Oliver Cromwell* (London: Camden Society, 1875)
Clarendon, Earl of, *History of the Rebellion and Civil Wars in England* (Oxford: Clarendon Press, 1826).
Clarendon, Earl of, ed. Roger Lockyer, *History of the Great Rebellion* (Oxford: Oxford University Press for the Folio Society, 1967).
Coe, Richard, *An exact diarie. Or the Brief Relation of the Progress of Sir William Waller since the joining of the London Auxiliaries with his forces which was the twelfth of May until their return homeward on Thursday the 11 of July following ... by Richard Coe under Captain Gore of the Tower Hamlets Regiment.* (London: Humphrey Tucker, 19 Jul 1644)
Firth, C.H. and Rait, R.S., *Acts and Ordinances of the Interregnum, 1642–1660* (London: HMSO, 1911)
Hamilton, W.D., *Calendar of State papers Domestic, 1644* (London: HMSO, 1888)
Hamilton, W.D., *Calendar of State papers Domestic, 1644–1645* (London: HMSO, 1890)
Hinds, Allen B. (ed.), *Calendar of State Papers relating to English Affairs in the Archives of Venice, 1643–1646* (London: HMSO, 1926), vol. 27.
Hopton, Sir Ralph, *Bellum Civile, Sir Ralph Hopton's Narrative of his Campaigns in the West, 1642-1644*, ed. C.E.H. Chadwyck Healey (Taunton: Somerset Record Society, 1902), vol xviii
Howell, T.B., *A Complete Collection of State Trials and proceedings for high treason and other crimes and misdemeanors...* vol. 4, 1640–1649 (London: Longman, Hurst..., 1816)
Ludlow, Edmund, *The Memoirs of Edmund Ludlow, Lieutenant General of the Horse in the Army of the Commonwealth of England.* (Oxford: Clarendon Press, 1894), ed. C.H. Firth, vol. 1.
Luke, Sir Samuel, ed. I.G. Phillip, *Journal of Sir Samuel Luke*, vol. 1–2 (Oxford: The Oxfordshire Record Society, 1947–1950)
Ogle, Rev. O., and Bliss, W.H., *Calendar of the Clarendon State Papers preserved in the Bodleian Library* (Oxford: Clarendon Press, 1872) volume 1
Rushworth, John, *Historical Collections of Private Passages of State,* vol. 5 (London: D. Browne, 1721)
Symonds, Richard, *The Diary of Marches of the Royal Army during the Great Civil War kept by Richard Symonds*, ed. Charles Edward Long (London: AMS Press, 1968)
Tibbutt, H.G. (ed.), *The Letter Books of Sir Samuel Luke, 1644–1645* (London: HMSO, 1963)
Venn, Thomas, *Military and Maritine [sic] Discipline in three Books* (London: F. Tyler and R. Holt, 1672)
Vicars, John, *England's Worthies under whom all the civil and bloudy wars since anno 1642 to anno 1647 are related,* reprinted (London: Benbow, 1821)
Walker, Sir Edward, *Historical Discourses upon several occasions* (London: Samuel Keble, 1705)
Waller, Sir William, *Recollections in the Poetry of Anna Matilda*
Waller, Sir William, *Vindication of the Character and Conduct of Sir William Waller Knight... Explanatory of His Conduct in taking up arms against King Charles the First* (London: J. Debrett, 1793)
Walsingham, Edward, *Britannicae Virtutis Imago or the effigies of true fortunate expressed to the life in the famous actions of that incomparable knight, Major general Smith who is here represented, June 1644* (Oxford: Henry Hall, 1644)
Walsingham, Edward, *Hector Britannicus or Sir John Digby*, in *Camden Miscellany* vol. XII (London: Camden Society, 1910)
Washbourne, John, *Bibliotheca Gloucestrensis, a collection of scarce and curious tracts relating to the county and city of Gloucester illustrative of and published during the Civil War* (Gloucester, 1825)
Webb, J. & T.W. (eds.), *Military Memoirs of Colonel John Birch, written by Roe, his secretary* (London: Camden Society New series vol. vii, 1873)

Secondary Sources

Anon., *English Heritage Battlefield Report: Cropredy Bridge* (English Heritage, 1995)
Adair, John, *Roundhead General: a military biography of Sir William Waller* (London: MacDonald, 1969)
Adair, John, *Cheriton 1644: The Campaign and the Battle* (Kineton: Roundwood Press 1973)
Bayley, A.R., *The Great Civil War in Dorset, 1642–1660* (Taunton: Wessex Press, 1910)
Bull, Stephen, *The Furie of the Ordnance, artillery in the English Civil War* (Woodbridge: Boydell Press, 2008)
Couper, Rev. D L *The Story of the Parish Church of St Lawrence, Alton* (Gloucester: The British Publishing Company Ltd, nd)
Dalloway, James, *A History of the Western Division of the County of Sussex*, vol. 2, part 1 (London; Bensley and Son, 1819)
Dixon, John, *The Unfortunate Battaile of Alresforde, being an account of the Campaign and battle of the Cheriton, March 29th 1644* (Nottigham: Partizan Press, 2012)
Edgar, F.T.R., *Sir Ralph Hopton: The King's Man in the West (1642–1652)* (Oxford: Oxford University Press, 1968)
Godwin, Rev. G.N., *The Civil War in Hampshire and the Story of Basing House* (Alresford: Laurence Oxley, 1904)
Hagedorn, Rosemary, *Arundel at War, 1642–1644* (Kibworth Beauchamp: Matador, 2018)
Holmes, Clive, *The Eastern Association in the English Civil War* (Cambridge: Cambridge University Press, 1974)
Hutton, Ronald, 'For King and Country', in *The Making of Britain, the Age of Expansion,* (Basingstoke: MacMillian Education Ltd, 1986), ed. Lesley M. Smith
Memegalos, Florene, *George Goring 1608-1657, Caroline Courtier and Royalist General* (Aldershot: Ashgate, 2007)
Miller, Amos C., *Sir Richard Grenville of the Civil War* (London and Chichester: Phillimore & Co Ltd, 1979)
Money, W., *The Battles of Newbury* (London, 1881)
Peachey, Stuart and Turton, Alan, *The Fall of the West*, volume 7 (Bristol: Stuart Press, 1994)
Peachey, Stuart and Turton, Alan, *Old Robin's Foot, the army of the Earl of Essex, 1642–1645* (Nottingham: Partizan Press, 2017)
Peacock, Edward, *The Army Lists of the Roundheads and Cavaliers* (London: Chatto & Windus, 1874)
Roberts, Keith, and Tincey, John, *Edgehill, 1642, First Battle of the English Civil War* (Botley: Osprey Publishing, 2001)
Scott, Christopher L., *The Battles of Newbury, Crossroads of the English Civil War* (Barnsley: Pen and Sword, 2008)
Scott, Christopher L., 'How did Waller Lose Roundway?' in Ismini Pells, *New Approaches to the Military History of the English Civil War* (Solihull: Helion & Company, 2016)
Scott, Christopher L., *The Most Heavy Stroke, the Battle of Roundway Down, 1643* (Solihull: Helion & Company, 2018)
Scott, Christopher L., Turton, Alan, Gruber von Arni, and Dr Eric, *Edgehill, the Battle Reinterpreted* (Barnsley: Pen and Sword, 2005)
Spring, Laurence, *Waller's Army, The Regiments of Sir William Waller's Southern Association* (Farnham: The Pike and Shot Society, 2007)
Spring, Laurence, *The Campaigns of Sir William Waller's Southern Association, 1643–1645* (Bristol: Peachey Press, 1997)
Spring, Laurence, *The Battle of Cheriton* (Bristol: Peachey Press, 1997)
Spring, Laurence, 'For God Sake Come Home! Soldiers' Wives, 1620–1660' in Jones, Serena (ed.), *Home and Away, The British Experience of War, 1618–1721* (Solihull: Helion & Company, 2018)
Spring, Laurence, and Hall, Derek, *The Farnham Greencoats, Samuel Jones Regiment of Foot* (Leigh on Sea: Partizan Press, 1987)
Thomas-Stanford, Charles, *Sussex in the Great Civil War and the Interregnum* (London: Chiswick Press, 1910)
Tibbutt, H.G., *The Life and Letters of Sir Lewis Dyve, 1599–1669* (Bedford: Bedfordshire Historical Record Society, 1946)
Webb, John, *The Siege of Portsmouth in the Civil War* (Portsmouth: Portsmouth City Council, 1977)
Wroughton, John, *The Battle of Lansdown, 1643, an Explorer's Guide* (Bath: The Lansdown Press, 2008)
Young, Peter, *Edgehill 1642: The Campaign and the Battle* (Kineton: Roundwood Press, 1967)
Young, Brigadier Peter, and Toynbee, Margaret, *Cropredy Bridge, 1644: The Campaign and the Battle* (Kineton: Roundwood Press, 1970)
Young, Brigadier Peter, *Naseby 1645: The Campaign and the Battle* (London: Century Publishing, 1985)